To: Jane K. ♥

Thanks for all your support
And much Health
Read work

THE POWER FROM WITHIN
BUSHIDO

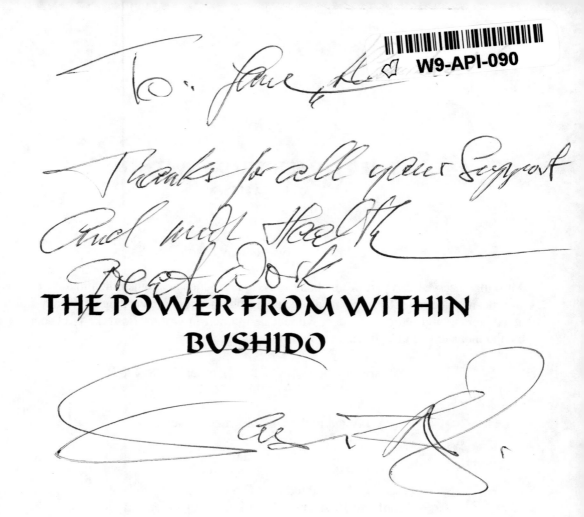

Sensei, Anthony Martin von Sager

August 30, 2014

THE POWER FROM WITHIN
BUSHIDO

Copyright © 2006 by Anthony Martin von Sager

Library of Congress Control Number: 2008940871
ISBN 978-0-615-26172-0

Printed in the United States of America

First Edition

Edited by Anke Cannon
Proofread-Revision-Adaptation-Arrangement-Layout
Scripts-Books-Screenplays-Stories-Letters
Translations-Lessons
English / German
cannon_office@freenet.de

Published by
Cloud Dancer Production–Media Division
18533 Roscoe Blvd # 272
Northridge, CA 91324
www.getfit4yourlife.com

Produced by
PPC Books
Redington Shores, FL

Dedication

This book is dedicated to my family, Ingeborg Schiel/Sager and Rolf Sager, my brother Anthony Martin, and to my original Grandmasters Geert J. Lemmens and Toni Bader. They elevated and motivated me from day one and ensured that I would reach my full potential and set my goals high, but within reach. Also to my lifelong friend and brother from early childhood days, Renshi Mihran "the Armenian Lion" Aghvinian, (and his Hye-Katch-Do team) who has been by my side many times, gently pushing me to and beyond my limits, ensuring my complete victory against all odds. Thank you all, and if I have not mentioned one or the other within these pages, be assured, your support and love over the years are certainly appreciated and not forgotten! God bless and good health to all.

Sensei, Anthony Martin von Sager
www.getfit4yourlife.com www.hyekatchdo.com

Anthony's brother

Ingeborg Schiel

Family Crest

Contents

Foreword

There are two essential qualities that lead every human being to success: The ability to focus on a goal and an 'I never give up' mentality.

When Kai Anthony Sager came to my dojo at the beginning of the 1980's, his goal was to learn Karate. But he had a severe handicap: He was disabled by cerebral palsy, had spent most of his childhood chained to a wheelchair and still needed to use a cane.

Anyone else would have failed before actually beginning, but not Kay Anthony Sager. We started to work: Stretching-, muscle-build up- and coordination-exercises…and Karate. The path was steep and rocky, but Kai Anthony never gave up. Despite difficulties, despite set-backs, despite people's unfavorable opinions, despite rejection by uncaring pseudo-Karate Masters, who would only have a weak smile for his efforts instead of encouraging him, Kai Anthony carried on and reached, with 'sweat and tears', his first goal: First degree Black Belt!

This was not enough for him. He wanted more! He wanted to open the wonderful world of Martial Arts to others, first and foremost to people who were disabled from birth like him or through an accident. All his energy he aimed at this goal. And he accomplished it! Many of his students walked and still walk the path of Martial Arts to success like him.

The humanitarian qualities of true Martial Artists are courage, perseverance, willingness to make sacrifices, truthfulness, thankfulness, loyalty, and love for their fellow humans. Kay Anthony unites all these qualities within himself, and he has always proved them to me. I thank him for that!

One more highlight of Sager's career is his book, ***POWER FROM WITHIN BUSHIDO***. It reflects the essence of his life work.

POWER FROM WITHIN BUSHIDO can and will be a great help. Not only to handicapped people, but also to all those who walk the path of Martial Arts to unfold their personality and to reach excellence or who help others to follow this path.

For his achievements within and for Martial Arts, especially for his work with handicapped children, Kai Anthony has more than deserved recognition, admiration and thankfulness. He is an example for all Martial Artists.

Kancho Geert J. Lemmens 10th Dan

Heide, North Germany, Sept. 2008

About the Author and Shin-Tora-Do Karate

When Anthony Martin von Sager was born with severe cerebral palsy (CP) in 1963, his parents were told their son would never walk, let alone engage in any sportive activities. So he spent the better part of his childhood in a wheelchair, living through the nightmares of a handicapped kid and his personal horrors brought about by society and the government regulations of those days. When he was 6-years-old his mother found a German Professor who performed a barrier-breaking operation on his legs, followed by three more before he was 10-years-old, enabling Anthony to exchange his wheelchair for a walker and canes – the first step to independency. With extraordinary determination and will power he began to move obstacles and barriers out of his path, but it was not before he, already in his teens, met Geert J. Lemmens – a touch of destiny – that his life began to change rapidly.

Geert J. Lemmens, true founder of the European Kickboxing and Free-Style-Karate Systems, brought to life in the late 60's, and the WAKO Kickboxing Association in Berlin (1977), the world's oldest (and one of the largest) Kickboxing Organizations, became Anthony's original Grandmaster (Karate), besides Tony Bader (Jiu Jitsu, Judo), father of the European Jiu Jitsu. Living and learning under the watchful eyes of such strong and legendary Grandmasters as their true student, Anthony understood the importance of harmony between styles and of blending different approaches and training methods from the start and made his Masters' concepts to his own. The 'Art of Old School Teaching' played a major role during his training with Grandmaster Lemmens, and together they developed a Karate fitness and rehab program to be integrated in the traditional methods that had proved to lead to success for many centuries. Moreover, during his extensive travels across the globe he attended countless seminars and workshops to further his skills, knowledge and wisdom and was trained under numerous Grandmasters among whom such legends as Hirokazu Kanazawa, Carlos Manchado, J. Pat Burleson, Benny 'The Jet', Bill 'Super-foot', Jon Bluming, Dan Inosanto, Emanuel Bettencourt, Michael Wuebke and Prof. Dan Baker are to be found, just to name a few and most influential. From early on the aspect of teaching, mentoring and especially healing within the Martial Arts took a major part in his life and is reflected in his own style Shin-Tora-Do, which he began to form in 1980.

After 11 hard years of painful battle with his physical limitations, he was finally able to reach one of his greatest goals and became a first-degree Black Belt, which dramatically changed his life forever. With determination and will power he went on, and his efforts were rewarded by reaching the status of fourth-degree Black Belt in Jiu Jitsu and third-degree Black Belt in Kickboxing and second-degree Black Belt in Karate, and became the highest-ranking tested Black Belt with a physical limitation in the world.

Starting his career as competing athlete in Germany, Anthony was soon found at various northern German state championships gaining several second to fourth places despite his handicap before emigrating to the United States, where he moved on to win a number of state and national championships in the handicap- and several places within the non-handicap division. Between 1997 and 2002, he became World Karate Champion eight times (handicap- and non-handicap division) besides gaining six second/third places in the Kata and self-defense w/ partner category and third and fourth places in the semi-contact category in +75 Kg. divisions, before he retired from competition. He has also established two World Records. On May 15, 1999, Anthony was awarded the Lifetime Achievement Award in Los Angeles, California, and in 2000 he was honored by being nominated to join Tony Bader in conjunction with J. Pat Burleson and Jim Harrison, earning his third degree Black Belt and so be nominated for the Hall of Fame of Jiu Jitsu. Later he earned his Black Belt in CA, under Pat Burleson in 2002.

During his outstanding career as an athlete and teacher, Anthony staged countless seminars, made speeches and appeared on television and radio passing on his immense knowledge and motivating thousands of people, besides teaching and mentoring innumerable students. As a 'sideline' he was also an active stunt- and fight-coordinator for a number of years having worked with such professionals as Chuck Norris, Aaron Norris, Stuart Whitman, Rod Steiger, Pamela Anderson and Drew Barrymore, just to name a few. Moreover, he is author, producer and director of three short films: ***Close Quarters Combat*** and ***The Power from Within,*** as well as his DVD ***Get Fit for Life***.

After Anthony retired from competition, he devoted the major part of his life to teaching and helping people with limitations even more, especially handicapped children and youths, achieving changes in their lives nobody had thought possible

Endorsements

"In the old days, it was very hard for Anthony to become accepted. He was denied enrolment at the German Sports College at first. Luckily, however, I was able to help him, and he graduated with best results. Moreover, two teachers declined to permit his participation as a student in our Jiu-Jitsu classes. I could intervene and Anthony, again, although handicapped, passed his exam with best marks. I am very proud of my Jiu-Jitsu and Judo student! His work, more so with handicapped kids and youth are outstanding!"

Shihan Tony Bader (German Judo and Ju-Jitsu Pioneer)
9. Dan Jiu-Jitsu, 8. Dan Ju-Jitsu, 8. Dan Judo, 4. Dan College Internation. Dan
2. Dan Judo Kodokan Japan, 4. Dan Jiu-Jitsu Diploma Rukopashiny-Boy Ukraine

"Anthony and I were schoolmates and good friends. We looked after one another and helped each other in many ways. We often trained together, and while I could teach him some moves, he introduced me to 'body building'–power-workout for muscle growths which he liked a lot in those days. There is one little story, I will probably never forget: At school, there was a gang of bullies who tried to intimidate us and push us around; Tony, because of his handicap and me, because I was not a 'big guy'. That was a big mistake! Anthony took two of these bullies aside and told them to leave us alone, if they were concerned about their health. Full of themselves they looked at him like 'what does this cripple think he is' So, we invited them to the gym that was part of a youth-centre where some friends and Tony helped me to teach 'the inner-city kids', as we called them, in the weekends. The fools agreed, or rather, they threatened to come along. And they did. We were just in the middle of our training, when the large swing door was opened and a few heads appeared. We pretended not to have noticed and carried on with our class. Within minutes, the bullies were gone and, needless to say, never bothered us again. For a change, we had been able to dissolve a tricky situation without being punished by the school authorities, which made our victory so much sweeter!"

Sensei, Jo Jacobson – Gojo-Ryu Do–Flensburg', Germany

Mission Statement
Anthony Martin v. Sager

"Sounds extraordinary, I know. But it is not! The strength I discovered, the wisdom I gained and the intensity of focus I applied day in and day out lies within any human being! It is in you, too. When I started my journey over 25 years ago, I had no idea that I should actually become a trail-blazer for anyone with the need to be in a better place in life, particularly for our 'Rock Stars', our children with special needs!"

This is the only comment to his outstanding achievements by a great and kind character who has always stayed with his two feet on the ground to be there when he is needed!

And comments are not really necessary; his remarkable record and impressive trophy collection speak for themselves!

Other Media Works by the Author

Daydreams Poetry Collection
Get Fit for Life DVD
The Power Within Commercial
Close Quarter Combat DVD

Introduction

L ife is a wonderful thing. And there is so much loveliness in our world–like this amazing sunrise I am fortunate to witness just now...

Life itself has always been like a drug to me, an unceasing flow of energy. I live, I breathe, I love and I dream...full-blooded, day in, day out. And to experience true love and friendship (Shinwa: Truthful, loving heart) has always been my greatest goal in life. In order to accomplish this, I try to treat my friends and loved ones the way I want to be treated by them. And I try to do positive things every day–not just for myself, but for others, too. If I am needed, I will be there. Never in my life have I denied my full attention and full force of action to someone in need.

Now, what does full force and undivided attention mean? Well, it certainly does not mean giving only half or even less of yourself but expecting at least a 100% payout in return! Be sure, people will soon realize that you are after the quick fix. Or, as a dear friend of mine would say, that you are an 'energy vampire' out for the take. I promise you that in my experience the only way to get a 100% return of any emotion investments is to be willing to give all you got first! In anything you do. It is as simple as that.

I have been a mentor, teacher and competitor for a long time; and I have been fortunate enough to be able to travel this wonderful world. But do not think I was born with a silver spoon, or born a male version of Mother Theresa; far from it. So how did I find my true path, my calling and life goal? Not by crying or by blaming others or sitting in a dark corner complaining about God and the world. And certainly not by letting others do the job for me. No, it was by good old-fashioned 'do it yourself'! Get up and fight for what you want to come true! Your one way of life! Then, amazing changes will begin to happen, and fast! Before you know it, you will be in a current that grows and grows until it turns into an immense wave. Before you realize it, you will be in control, like a captain on the bridge facing any storm and hurricane and rough waters ahead with a smile.

THE POWER FROM WITHIN
BUSHIDO

Chapter: 1

Yourself, Family and Friends—Interactions

A partial quadriplegic as a result of cerebral palsy, my parents were told I would never walk; let alone engage in any physical activity.

So how was I able to become a pro athlete? First, I need to say thanks to my parents who provided me not only with some natural abilities, willpower and determination, but also with what the scientists call the "Super-gene delta 32". I inherited it from both my father and mother whose families can be traced as far back as the 14th century (one of my ancestors was even knighted by the King of England). This amazing gene makes your immune system extremely strong protecting you from AIDS and even to most types of cancer. It is the perfect antidote. Why the scientists have not been able to use it to save millions of people around the world is beyond my understanding! So, I have been lucky in that respect.

But if you think for a second that your ancestors, your family, your cultural or financial background is responsible for your journey through life, for your life's failures, well, I am sorry, you are all wrong: It is in your hands and your hands alone. How did I find that out? Very simple: I was born a 100% disabled despite such wonderful parents descending from an old aristocratic family; and when I was growing up, people even in Europe thought that anyone with a physical or mental disability had to be put away. For the greater good of all!

Young couples like my parents were pressed by the public, by officials and by their families to give up their crippled or retarded child and submit him or her to government Child Services. My mother, however, would not be subdued. She ran from one doctor to the next—only to be told there was no hope. She was even smiled at and pitied, her state of mind questioned. But she remained unmoved by the desperate situation and hardship put on this young couple. Finally, she found a professor in Germany who would perform several ground-breaking operations on me. Thanks to him and my mother, I was able to begin my new journey.

However, there was a bitter tear in those turbulent years filled with the search for answers: The pressure family members and city officials put on my parents broke their marriage. My father and my mother had to lose the love of their lives because of a child supposed to be too difficult and probably too hard to care for. Because of a child that had absolutely no place, then, in the sophisticated culture of a leading nation in Europe!

I was locked away in various orphanages, because I was 'disabled'; hunted like an animal, because I ran away to find my brother; thrown into jail, transported back in handcuffs. There were the fights against authorities' orders: As if cerebral palsy (CP) also was a 'mental disability', the officials tried to classify me as 'retarded' to be sent to a 'special school'; and later, I was–at first–denied enrolment at the Sports College (Olympic Center) Germany, considered 'unfit'–I got there in the end, helped and supported by the one and only Tony Bader, one of my wonderful Grandmasters. However, would I be asked to go through all this again, I would. If only for all these wonderful young children, youngsters and adults I was honored to help together with my Master Students!

So, how could a young kid, born with severe CP, end up against all odds in a normal high school and later graduate with honor at the sports college in those days? And as if that wasn't enough, become World Martial Arts Champion–in the handicapped as well as non-handicapped division–undefended eight times, even become a sports icon, some kind of a legend, equipped with a Lifetime Achievement Award and recommended to the Jiu Jitsu Hall of Fame, and finally, following my greatest passion, turn into a teacher and mentor? Ah yes, let us not forget the two world records!

It was not easy, to say the least! Believe me, I am just an ordinary person–only perhaps with an extraordinary life story! The strength I found, the focus I applied day in day out, and even the intensity of focus I discovered, lie within every human being! And one of my greatest sources of energy is and always has been a loving open outlook on life! And with a big smile on my face, I try to draw even my hardest critics over to my side. 'The Power from within'–always with a smile. Believe me, it opens doors!

One of my very personal goals is to give assistance to any man or woman–no matter what their background may be–who needs or wants to find a better way to lead their lives. Perhaps there is even someone out there who will get enough out of reading this book to become a pro athlete or an advanced Martial Artist. Or whether it is just the young woman next door, the single mother who is looking for some answers, some kind of guideline to live healthier, raise her teenage son. And if there is only one reader who makes me reach my goal, I will be the happiest and luckiest man alive.

I did what no one ever thought possible, and so can you! If you realize it or not, you have it in you. All you need to do is get started. Today. Not tomorrow! Change your life, step by step, day by day. You will reach a very special place inside yourself. Make it your personal home. Trust yourself; you are stronger, smarter, more powerful and more resourceful than you might think.

Now, let us begin. From personal experience as well as from being a teacher and mentor to many people, I can tell you: Begin slow and keep it simple! Take one step at the time, change a little more every day and position your personal goals within reach!

But if you know it all–stop reading here and now. Give this book to someone who is in need; he or she may thank you for that. And carry on with your life; be as happy as someone can be. However, I believe, no matter how successful you may be, perhaps even born with a lot of privileges or a silver spoon, I am certain you, too, will find some useful material in this book. Maybe it simply widens your horizon a little more or helps to deepen your wisdom. It may even inspire you to donate not just money but your own time to help and put a smile on many little faces, especially on those who need to be in a better place in life. Not all the money in the whole world can buy you this wonderful thankful smile you get, after you have been there for them. It is so little and yet so much that is needed. Or give this one smile to me, and I am paid in many ways. However, that is me.

Let us see what we can do for you!

Before you are able to go out and 'rescue the world', you have to take care of yourself first! But, again, keep it simple, do not under- or overestimate your problems or the changes you want or need to make. And, do not lie to yourself! If you cheat or lie about them, you will only hurt yourself in the long run and maybe even your loved ones and close friends as well. So do not do it! It is only a waste of time. You and you alone know best, where or why you need to make these small or not so small changes in your life–in many cases, this has long been put off. And be aware: it is already cheating to postpone the starting moment! "I would if I could; I will, when …; I might, after …; I should perhaps, but…" This simply is not good enough. If you are in any of these stages or that type of person, leave it! Better do not do anything at all! And if you are looking for someone to sell you a game, a gimmick or a magic pill that makes you to feel better and keeps you going as if everything was okay; sorry again. This book is not for the faint hearted.

However, if you really want to become active, be aware, there are no shortcuts–but you do not need any!...Hang in there...I will guide you through. It is vital to start with small things, no matter how simple they may seem. That way it will be less intimidating to yourself and to your loved ones. More often than not, the most effective way to reach your destination is to break it down into small steps: Achieve at least a tiny success daily, weekly or even monthly, keep your goals within reach. Take one step at the time, and you will be less easily discouraged and less often tempted to quit.

Draw up a list. Whatever bothers you, whatever you need, whatever changes you want to make: Write it all down. This list may just be a scrap of paper taped to your fridge: 'Get more fresh fruit from the market. Improve your vitamin intake!' Of course, there are no limits. But do not get discouraged if your catalogue becomes quite long; that is fine. Finally, outline your life goals–in the shape of a letter, perhaps, addressed to your self. In the business world, this is called a five to ten year goal projection. So why not call your outline a life goal projection? From experience I can tell you this works like a charm. So far, I have written down four life goals; and three of them I have been able to mark as accomplished. You can attain the same. Believe me, it is not that hard!

So, take a minute, take a pen, and take some paper. Choose your items. Begin with ordinary 'day-to-day' things: 'Get a new hair cut', perhaps–that can be ticked off within a day or two. Carry on with more complex matters you need to work on and so proceed down the page until, perhaps, you come to the large goals or changes you want to achieve, say, by the end of the year or even later. Let me tell you, it feels like a homerun when you start to get the hang of it, and even more so when you begin to mark the big items on your list as done! Remember to be honest to yourself; you know best what needs to be or should be on this list.

Surely, one person's problems and the personal ways of dealing with them cannot be compared with the problems and ways of any other person, even if the problem or problems seem the same. Therefore, a completely different approach is necessary in most cases to find the origin of a problem. Moreover, speaking out of personal experience, the approach to help or heal that works for me does not necessarily work for someone else as well, not even for my friends close to me. And finally: The things appearing unbearable, unmanageable or unforgivable to one person do not even exist for another! Right at the beginning of my years of teaching and mentoring, I learned never to underestimate or trivialize someone else's problem. Ever!

So please, do not be intimidated or discouraged by my personal life story. Maybe you can use it as a compass for your journey. And it is absolutely your journey, regardless of status, money, wealth, social or cultural background! You are the one who must walk your own path. Let me be a tour guide in a different new country, a strange town; on a winding road up a mountain to the top. You will get used to the new culture and strange words and voices around you more and more. You will get surer and surer of yourself finding your way around town. You will slowly start to explore the mountain, and before you know it you will be up there on the top with a smile on your face waving down to the world and declaring victory.

*

I remember the first time I rode a bike. It was one of my greatest achievements in those days! My brother helped me, God bless his heart. I was almost 12 years old then, and for about a year my mother, my brother and I had lived–at last–together under one roof. My mother had finally been able to convince the Child Services that it was a lot better for all of us if I lived with my family and not in one of these horrible places where they dumped children, simply because they were born physically or mentally handicapped. The Child Services put those kids in there even against their families' will; took them away from their families even by force. So that the 'sophisticated' population could go on with their daily lives without being disturbed by 'unpleasant' sights. This happens even today, over 30 years later!

Let's take the U.S. From 300 million people living in North America, we have close to 25% with a handicap! Of course, there are many elderly people among them. However, we still have over 15 million handicapped or disabled citizens all in all. So if these numbers are just remotely accurate–which they are, I researched it–then it means every fifth person in the U.S. has some sort of handicap! Therefore, you should see people with a disability everywhere: At the laundromat, the gym, the supermarket, the post office, the school, the park or just on the street or on the bus. Well, do you? I think it is safe to say no, not really! Why is that?

It is, because we definitely have an 'emotion problem', when we are confronted with, or are in a situation involving, someone with a physical or mental disability. So nothing has really changed yet. Maybe the places where they dump someone like me when I was only two years old are not so lonely, dark and impersonal any more as they used to be in my time, 40-something years ago. But the culture? The personal approach of people? Is it not rather like this: "I don't have time for anyone in my way. I am not to be held up or bothered by anyone who does not contribute to further my career. I am not to be disturbed in my personal life!"?

I am quite convinced too many members of our western industrial countries have a rather superficial interest in their fellow humans. And they join all kinds of fast developing clubs and institutions, as an example, because they only think it 'cool' to be part of these communities, nothing else. They do Yoga in crowds not knowing, not even wanting to know, what Yoga is about.

My Grandmaster Geert J. Lemmens was one of the first, if not the first, who taught Yoga and Martial Arts in a unique combination. He was laughed at and called a 'girly man' when he was practicing Yoga. Today, he is considered one of the leading authorities on Yoga in Europe! With his knowledge, he changed and more or less saved my life; and he changed the Martial Arts landscape and understanding. Today, I am able to do the same for others, especially for our "Rock Stars"–how I describe these children and youths with any form of handicap.

Most people do not want to be different, 'originals', outsiders. But think about it. Someone different, someone 'original' may become a trendsetter! However, the point is, be your true self, be **original,** never a copy-cat, no matter what! Be **authentic!** These are most important personal qualities! The case of Grandmaster Lemmens shows clearly: Sometimes it is only a matter of seeing things in the proper light! So, do not swim with the mainstream! Do not get discouraged by people who laugh at you, because they think you are different from the crowd! Stick to your personal **authenticity**! In time, you might even be known as the 'one' to see, the 'one' to ask and even the 'one' to be measured by. It is a lot like learning to ride a bike: after you get the hang of it, you will always remember.

*

This brings me back to the day when my older brother Anthony Martin took me up the hill near our house: Only for a few years had I been able to walk without help; I was still falling down often and had to use my hands a lot to balance myself. As Anthony and I finally reached the top of the hill, I was quite afraid. To be honest, it was a rather steep and high hill! My brother helped me on to his great 'Bonanza 3' speed bike and told me to turn the handle bar to the right or left, whichever way I wanted to go. I was listening intently to his explanations–my heart beating like thunder–when, without warning, he pushed me over the edge of the hill. Heavens, was I frightened! Gathering speed like a launched rocket I shot down that hill towards a large cornfield beyond the end of the path I was on. That field came closer and closer, and I had completely forgotten what I was supposed to do. Before I knew it, I was flying high in the air and landed–by pure magic– safely on my butt among the corn! I heard my brother yelling as he came running down the hill. And I started yelling, too, asking how the hell I had done it! Anthony Martin just picked me up and hugged me. It was a wonderful moment, and I miss him a lot.

I was back on top of that hill in no time with a smile of course–we named it "Hill of Horror". My brother pushed me off again, yelling not to forget the breaks and to turn left at the bottom. You surely guessed: It took me a long time to get the hang of it and not to land in the cornfield! When we finally came home by sun set, my skin was bruised and broken all over, and my brother had to drag me through the door. You should have seen our mother's face! At first, she was angry to say the least, but after telling her about what we had been up to, she gave me a big hug and was very proud of both of us. I guess she couldn't really believe that it was me who had gone through this ordeal. I felt great and did nothing but smile; and later that night my brother and I told her the whole story again with relish–in later years we all laughed a lot about this adventure and mother's first reaction about it. From that day on, I felt a true risk taker, an explorer, determined to take on the whole world!

I am sure you can remember such an important event in your life, too. Who was involved and how did you feel then? Also, think about the positive influence this childhood or young adult experience had on your later life. Where did it lead you from there?

Remembering such events will help you to tackle your difficulties of today more at ease. And once you got started and your new path is beginning to take shape more and more, you will find yourself in a momentum of your own, like in an underwater current. Before you know it, you are sucked into a different world with dynamics of its own.

The next point for most of us is nutrition assessment. I know, our busy and hectic modern lifestyle makes this a real challenge! However, it is very important! Especially for those who need to change their diet for health reasons. Let us be honest, who doesn't? There is a lot of obesity, high cholesterol and high blood pressure due to the lack of exercise and wrong food in our daily lives. At the end of this book I will devote a full chapter to nutrition, which I called: "Soul food to go".

Now, let us apply a simple technique I used to exercise with my students for many years: Write down everything you eat every day for two weeks! And everything means everything! Every meal, every snack, every mouthful. Do not cheat! It wouldn't do you any good! This 'food record' will show you a pattern of habits and behavior and will be a useful tool for changing your life.

So what food is good for you and what food should you stay away from? Well, look at your list and ask yourself: Do I get enough vitamins and minerals with my daily nutrition? Do I consume mostly 'good' or 'bad' calories? What about protein and carbohydrates? And, last but not least, what sort of fat do I eat? Is it saturated or unsaturated fat? This is very important for a healthy cholesterol level. And, does my daily fat-intake add up to over or under 10% of my daily food? These are the major questions you need to ask yourself. It may sound confusing at first, but in no time at all you will become a nutrition expert. You will find and pick the healthiest items even at your neighborhood shop so that you don't need to make a long trip to the next 'Health Food' store. And when you are on the road you will easily find the 'good stuff' in the cooler of the gas station as well. It really is not that difficult, or different from what you have done in the past. You only choose one item instead of another. Last, but not least, not only the kind of food you eat is important, but also the amount and the time of intake.

In 1982, I opened my first dojo in the basement of a fitness studio in North Germany, where I was working as fitness instructor. It was a box and kickbox gym. I was 18 years old, and my two best friends were also instructors at the studio and helped me around the gym. We were ignorant of any book about diets, and yet we separated as well as we could the three major ingredients of our daily food, which are carbohydrates, protein and fat.

Why is this so important? Well, I for my part, want to celebrate at least my hundredth birthday as healthily and happily as possible! The 'modern lifestyle' of today leads most people to overload their bodies with 'bad' carbohydrates, saturated fats and sugar (fast-food) almost leaving out protein, vitamins and minerals. That is why so many people suffer from obesity and overweight, heart diseases, high blood pressure and blocked arteries, and their life is a lot shorter than it should be.

As we all know, our health problems do not appear over night. They build up during years of bad eating habits and lack of exercise. Therefore, you cannot change this overnight, either! A little patience is required, but with the 'step by step' technique you will see it works. Before you know it, you will be in great shape and feel healthy and wonderful. And if you do already, you can improve, and improvement always is a good thing–on your way to become an athlete or coach perhaps?

There are two rules. First: Stay away from fried food, greasy burgers and French fries, chips, chocolate and such as much as you possibly can. They should only be consumed in moderation. If you follow this rule, you will be surprised how much healthier you already live! Second: Control and separate your protein and carbohydrates intake. Separate means: don't eat protein and carbohydrates at the same time. It sounds perhaps complicated, but it is less difficult than you might think, and you only need to do this as long as it is necessary. To find out about the ingredients of packed food, simply read the label on the containers. It should tell you the amount of fat, carbohydrates, protein and other ingredients. Separate as much as you can or need, but do not get too technical to start with.

Here is a simple example: You pick a ready-to-eat-turkey meal and compare the ingredients with the ones of a turkey meat package. You will instantly see the dramatic difference in the fat and protein contents! Needless to say, the turkey is much healthier for you: A lot more protein, almost no fat! The same applies to cheeses: Pick cottage cheese–it tastes great with a fresh bagel–instead of these plastic wrapped fat-bombs. Or tuna fish in water: Close to 40% protein, low fat, low Carbohydrates and a great meal with a salad of fresh green lettuce and tomatoes! Well, I could fill page after page with similar examples of good and bad food, but we want to keep it simple. So, just make sure from now on to keep your fat intake per day under 10% as often as possible, keep the carbohydrates lower and the protein higher. And next time you do your shopping and remember to pick up some fresh lettuce before leaving the store, you have won half the battle.

Here is another 'little secret': Your body is able to break down protein at night! But not fat or carbohydrates! So, for anyone who needs or likes to slim down, try to have your last meal about three hours before you go to bed. This gives your body time to work on the food, and a bit of exercise as well. It will thank you for that by not (!) storing away so much fat on your hips and belly. And if you remember to eat your tuna and salad instead of the beloved big fat pizza for dinner, you will be well on your way! One more thing: Leave the sweet soda in the fast-food store, drink milk (plenty of calcium, protein and 'good' fats) or orange juice, fitness water or tea. So, again, it is not difficult. All it takes is a little awareness. There is no need to be upset about a–former–lifestyle. That is the past. And the future is in your hands!

Before long, you will have lost a lot of weight simply by following those little rules. And, even more important: By following the guideline you created step by step, major changes will happen in your life. Perhaps you will even establish a new **'Way of Life'** altogether! Like me. At first I needed to become healthier and improve my quality of life as well as my level of activity. But then, this grew into a new way of life and changed it forever. I became a pro athlete eventually. Of course, you do not have to go that far; however, it would be nice to know you could! So, do not waste another day. Besides, if you have your day-to-day life under control, you can treat yourself once or twice a month to a rest and have a really 'bad' meal without regret! I love those days: Ice cream and soda as much as I want, or the fried chicken with a good old fashion milk shake. If you are that well under control **the whole month**, you deserve and need a 'food party' like that once in a while. It doesn't do you any harm!

*

That reminds me of a great experience: When I had just started to exercise with

Grandmaster Lemmens, I noticed a flyer on the looker room door one day. It announced the annual 'City Run' in our town. I quickly found my teacher and asked him if I could take part in it. He raised his eyebrows and asked: "Do you think you can walk that far?" The question was well justified, because I had hardly ever walked a distance longer than the way from my bike to the dojo and back–and that was a rather short distance! Also, I had no idea the 'City Run' was five to ten kilometers to go! "Yes, I do, and I will!" I answered quickly! Lemmens raised his eyebrows again and looked over to his wife. Eventually he said: "Well, if you think you can walk that far, put your name down on the list". I was very proud then and happy to be able to take part in such an event. During the following weeks, I trained harder and longer than ever before. I wanted to be as fit and strong as possible. Somehow I felt a good deal of my future as an athlete was at stake. Besides, I did not want to disappoint my teachers.

Soon, the day came. Oh boy, was I intimidated by the whole scene: The run was an event organized by the town's sports club. Everybody seemed to be out there, and I think the whole dojo had come to the start, at least all those I could remember: Geert and Vera Lemmens, all the Masters and students! To make matters worse, the sun blazed down from a clear sky on this summer day, and the temperature was close to 30 degree Celsius.

However, I was determined to get through this run right to the finishing line. I can tell you, it was really hard, every single step of it. I got dizzy several times and my knees were hurting incredibly from beginning to end. Half way through the distance, when I was dragging myself along, lightheaded and about to see stars, Marwan Abu Khadra was suddenly by my side and said: "Lighten up, champ, everyone is watching you. Pull yourself together, you are half way there!" I managed to look at him nodding my head thankfully. He and Mihran Aghvinian had a forceful influence on me in those days of growing up, especially because they stood up for me so many times. They were captains of our full and light contact kickboxing teams and also taught in the dojo along with G. Lemmens. You can imagine I did not want to let them down. Besides, I knew a lot of people had a bet running that I would not make it to the finish line; that alone would have been motivation enough to keep going, no matter what! So, after Marwan's pep talk I pulled all my strength and energy together and put one painful step in front of the other.

Later, he handed me a bottle of water and gave me an encouraging slap on my back. Glancing over my shoulder once in a while, I saw Geert and Vera Lemmens walking near by, and Vera had a worried look on her face. That made me even more determined to finish the run, what ever it took. When I eventually saw the finishing line in the distance, I was about to pass out! And to this day I do not know where I found the strength for the last kilometer. Immediately after crossing the line, I collapsed on a bench, not able to move for nearly an hour. My Grandmaster and his wife came and congratulated me on my tremendous accomplishment, and I was so happy and so exhausted at the same time, you would not have believed it! Later, Mihran and Marwan took me to lunch; and I remember sitting at the table, completely speechless, holding on to my water. Both kept congratulating me on my triumph and told me how proud they were and glad that I was part of the dojo team. They encouraged me to keep up my training and not to give up. I was very happy, and both men still mean a lot to me today. Of course, I had no intention to stop. But to be perfectly honest, I had not been sure at all whether I would be able to make it through the run. I would never have known, however, had I not tried. It was a milestone, a springboard to further success.

I am certain there was a springboard in your early life, too. Think about it, and you will surely remember. It is quite amazing to see just how support and help from others shape our future and set stepping-stones! Quite a few youngsters today, however, focus on people who influence them in a bad, destructive way. There are so many around who call themselves teachers and mentors. But the only thing they ever do is concentrate on the things their students do not have instead of focusing on their abilities and how to develop them. This, of course, applies to you, too. If you concentrate on the negative aspects of your life and/or body, you will be stuck with them. I had plenty of negative aspects I could have focused on throughout my childhood and even young adulthood. But feeling sorry for yourself and moaning about things only make matters worse; they bring you down. That has never been my manner. Instead, I take the bull by the horns, so to speak, and tackle the problem! If you just think like that, you will be surprised how much stronger it will make you! You will find you are halfway through the trouble already. Moreover, others will notice your attitude and will be more than happy to help you.

There are so many different ways to lighten up your mood, to give your life a new positive meaning: They can be as drastic as changing your eating habits or as simple as buying a new plant for your apartment. As radical as to stop taking drugs, smoke or drink too much alcohol or as plain as getting out of the house more often and mix with people. Whatever it is for you, again, start slowly, do not push yourself too hard, but keep going– step by step, one day, one meal or one exercise at a time, five sit-ups today, six tomorrow.

*

So let's do a little check-up before we dive into deeper waters: a healthy or healthier view on life, better nutrients, and regular exercises. And do not forget to smile a lot...

One of the most important conditions on your way to self-success, as I call it, is the ability to love yourself. Sounds strange? Not at all. With this ability you will find missing answers much faster; and there is a lot more fun in the search as well. So give it a go. There is an amazing new journey ahead. If you love yourself in a healthy way you will automatically start to generate that feeling all around you, and people you meet will return the favor! Soon, there will be hardly anyone who will not notice you walking into the room. People will open up to you as you open up to them. This has very little to do with sex! If you think sex and love, especially 'self-love', are one and the same thing, you make a big mistake, and it is not surprising why you keep being shut out. You need to change your frame of mind.

In order to achieve self-love, we walk inside ourselves and search for the natural **"Power from within"**, the power of love from within! We all have it within ourselves. First, search and find it for yourself, for you alone and then for the ones close to you. Concentrate on your feelings, your hopes and wishes, and ask yourself: What do I like, what don't I like? What are my fears? How would I like myself to be? How would I like to be treated by my fellow humans? How do I want to look? Please do not forget: one step at the time. Material things, superficialities and money are secondary, which you will find to be true when you lose your health, a close friend or a family member. Let us hope you will not need such a harsh experience before you wake up. Once I told a woman I loved her for her amazing eyes, warm wonderful smile, and loving heart. She looked at me in astonishment; I do not think she believed me. Considering her outstanding beauty, she was most likely used to this stereotype of man that would stare down her body and think about sex. Instead of getting to know her for her outstanding, loving heart.

In our fast moving world most of us focus on superficialities and on material things. We do not look at a personality, at a character. We focus on clothes somebody is wearing, we look at the car he/she drives, at the house he/she lives in. We judge a person by the club, by the crowd he/she is a member of, by the looks. Moreover, we seem to believe that only material things can make us happy and, consequently, the lack of them will make us unhappy. What a mistake!

There are many different opportunities that can cause a feeling of wellbeing, of love and comfort: A treat at the hairdresser's, a manicure– I like to go to the spa and wallow in a tub filled with hot scented water, for example, or to the gym for relaxation and not only to train. And once or twice a month I am just fine to get a great massage by my wonderful therapist.–every man, every woman has a different idea about relieving stress and relaxing. Important is that you create a comfort zone or get away after a hard day or week of work. Some people may go fishing, others may like to sit comfortably on the sofa with a newspaper, do some gardening or play with the cat. And, the more you think about these ways to relax and feel well, the more you will enjoy them later.

What about the experience of reading a great book, a walk on the beach or in the park with a dog, perhaps–and if you don't have one, it might be nice just to imagine you had– the smile on the face of a stranger. Go out and take a minute to look around. You will see so many different wonderful things, so many possibilities to join enjoyable happenings for free, a concert on the pier, for example, and with the beautiful sunset on top. Is this not something that can make you feel happy? Is it not much nicer than sitting alone at home, watching the same meaningless TV show evening after evening, and worrying, perhaps, where to get the money for a bigger, shinier car to impress people? This invites you to consume all this terrible junk food as well!

If you would like–and I believe, most do deep down, unless they already are happily married–to find someone special in your life, then think at first about what makes **you happy** and contented, and not about what others may consider important to get into the 'game'. Then imagine you are attracted by someone. And that person feels your comfortable self-esteem, loving attitude and confidence, likes you for that and returns the same signals instead of looking at your 'Gucci-clothes' or gold watch. There will appear a great smile on both your faces, before you know it! And in my opinion, this kind of smile is one of the most attractive features on a woman–or a man, depending on the point of view.

So, let's have the essential issues once again: Think about yourself, your feelings and emotions. What is it that you really want? Draw an outline of your life the way we have discussed. Reflect on what you have already achieved and found out about yourself through those simple steps. Be **truthful to yourself, always!**

Now you need to start and live by those insights you have gained. A fine method to help you with this is to keep a journal. Many of my close friends do it with great success. Take one day at the time, I can't say this often enough! Life is beautiful, and so are you! You set the standards for anyone to follow. You determine the speed, you are in control! All you need is a loving attitude whatever the reason is for your search. With a loving heart and a positive loving outlook on life you will accomplish anything!

And for the more experienced Martial Artist, you might ask yourself: "What does that have to do with me; I am there, aren't I?" I have heard this more than once. Well, it is my conviction that you, no matter how experienced and successful you are, should go back to the beginnings, to the basics once in a while. Not a bad thing at all to go through lessons learned a long time ago, for example. It will provide you with a better understanding of the needs and fears of the beginner standing in the dojo for the first time. And this understanding will make you a better teacher and partner. Working through old books or seminar papers keeps my mind sharp and makes me challenge myself. And from experience I can tell you: No matter how accomplished you are, reaching down is far better than pushing or looking down. Being a true Martial Artist, teaching and healing humbles me. And a true teacher **never asks**: "What is in it for me?"

There is a saying in one of the old Budo legends: 'From white to black belt you only go one step. The beginning is embedded within the end, the end lies within the beginning'. And all begins with loving and healing yourself.

Take another look at the list you wrote earlier on and check once more how far you have come. How many steps do you have left to reach your first goal? Maybe even reached some of your bigger aims already? Remember: "K.I.S.S." That is what they say in show business. It is short for "keep it simple, stupid!" Do not overdo it, do not overload yourself! You realize I keep repeating myself, but this really is important because overdoing is the number one reason people get discouraged and quit. However, you will not be alone on your path. There are always people who will give support to someone trying hard to change his/her life for the better. Even if it is only with nice 'motivation comments'. Most of them will even get involved and help you along the way. However, you may have to face critics that put obstacles into your path.

*

I probably was the first 100% handicapped youth to become a Martial Artist and, for sure, the first 100% disabled kickbox fighter and champion that has ever lived. But I had lots of barriers to overcome, not least my own physical limitations. My Grandmaster, a few close Masters and students as support group were about the only ones who believed in me! I was thrown out of tournaments several times because the promoters and judges were afraid I could hurt myself. Well, that was not the worst of all reasons to keep me outside the ring. But they were also afraid my taking part could establish a precedent for any handicapped competitor to follow in my wake! And, I was invited to my first degree black belt test five times–only to receive a 'friendly' letter just before the event telling me not to show up! It takes a lot of inner love and strength to keep going, a lot of passion not to give up and find a different sport. But had I done that, it wouldn't really have been me. Besides, Martial Arts are a way of life, not just a sport. The more they told me that I could not have it, the more I wanted it. Anyway, believe me, even today it is more than difficult for someone with limitations to take part in sportive activities of any kind!

Determined to succeed, no matter how high the mountain of rejection was that I had to face, I opened my second dojo with my childhood friend Bill Leone. But this time with all the extras that a sports and Martial Arts fan wants to find: 5000 sq. with dojo, weightlifting gym, fitness bar, showers, tanning. Many of the other gym and dojo owners in my town became annoyed because a handicapped person in those days was not supposed to work in the sports and fitness sector! I was called names, my signboards were broken, rumor was distributed around town that I would shut the dojo doors within a month. But all this did not stop my friends and me. And as the actions against us didn't cause the expected results, they gave up eventually.

I never concentrate on any bad thing happening to me, but always on what I love and where I want to be instead. And believe me, I have had many more bad experiences that could have given me enough reason to blame myself or others for my shortcomings. My Grandmasters told me from the start that it is all up to me and me alone. I took it to heart.

So, the beginning was anything but funny, for sure not a picnic. But all this trouble made me stronger. And it strengthened the bond between my friends and me! Within a year, not only did most members of my team become North German Champions several times but also the 'Top Four Hurricanes', as we called our team. The following year we won the German Team Championship of the WKA. Not long after, we started to dominate the German kickbox scene. Between 1990 and 1993 the 'Top Four Hurricanes' was one of the most successful kickbox team in North Germany.

The more critics I got through my career, the more I became determined to show them what I was made of. So do not let critics discourage you. There is no need to be a Martial Artist, only think like one. You will succeed. By the **Spirit of a real Martial Artist and with the 'Power from within'**.

Chapter: 2

Love and Peace within You, Friends – Neighbors

Those dojo-kids of mine were a wonderful crowd! Remembering the events we have been through never fails to make me happy, like this one: Our team had just won both North German Kickboxing Championships which qualified us for the South West Kickboxing Championship. A victory would take us straight to the Int. German Kickboxing Championship in Berlin, and a dream would come true. Jan, Helge, Uwe, Kim, Ingolf (my biggest sparing partner besides Uwe), Andy, Mikosh, Andrea, Heiko, Olaf and the others had trained like never before and were ready for anything that would come their way. So partying was due before the take off to Bavaria. As usual, Jan, Bill and I went around the harbor bars at about 2:00 in the morning to draw some of our youngsters gently away, bring them to the dojo and let them sleep it all off to make sure we got the whole team together for hitting the road to the south of Germany at 6:00 o'clock. We still laugh about what happened on the way.

After a long drive we stopped at a gas station close to Bavaria. While Jan was filling up our van, the rest of us went to the cafeteria. Now, Helge–known throughout his career to often win a tournament after a strong hangover finishing the fight quickly to get back to sleep, literally–and especially Ingolf had problems to keep their weight due to partying and too much junk food. I do not have to tell you that a kickboxer, just like a boxer, has to be on a strict diet, lifestyle and training program in order to keep his weight, especially eight to ten weeks before a fight. Helge and Ingolf kept their weight only just about to stay in their weight division, so that the days and hours before a competition always were the most critical for them.

Back to the cafeteria. We were all slowly moving in line towards the checkout passing these glass cases filled with pastries, chocolates, sweets and other 'goodies', when I noticed Ingolf, starved as he was, eyeballing hypnotized a large chocolate cake by the till counter. Before long he opened the glass case, grabbed the whole cake and off he went. I knew he would lose his weight division if he ate that cake. Besides, we didn't have the money to pay for it either! So what was there to do? On top of my voice I yelled across the whole restaurant: "Go and get him, block the entrance! Don't let him out!" We all started to run, Helge got hold of him from behind and I was luckily able to talk him out of the business. Slowly Ingolf handed over the cake. You should have seen the faces of the people in the cafeteria! They were probably thinking we had just escaped from a state mental home. Giving back the cake we apologized and left the place as fast as we could before the cash register lady could call the police.

Poor Ingolf lost his fight closely to the referee on points that day. I believe, he was thinking too much cake… The others all won their fights, but I was–as so often–stopped at the scales by the ring doctor. He would not allow me to fight, although I presented a letter by my MD stating best of health. So, I could only carry on with my hard training and prepare myself for the next tournament hoping, that prejudice would not prevent me from stepping into the ring again. Finally, however, I was able to convince most officials and promoters that I was fit to compete, with loving support from my team.

I think this story about Ingolf's encounter with the cake is a good example for what can be achieved with the right amount of motivation: Although my old friend did not win this particular fight, he kept his weight under control with great determination because he wanted to succeed. And he did! Next time, you feel like taking the whole cake, you may be able to find the strength to slow down a little, with a smile. Your reason could be your health, family, friends, an upcoming high school reunion, a new dress or simply a better feeling about yourself. After all, it is your life: Lead it as healthy, caring and happy as possible and there will be nobody in the world to stop you, a true champion at heart.

Did you pick up a new hobby by now? If not, get out there today. It does not really matter what you do, as long as it is healthy and makes you feel great. As long as you get out of the house a little more often and become more active. Go fishing, go surfing, take a walk in the park, ride your bike. How about a very often free evening/weekend community college class in art, English literature or painting? Isn't that, perhaps, what you have always wanted to do? Leave your loneliness behind and mix with people? One great method I used sometimes, when I felt like company, was to take my business out of the house: Instead of laboring along for weeks on end at home, I grabbed my laptop, went to a friendly coffeehouse close by, preferably with a terrace or garden, and worked there among people on my new book or a story enjoying the great Southern Californian weather with a coffee close by. More than once I got to know some interesting people on these occasions, found myself at a quick game of chess or backgammon during my coffee break. It is simple enough. You do not know how well it makes you feel, unless you try!

*

The members of my team had never really thought of setting an example. What held us together—with some it still does to this day—was the love for the sport and the friendship we felt for one another. Most of my youngsters came from low-income families or what we call in the U.S. the 'projects housing'. Some didn't have a family at all, came from an orphanage or had just gotten out. It always was tremendously satisfying to help and heal these kids. Most of them didn't have money or a place to go to. Some stayed at the dojo—literally—all day in order to keep off the streets. My friends and I always felt like family towards them. We had created a safe haven, and a lot of them became great Martial Artists and athletes.

During the week, we all trained hard, and on most weekends we went to competitions. Since we had very little money, my master students and I also worked in various night clubs so that we could afford to help and teach those kids and keep the female students safe who worked as waitresses and bartenders. But, of course, being young, we had also fun and quite a few parties that ended on the beach at dawn! I never drank any alcohol or took drugs, but that did not keep me from having a great time all night long: Dancing and then driving to the nearest beach to watch the sunrise. There is nothing wrong with having a great time. It even is essential for body and mind to have a rest in between hard work. However, it was not always an easy task to keep everyone on the lead, but we all looked after each other. And here I must pay my respects to Bill Leone, my friend since childhood, a lot like a brother, a supporter and advisor. He looked after me in his special way.

One day, for instance, he came to our dojo to check on things, when he saw me training my class of children, whose foot techniques were not the very best to put it mildly. After class, Bill took me aside and asked, why I was teaching so sloppily. I could not give him a proper explanation, so I tried to get out of it with a smart reply. He then called on our close friendship and told me off: "Just because you don't kick high and use your feet a lot, your students can have sloppy foot techniques? A student always is the reflection of his master's abilities and his character; get some books on kinesiology, body mechanics and anatomy. You know they judge yours twice as hard as they judge my students!" I took it as a challenge. After all, he was right! I read every book I could find. Through the knowledge I gained by them as well as through Geert J. Lemmens' continued education, I was then able to teach my students properly. And eventually they turned out to be great foot-technicians, which became my group's trademark even. I was really proud to hear people say: "How in the world can he teach this so well? After all, he hardly kicks, and yet his students are more kickers than punchers!" Thank you Bill, you have been a great friend.

*

Many of you are no Martial Artists or even train Martial Arts. That does not matter. There is so much more to the Arts than just fighting. The **Philosophy of Martial Arts** provides some remarkable principles and guidelines–personal rules you might call them– we live by. Through them we define ourselves, set examples for others to follow and are recognized. It is **Bushido, 'The Code of a Warrior',** handed down the generations from the old Samurais to the Masters of our time.

To become a true Master, regardless which style he practices, the Martial Artist needs in all areas of life to follow Bushido, learn, deepen his wisdom, and combine the five essential elements of Bushido in harmony. The following is my personal way of interpreting these to succeed:
LIVE (meditation) LOVE (fighting) PEACE (kata, nage) WISDOM (weapons) ARTS (rehab/herbals).

There are different techniques and forms of training–some of them thousands of years old–to deepen the Martial Artist's 'Inner Chi', wisdom, strength and therefore Shinwa (truthful/loving heart). Some of these forms and techniques date back to the old priesthood of the Shaolin monks in China or where developed in Okinawa in Japan, like the famous 'Sanshin Kata'. Other forms are: Kendo–one of my favorites; Katana–for the more advanced, sophisticated practitioner; Anis and Escrima, Sai, Philipino Knifes or Bow and Arrow. In my Karate style, 'Shin-Tora-Do' means **'The Truthful Heart of the Tiger'.** All these words have a very deep meaning for us, and we truthfully live by them every day. The Martial Artist, for sure the Master, must train professionally and with deep dedication. Furthermore, writing, reading and traveling are also essential to widen his horizon and to spread his own Master's lectures and wisdom, learning at the same time from others along his journey. Traveling and teaching have been two of my favorite parts of Bushido. When I was about 18 years old, for example, I traveled to France and had the honor to visit the dojo of Dominique Valera. And before I retire, I would like to visit

Japan at least once and walk on the paths of our legendary Grandmasters: Gogen Yamagushi, H. Kanazawa and others. For someone else the destination could be Europe or another country in Asia. Once, I rewarded my German team for their great achievements with a trip to Thailand to study the art and culture of this country. Jan, Helge, Uwe and Mikosh were among the members. It was a memorable trip! There are many great legends and wonderful stories to be found in the world of Martial Arts to learn from. One of these–a very old one–inspired me to write a story:

Bushido

One morning, Samurai Macura decided to take his son high up into the mountains, to teach him in combat. After reaching the foothills of the mountains overlooking the valley, he asked his son, "Can you tell me son, what you would do when you were surrounded by an overwhelming army!"

The son looked at his father and was quick to answer: "Attack, dad, attack!" The old Samurai smiled and shook his head. "No son!" "But dad, a Samurai will never be captured or surrender!" "That is true my son, but think of the mission that is so important to himself, to his honor and pride and to any of his family and Sempeis!"

He continued... "If the mission is of such a great importance, to himself or his shogun, remember our code of honor? Bushido...Son... he will hide, away from his loved ones. Through the high grass by the river he will make his way into the mountains, outsmart his enemies...Protect you at all cost, with his life...so be it.

"He will find his way in complete darkness, and through any enemy line, all the way up the mountains, to the small river fed from the spring of life high in the mountains. He will cross over, sit and meditate without food or water! Patiently waiting until most of his enemies have flooded by...Fast he will return to the village and complete his mission at heart.

"Shinwa! Bushido is our way." The son just looked amazed at his dad, and with a loving hug, they walked slowly down the mountain, smiling, back to the village...where many lessons waited to be learned.

Dedicated to and written about my Grandmaster, Geert J. Lemmens. L.A., CA, 06

When I was about 16 years old, I heard another story that helped me and lifted me tremendously in those difficult times. Only a very few people stood by me besides Geert Lemmens and his wife. Bill Leone was one of them. During the years that followed he helped me on my way through all the belt tests and was by my side when I finally prepared for my Black Belt test. There was quite a risk involved. After all, the JKA (Japanese Karate Association) hadn't wanted me for many years; not as a Martial Artist, not when I was going through the ranks, not even when I became a Black-Belt and teacher....

In 1945, just before the end of World War II, thousands of Japanese prisoners were transported to detention camps throughout the U.S. In one of those camps Grandmaster Gogen Yamagushi and some of his Senseis who belonged to an elite troop were detained. The wardens of this camp noticed straight away that Yamagushi was a somewhat exceptional personality: He always sat in the middle of the courtyard surrounded by his fellow prisoners who formed several circles around him; and every time he got up to leave, the others would follow. The camp's captain was uneasy about this–for him–strange behavior and told his wardens to keep a close eye on the men. This did not help, of course, to relax the extreme tension between guards and prisoners. On the contrary, the prisoners were beaten daily, were starved and got hardly any water.

The situation became unbearable and Yamagushi went, together with his Senseis, into silence as a means of protest against the treatment of his soldiers. For weeks they did not speak, perhaps only whispered to each other when necessary. And every day the camp captain watched the same routine: Yamagushi came into the courtyard, sat down and was surrounded by his men. Not a word was spoken, and when the time was up, they all disappeared in utter silence with Yamagushi in the middle. One day the captain decided to go and talk to him. As he was about to penetrate the outer circle several Senseis jumped up ready to fight! The wardens responded of course, and after a short scuffle Yamagushi raised his arm and waived the captain through to his inner circle. They sat down and Yamagushi declared the reason why he did not speak and asked for a better treatment of his soldiers. The captain nodded his head and asked for a day to consider. Yamagushi just nodded, too, and the meeting was over. He got up, they all left.

The following day the captain came to see him again. He pointed at an old but fully intact wall nearby that had once been part of a building, now ruined. "If you are able to break down this wall I will ensure better treatment and food for you and your soldiers," he said. Yamagushi nodded quietly, walked over to the wall and sat down in front of it. He stayed there, hardly moving, for two days! On the third day, after all his men had formed a semi circle around him and the wall, he suddenly jumped up, and with one Elbow-strike upwards and a loud 'Kiai' he broke down the entire wall! Needless to say, everybody was speechless. The captain stood to his word and the treatment and food became better. Later on, the captain was transferred to a different camp, and on the way out he greeted Yamagushi and his men....

For the young single mother and her teenage son, the middle-aged factory worker, the ordinary person from next door, the story about Gogen Yamagushi might seem quite unbelievable, intimidating even. I have been told sometimes my own story had a similar effect. But this is not about Yamagushi or me. This is about you! Every person, any person, has the means, the make-up, the basics, to accomplish similar things, to reach goals. And in Martial Arts you can find the means.

For many years a special training technique has been established in the business world which is called 'Keno-speaking'. The first Keno speakers came to Europe and the U.S. mainly from Japan about 15-20 years ago. Many laughed about them, then. But today, almost all 500 fortune companies employ a Keno-speaker or coach with numbers rising who teaches their employees a deeper understanding of themselves and how they can improve their productivity as well as the quality of their own life through this. A Keno-speaker and a Martial Artist use the same techniques, have the same approach; not surprising, they come from the same division! Only the Keno-speaker exercises mostly your mind. I attended several of these amazing workshops and was impressed. Every high positioned manager and CEO of any large '500 fortune company' today, world-wide, goes through Keno training and even through physical and emotional boot camps!

The Keno-speaker uses those guidelines as a tool to teach, motivate and shape any future CEO or to re-motivate CEOs and general managers (GMs), to protect them from burnouts and to cure collapse-patients around the world. Before this movement started, the average CEO- or GM-life/career limit used to be 45-50 years, early retirement and/or burnout was the rule. Nowadays the limit is almost doubled in many cases. And the productivity and motivation has improved tremendously all the way down to the average worker. Also, stock-options and pension schemes, health care 401 plans and the like have been established–all powerful incentives for better team work and productivity–which secure long term jobs and a company's future.

The philosophy of Martial Arts, its guidelines, can, of course, be applied in our day-to-day life. The guidelines can help to set aside fears, troubles and barriers, and accomplish dreams. And we can even make use of this powerful story about Gogen Yamagushi. It is not quite as difficult as you might think.

Let us take a pupil, as a first example, afraid of failing in the mid term exams. Growing up, I failed in these mid term exams lots of times, but not because I was a bad student. No, I was truly a high school junior despite being a rebel without a cause and searching for my true self. I had quite a few A's and B's across the board, but when it came to the exams I could not concentrate, even walked out a few times, before the time was up. My teachers knew and one of them helped me to break this vicious circle simply by boosting my confidence: He appointed me to the theater/drama and to the writing/reading classes. Within months I lost my shyness, became a powerful reader and, at the end of the summer, I performed 'the Angel Gabriel' before hundreds of students. My teacher hadn't been able to find anyone better suited for this role... I got over my stuttering and through that I gained confidence and, needless to say, I didn't fail the exams any more.

So, my teacher and the theater/drama coach knew exactly what I needed: They understood from the start that it was an emotional push to lose my blockade. And this is exactly the method of the professional Keno-speaker teaching the employees of a 'Fortune 500 company': Use all your resources to the best of your ability and learn within minutes from your surroundings, your family, friends, colleagues and superiors.

In every true Martial Arts style, the truthful Master always needs to teach the five essential elements of Bushido. He must widen his knowledge and wisdom and, with open, loving heart, pass them on to his students. And soon his students will do the same. If you sit back for a minute and think about your ideas and dreams, your desires and your knowledge about your own live, love and work, you will find out that there are dots you can connect. This is a simple but powerful way of analyzing your own position and of finding the right tools and paths to achievement.

Write down your first plan for the road to success. If it is not the first, just write a new one; it does not matter. And remember: This is only the beginning. To understand the meaning of those elements better, let us phrase them differently: Self-respect, self-esteem, self-confidence, self-reliance; and, at all times, truthfulness and integrity to yourself, to your GM, CEO, your company, to your family and friends. Write that down and see how many of these five elements you have already. If there are some missing, we will find out why; and in no time we will have a way that helps you to get them. I found out that nine out of ten people who come to my seminars and workshops for the first time already have all these components within them! Yet they are 100% convinced they haven't.

Through this most dissatisfying feeling they have more or less forgotten or dismissed their true potential, their dreams and desires. And not to use your full potential, simply because you don't realize that you have had it within you all along, would be a shame.

Now, imagine you have been working for a large insurance company for years; and you should have been promoted at least twice, but you were passed over. Now, due to the company's expansion in about, say, 6 months' time a fresh opportunity for promotion is heading your way. Take a moment and draw a line down a piece of paper. On the left of it–headed 'Contra'–write down the reasons that you think are responsible for being over-looked in the past. Be honest to yourself down to the bones! On the opposite side of the line–headed 'Pro'–write down why you 'know' you would have been the perfect candidate. Now compare the two columns and find what you have to look out for and what you have to work on, which of the five elements are truthfully missing and why. Do not become frustrated, if the outcome is not quite satisfying. Again, it is only the beginning. Before long your list will have changed and you will be in control of your destiny. As next step you need to know as many features and advantages of your team players as possible without any hostile looks, of course. Write them down. Make mental notes about the person in charge of the office and why he/she is the superior. Finally make a truthful assessment of what you need to do in order to get a higher position in the team.

Then, go over your 'pro/contra-list' once more and consider your most important asset: Your skills. Furthermore, think about your personal appearance, your professional attitude, the way you carry yourself. What about your social skills; how do you behave under pressure, in stress situations? These are all criteria your GM, the upper management, will consider when it comes to promoting a member of the team. So if you give them the wrong picture of yourself, you will not be promoted and therefore you will not be able to prove your worth and show everyone your strong points. That would be a shame! And this, of course, can be very frustrating. So, if you want to keep up with this fast-moving upper management circle, especially if you want to break into that circle, you should better present yourself as best you possibly can in the office and at meetings, and let the upper management find out that you are the right choice. Besides excellent skills, it is the way you handle yourself that makes the difference. It establishes a certain preconception about you on a daily basis, which you might have to overcome in order to succeed. In many cases this preconception is totally wrong, and it is completely up to you to prove who you are and what you are able to do!

A great opportunity to show your GM that you have what it takes is **not to be a 'yes-sayer'**, a conformist, a 'here-is-your-coffee' kind of person. Nobody likes this type. So, be your self. And if a problem occurs that you are convinced should be tackled in a different way, do not bend under pressure, do not shy away! Instead, find a solution and present it at the right time, at a staff meeting, for example. In other words: Be a man, be a woman! Stand up for yourself, be authentic, be original. That is how you will become a leader! And at your next presentation or semi-quarter audit you will look much stronger; you will be well prepared and therefore in better shape. And you will have a much better chance to get promoted or move closer to it. Simply by using your resources more effectively, by being much better prepared for a coming curve ball. And that is half the battle! Every good fighter prepares himself like that. Before he steps into the ring he trains hard using all his resources as best as he is able to. Not just to ensure his victory, but also his health and to eliminate as many opportunities to be defeated as possible.

A few thousand years ago, it was compelling for the Samurai to know his opponent's next move. In a sword fight, the Samurai who moved first to place his final blow was mostly the one who lost, giving his opponent a split second advantage to react, counterattack, and secure his survival.

Think like a warrior, a Samurai. Your weapons are your skills; your sword is your words, razor sharp and right on the money. Your amazing outfits and great looking suits are your shield. You are ready for any opponent. Let them make the first move; with a smile you will predict their course of action, and with brilliant accuracy you will execute the 'deathly blow'. Without injuring them, of course, only hurting their pride a little, letting them know through your unmistakable course of action, they should better count on you when the promotion is due. Believe me, your GM will notice, whether he shows it or not.

Of course, there are many mainly smaller companies and firms around that are run with the motto: "If it is not broken, don't fix it", or that are run by GM's and CEO's who think they are a class of their own and are therefore not interested in the forthcoming of anyone 'down below'. In these cases it would be very difficult, if not impossible for you as an ordinary employee to develop and climb the career ladder. But this surely also applies to those companies and firms, because 'non-development' in any department doesn't lead to a successful future in the long run! At least that is what I believe. If you are in such a position, there is little you can do, except perhaps gain as much knowledge and experience in your field of work as possible and then move on to a more suitable employer.

I am well aware that this is not easy. However, there are a number of possibilities available to put your career into your own hands, to further your education in order to improve your chances, and, of course, this applies to the 'promotion seeker' as well: Weekend community colleges, for example, or tech-colleges, educational and motivational seminars and workshops. You will find out quickly that attending one of those takes care of several things at once: Education, self-motivation, self-appearance and self-confidence. After you successfully completed one or more of these exciting seminars, classes or workshops, make sure you include them in your personal profile. If you do not have one, draw one up before the end of today and have it ready for anyone–may it be a superior or a prospective new employer–who wants to check your educational background or special skills. This is another fine way to separate yourself from the crowd. You will look good, much better than last year; and soon you will become a hot-handed person for the upcoming promotion or the vacancy to be filled. And with it comes a totally different outlook on your career; it opens new possibilities: More interesting job, higher position, better payment, better life.

There is an old saying in Martial Arts: 'If the prophet doesn't come to the mountain, the mountain will move and come to him, if his beliefs are true of heart, without a price. So, most of the time, it is just a question of how badly you want that particular change. With strong motivation and the right view on life, things come together, changes happen and family, friends, even colleagues, encourage you, lend you a helping hand, before you know it.

Gogen Yamagushi would never have earned respect from his men and the captain without will-power and determination. He would surely not have been able to break down that wall, protect his fellow soldiers and save the lives of some of them. Whatever ability it is that lets you choose your actions, the important point is that you do it! Without hesitation or second thoughts. If you don't, you will lose or simply be forgotten in our fast moving world. Small and big problems, tiny and large goals appear in a micro-cosmos which we call our own life. We share it with others. Therefore we depend on one another, and need interaction. Have you ever tried to play a soccer or basketball match all by yourself? It is quite silly. And, be truthful to yourself, wouldn't you have a lot more fun playing with a handful of people or, even better, with the whole team?   .

To summarize: You can go far, if you put your mind to it! 'The Sky is only the Front door' regardless what anyone else says or thinks! You are the one who decides! The success stories of some of my students and Master Students are fine examples. A number of them were severely handicapped by birth or by an accident. Eden, for instance, or Master Student Jessica, who had removed tremendous obstacles from her path. Michelle is another, or World-Self-Defense Karate Champion Marine Clinton Cloudle who is 100% disabled and bound to a wheel chair due to a car accident, an amazing person and athlete from Mid Cities, TX. They not only show that anything is possible; they also contribute to a good reality check. They have continuously done this to me and I have always felt privileged to teach those remarkable youngsters and athletes. But it would not have been half the fun without my wonderful assistants.

Or take even my example. About 25 years ago, when I started my journey, it was not my intention to become a 'trail-blazer'. The reason why I decided to walk this path simply was: I wanted to be accepted and respected. And the more they told me I couldn't have it, I couldn't be part of the Martial Arts circle and compete, the more I wanted it, the harder I worked. And finally, I was able to clear the way for the ones walking after me.

*

The following is one of my favorite quotations that I relate to my beginner students:

Choice
Winning or losing is not a maybe or a sometimes. Winning is a lifestyle, which you are the one to become accustomed to, if you decide to do so! In anyone lies a born winner or loser. Which one you are, is your choice to make!
Peace–Love–Wisdom is Shinwa! Sensei, Anthony v. Sager LA CA 05

There can be situations in life, however, when you feel there is no such choice to make: I was about 13 years old, when I lost my mother, one of the most wonderful women and mothers who had ever lived, if you ask me–Ingeborg Schiel, former beauty queen from Vienna, Austria (Miss Vienna, runner up Miss Austria), an amazing pianist and painter. And yet, life had not made it easy for her. In 1958, she had become the rape victim of a famous former actor in New York, a horrific crime that left her deeply scarred. And despite her struggles to overcome this terrible experience, despite her kind and caring heart, despite her outstanding talents and beauty, she was hardly ever treated with love and respect. Why perfidious males, radicals and terrorists always pick helpless women and people who are unable to defend themselves is beyond me! Weak small manhood! Later, this has given me a life-long motivation to help those people and to be as strong and powerful as possible to be able to put anyone in need in a better place in life.

In the spring of 1977, my mother went on a business trip to South Africa to buy jewelry. She was tricked into this, out of the blue, by her former boyfriend, an abuser, a wolf in sheepskin, Gerd K. She trusted him…and was kidnapped and dragged back to Europe, where her trail of suffering finally disappeared forever, leaving her children, she had loved so much, alone. Needless to say, this tragedy put my brother and me into hell's fire and we could hardly cope. Before this, we both had already gone through difficult times: My brother was highly intelligent, even skipped a whole year at junior high school, but was extremely sensitive and hard to be kept within reality. The fact that he had never met his natural father added to his vulnerability. And I had difficulties through my handicap.

So, it is not surprising that we turned into rebels. Rebels without a course revolting against everything and everyone just to give air to our despair and frustration. Our grades dropped quicker than the thermometer in the desert at nightfall. We behaved horrifically, and although we didn't bully anyone around, we were glad when we were picked for a fight. By the end of the school year both of us had become regular visitors at the dean's office and numerous meetings had been held in our honor. About me, opinions were voiced like: 'What the hell is this crippled worm thinking he is; he can call himself lucky to be allowed at this school; if it was up to me he would be put away into an elementary school for retarded cripples; they should never have let him out in the first place'. Too bad I heard all this; they must have thought me deaf! So there we were, close to Christmas and about to be thrown out of school. Our father wanted to take us home, but the woman that lived with him hated children and put a lot of pressure on him to give us away. The Child Services took over and we found ourselves in an orphanage….

Tragedies happen far too often. Very personal ones, and tragedies involving many people. Lives are lost, destruction spreads. Think of Chernobyl, of Columbine, 911, Hurricane Katrina, of tsunamis in Asia, volcano outbreaks and of wars. We face these helplessly and hope for a miracle to happen. However, faith and inner strength are among the greatest qualities of human kind. And I am a firm believer that we are all connected to and influenced by each other in many ways, but most of us don't realize this anymore, and are reminded, perhaps, only when disaster strikes and the walls and borders we so successfully built, disintegrate. It is just too bad that it often has to come to such harsh measures before we get together and interact.

Even more so, when disaster, violence and destruction could have been avoided, could have been prevented. Like the LA riots in the early 1990's, for example. They supposedly started with a sandwich thrown into an Afro American man's face; rude words followed, then a scuffle and the rest you could see on the TV news. So sad and unnecessary. Every time I hear about such terrible events, I hope it will not happen again. Surely, we learned from this one? I cannot provide an overall solution; I am far from it. But I am convinced we can all do something about it starting in our own small world.

It is a matter of our own personal choice: We can stand aside and watch things taking their course, afraid to become active, get involved or, even worse, become part of the negative happenings. Or we can walk a different path. This was done, as an example, in a big sense, when the Geneva Statutes of Humanity were established to bind our modern democracies together. However, things sound great on paper, but it is up to the individual to bring them into the day-to-day life. How about you? When did you last visit your father or grandmother, a sick friend? When did you last volunteer your time for any kind of charity organization or activity? Been a long time? Never happened? It is a wonderful way of catching two flies at the same time: You get yourself out the house and become part of something very special. Many of my Master Students and I have been involved in various charities for many years, and there has never been a reason to regret it! On the contrary!

So, we can change things for the better and help the ones next to us with compassion and with inner strength. As a result–this will spread like a flu infecting everyone around us, because it generates a positive air. We can create peace within ourselves, and inner peace certainly also means world peace.

World – Love – Peace
Words alone do not hurt! Hateful people using them do...
If you love people; choose to not hear their words...
Therefore, with loving heart, peace to the world!
Sensei, Anthony v. Sager LA, CA 05

And this brings us back to Martial Arts and Bushido: In every true Martial Arts style, the truthful Master does not only need to follow Bushido and combine its elements through-out his life in complete harmony, he also needs to teach these elements. He must widen his knowledge and wisdom and, with open loving heart, pass them on to his students. And the truthful student needs to learn from his Master continuously combining these ele-ments in order to achieve the complete harmony between them. If he concentrates on only, say, one or two, because he, perhaps, prefers them, he will become strong in these and can surely succeed when he competes, as a good puncher or kicker, as example. But not for long. Neglecting the other elements will result in an imbalance. And sooner or later, he will not only endanger his overall health, but also fail and be fast forgotten. He will certainly not become a true Master and reach 'Inner Chi', inner peace. Well, first Inner Chi is not a new cool 'Chi-Laté Ice tea. It is not something you can buy.

As a non-Martial Artist, how can I achieve inner peace, 'Inner Chi'? Can I lose it again? Can I regain 'Inner Chi' after I lost it? Of course, all of this is possible. The same applies to self-love and the feeling of being loved. It can be compared to a rare flower: It is hard to come by; as a matter of fact, it needs skills and research to discover this wonder-ful thing. Which doesn't mean, of course, it is unreachable for the ordinary person! It simply means it is not for sale, it cannot be gained overnight. You have to discover it, work for it and earn it. Do not bother yourself with 'ifs' and 'whens'. This is not the approach of a winner, surely not of a Martial Artist. It would only cause the emotional setup for an upset and a self-programmed failure; you would only prepare yourself for the fall-down in the end. In the world of a true Martial Artist, of a Master for certain, it is all about earning pride and honor. Do you like the reputation of our manufacturers here in the U.S.? The label 'made in the USA' used to stand for high quality products, and for pride. But over the last decades Asian and European producers have taken the leading role in the International market of quality products and have pushed the American manu-facturers down the ladder! Can this movement not be reversed? But how? I think it is simple: With pride and craftsmanship, just as it used to be. What does that have to do with 'Inner Chi'? More than you might imagine. If our workforce is unhappy, underpaid and overworked, 'Inner Chi' will be a hard thing to come by. And I believe in order to achieve inner peace; it is of great importance to build the foundation for it at your place of work and at your home to ensure as much harmony as possible in your life.

Did you know, by the way, that the Japanese car manufacturers Mitsubishi are descendants from an ancient Samurai family? Having Keno-speaking and Bushido in mind, this tells you a lot about why the company is extremely successful in our modern industrial world.

Remembering what was said about making changes and reaching goals, about the rules of Bushido, we close the circle. With all this pieced together you will find 'Inner Chi'. And with 'Inner Chi–and with pride–you will be able to make more changes and reach even your highest goals. Again, the journeys of many of my students, and my own, are good examples. They show that anything is possible. And let me assure you once more, we are all just ordinary people like 'you and me'!

*

Being handicapped, it wasn't easy throughout my career. Whenever I took part in a competition, I had to watch out for the judges and ring doctors, because prejudice and preconception were never far away, especially during the early years. Therefore, most of the victories I was able to achieve tasted like real triumph. These, for instance:

One of my biggest goals of those days I could reach in 1997 with the help and support from my dear friend Mihran Aghvinian–the ticket to the World Karate Championship in Colorado Springs, CO. It was at the 'Legends' in Dallas, Texas. That is one of, if not the oldest, Karate Championships in the U.S.. It was initiated in 1966 in Washington DC by Bruce Lee and J. Pat Burleson and supervised by Joon Ree as promoter. The 'Legends' was such a prestige event that all big names of the trade were on the starter list from Canada down to Mexico and Venezuela, even current world champions; it was actually more on the level of a world championship; a fact that made our taking part in it a real 'treat'!

I could win the self-defense-category in my division and–an absolute highlight–the second place in the self-defense, with partner, category (choreographed with music) with Mihran. We competed with 14 (!) Black Belt-couples; and it was only by a small margin we were beaten by one of my greatest Karate idols: Grandmaster Prof. Dan Baker. It was my greatest accomplishment so far; and to lose against a man like him really was more an honor than anything else. After all, he was already World Champion before I was born!

At the end of the competitions Prof. Dan Baker, Clinton Cloudle, Mihran and I found ourselves up on the main stage once again. The promoters would not let us go without a demo. Standing ovations accompanied our exit, it was an indescribable experience. However, as so many times before, the judges in my last category of this memorable event– Black Belt-men over 75 kg–didn't see my partaking in a favorable light. The first fight I won five points to zero before the two minutes were over, there was no room for doubts. But in the second the judges gave me only two of the five points I was quite sure I had made. So, I became second in the end. No matter! The event itself was a wonderful experience, and I achieved what I had come for: The qualification for the Karate World Title tournament. I can hardly describe my feelings that day; never had I wanted anything more than a shot at this title after all those years of hard training.

Naturally, the six months following the 'Legends' were filled with intense work. I trained three to four hours a day, six days a week, and on top of that taught my students and exercised with Clinton Cloudle, determined to take him with me. He is paraplegic through a car accident. Later, I will tell you more about this outstanding man who surely re-wrote history by his exceptional achievements! He was also qualified for the World Karate Championship in Colorado by winning the self-defense, with partner, category (with me as his partner) in Dallas as well as the National Hurricanes in Galveston, TX. So, the training was hard to say the least, but, after all, we prepared ourselves for the most important career mark in our lives. We met at his house four times a week, where we had built a complete gym and dojo on the back porch. The greatest pleasure was to invent self-defense moves and attacks that fitted Clinton's limited range of movement perfectly. I can truly say he was without doubt my best student in TX, ever.
Jonathon Wells, another member of our team, was, as always, a great help to me during those months as well.

My great pride throughout my career has always been to have never used a self-defense, Kata or Nage form, twice! For two reasons: Firstly, the judges would not get tired of my appearance; and secondly, even more important, my opponents would not be able to copy my style and/or make up a similar form to beat me at my own game–therefore I had the advantage of surprising them.

Another method of playing up opponents I used was to walk around by the ringside self-assured and confidently as if I was the one who had owned the division for the last couple of years. Quite often, this 'showing off' resulted in a moment's hesitation of my opponent before executing a move, because I was generally underestimated through my handicap. So, I had an advantage and I could finish him off or get ahead in points. Well, I learned from the best, from 'ALI', the greatest!

However, being underestimated is one thing, prejudice is another. More than once I was told by opponents I should not be in the ring in the first place. I believe hardly anyone can truly say that he/she has never prejudged a person. But categorizing people by their appearance, their looks, their cultural background, their nationality, without readiness to give them a chance, can only be wrong. Many justify this attitude with experiences of some kind or other they have or had with an individual. Sadly, history and the present are full of examples with fatal effects. There is a rather extreme case of prejudice, which worries me still: I was just about to leave an air plane carrying a couple of trophies I had won at a National, as a little boy of about five who was carried by his father asked me about those trophies. Since I never had any problems with children–on the contrary–I smiled and told him about the Karate tournament. The child looked at me in surprise and seemed to consider what I had just said, as his father whispered something like 'real bad ass, congratulations' into his ear whereupon the boy raised his hand, pointed it at me like a pistol and said loudly 'bang'. I was shocked and the father apologized. I told him that I was rather more shocked about what his son seemed to have in mind than about what he actually did; and that he should work on that, because it was clearly a reflection of his surroundings and his neighborhood. The man turned and left the airplane quite quickly with his son. Let's hope, that remark made the father think and do something about it! Otherwise his son might have a real pistol in his hand and use it, perhaps under pressure, in his later years and think it perfectly justified.

Not long ago, Harvard University conducted a study about human behavior and interaction with alarming results that reflect the little boy's manner very well: The scientists selected 15.000 men from all levels of society and asked them if they loved their wives/partners/girlfriends. They all answered with 'yes'! Further questions about their relationship and/or family life produced the following result: Of the 15.000 men, about 5000 were convicted for beating the hell out of their women and for raping them. About 5000 did not abuse their partners physically but emotionally, partly in a most terrifying manner. Only the remaining men never abused their women and had a loving relationship with them. And yet, all 15.000 men swore they loved their partner dearly! Do you think the love was healthy and truthful in all three groups? So, when does the vicious circle of violence start and how is it imitated? Think of that father's comment and his son's seemingly natural reaction to it....

Chapter: 3

Wisdom – within Yourself – for Others – the World

Desert Dream

Let me tell you, my friends, how it all began: One night I saw myself wandering thru the desert. After days I was still wandering, burning hot thru the day, freezing cold at night. One morning I was not sure, was I seeing a mirage or not...? So I pulled together all my strength, with my last breath and energy I could drag myself closer. I did not fantasize, it was an oasis. "Praise the Lord," I yelled out... Stumbling, running, falling, I made it into the outer circle of the oasis. All of a sudden I stopped. I began to recognize a lot of old friends, school bullies, enemies and some strangers I did not know. All seemed to live here, never moved, never left, just took up space. Drying out the well, the spring of life, the reason for all of us to be...

As I finally arrived at the well, I noted the dangerously low water level and just splashed a little on my face. Someone said from behind, "Don't you want to stay, relax, enjoy it while it lasts?!" I replied, walking away, "No thanks ...you guys need it most, much more than I ever will."

And so I continued my journey alone...thru the cold desert night...

Let the moon be my friendly guide...

Sensei, Anthony v. Sager 86/93 LA, CA

You have never seen a fitness studio from the inside? Let alone a dojo? Not even gone jogging? And therefore can't possibly compare your situation or life with mine? I believe you already know better. Every one of us has to, or wants to, move obstacles out of the way in order to reach whatever it is. And at the end of the day, it is irrelevant what sort of obstacles there are: For you it may be your feeling of inferiority; an unpleasant neighbor who has to be dealt with; your indecisiveness; a difficult relationship. You do not need to end up in a ring fighting for a world title. It does not matter. But what matters is that you handle your life as if you did and prepare yourself! You would not step into the ring to fight a heavy weight champion without being a 100% prepared. It would be a threat to your health if not your life. So, why would you walk through your career, your private life without complete preparation, willing and able to use your full potential at all times? To go all the way, no less?

It always makes me sad, almost angry, when I meet people who could be ten times more successful and happy, if they weren't so careless or if they would try to reach their full potential. What a waste! This applies to career as much as to health and love. You say, "I gave all I got and that's it, that's as far as I can go". But is that really true? Are your sources of energy exhausted? And can you truly say, "I am happy and contented"? Or is it only a compromise, a feeling of defeat, even? Do not think about trying to pin this on someone else or on certain circumstances. You are the one who is able to move and change things. You could be the leader, the champion of your own kingdom to come. So get up and get going. The finishing line is closer than you might realize! It is all within you! You are the one who can step on the road to success.

One of the favorite quotations of my Grandmaster Geert J. Lemmens is: **"A true fighter comes out of any possible defeat even stronger than before. He/she will learn to change from within returning stronger and more powerful than he/she was before. Like the true champion he/she is at heart".**

*

Let me take this moment to tell you a little more about my childhood. I can imagine it will make your feel much better about yourself, much stronger. And you might just count your blessings, perhaps become a better teacher, mentor or parent…

When I was 13 years old my brother and I were thrown into an orphanage at the northern end of Germany. I already told you how that had come about. To make matters worse the Child Services then decided to take my brother away from me and send him to another equally terrible place far down in the south. Confused, lonely and very angry, I did not want to get involved with anything or anyone; and I was so tight that smiling wasn't part of my face expressions.

There was a swim club at school and most pupils took part it in one way or the other. But since I was the only handicapped youth, nobody even bothered to ask me if I was able to swim or would like to learn. Convincing myself that it did not make any difference to me, I hung about only watching the fun in and at the swimming pool from a distance.

However, one day the kids talked the lifeguard into opening the 10-meter jump tower. Everybody went up there, of course, to have a go; and the older boys were showing off their skills trying to impress the girls. Sitting in my lonely corner, I could suddenly not cope with my isolation any longer; I needed to do something. And since I have always been a dare devil, no matter what the challenge may be–like 'move first, think later'– I simply got up then and walked slowly over to the tower The lifeguard was about to stop me, of course, but our coach signaled him to let me pass. So I scrambled up that metal ladder and it took me at least 5 minutes before I reached the top. In the meantime, the lifeguard had stopped the other pupils to give me some extra space. When I finally arrived at the jump board, holding on to the handle bars as if my life was at stake, I realized how high this tower was and how far away the water below! My legs began to cramp up straight away and I felt sick. Surely, this would turn into a nightmare haunting me for the rest of my days at that school, let alone the orphanage. So, I took a deep breath and dragged myself forward to the spot where the handle bars end. I probably stood there for 5 minutes or more trying to calm myself down, praying for my legs not to give up on me. Finally some youths who had come up behind me were shouted at: "Get him down from there". That was the kick I needed. I just let go of the handlebars and moved slowly out to the edge of the jump board and jumped, head first.

It was a perfect header. I dived into the water and all the way down to the bottom of the pool. Getting back up was a different story. I could not push myself off the ground with my legs and panicked. I am not sure how I made it to the surface; it seemed to take a lifetime. On my very last breath, I reached the edge of the pool and was helped up by the lifeguard. It then slowly dawned on me how much effort the adventure had taken and that I had only just escaped catastrophe. I was shaking all over with exhaustion and relief, but got an unexpected reward: The coach, and even some of the kids, came over and congratulated me patting my back. And later that week the coach who was also our PE teacher asked me if I would like to join the swim-class although without a real chance to become a member of the team; but that should not stop me from training with the other pupils, he added. So I was accepted in some way. But, even better, I was provided with a chance to get rid of all my anger and frustration, 'swim' them off as it were; and during the weeks that followed I began to feel like a member of the group. I still wasn't able or willing to make friends, not even to socialize in any way, which made it difficult for anyone to even try. Besides, many had problems getting used to me being a member of the swim-class, officially or not.

It was the coach I opened up to first. He always treated me with respect and kindness taking no notice of my handicap. Later on, I learned he was a Russian political refugee who had escaped the socialist regime through the 'Iron Curtain' into the West; and a high ranking Jiu Jitsu and Karate Master–a touch of destiny you could call this. He told me I was a natural swimmer and taught me the basics of free-style and breaststroke techniques and to use my immense arm- and upper body-strength; and soon the short distances of 50 and 100 meters became my specialty. We trained three times a week and my 'colleagues' began to accept me, even started to be quite nice to me. I forgot all my problems for a while and felt I was part of something for the first time in a long period of my life. But the greatest blessing of all was the fact that the swim-training got me away from the 'Rock' as the orphanage was called: 120 unfortunate children, 30 girls and 90 boys; three fights a day just to get enough food to go on.

Water was a natural element to me and since I had been a decent swimmer before, my coach's teaching turned me into a free-style specialist to be noticed; with the result of being invited to join the school competition-team but without a promise to take part in a tournament. What an improvement to my situation! It almost put a smile on my face. Now I had something to work for and to really look forward to; moreover, it meant as well to be in the swim-hall most weekends and away from the 'Rock' even longer than before.

All went well and I felt something almost equal to happiness until I received the first letter from my brother. He had always been emotionally unstable and easy to influence. And his few lines showed me in a terrifying way that he had become the perfect prey for 'punk kids' with no wisdom to spare, nothing to lose, a bag of drugs in the pocket promising a lost and lonely child the quick fix, the numbing of his pain. I was frightened and desperate, couldn't sleep, and when I did, had terrible nightmares. Sick with worry I needed to do something and wrote letters to my father, my Child Services caseworker and to my brother trying to lift him up again somehow. All this came on top of my never ending fight for a position at the dinner table in order to get anything to eat–and I mean anything–and the desperate efforts to defend myself against daily and nightly attacks from kids in the orphanage and at school who thought me a useless and worthless cripple and therefore easy prey. This is, perhaps, difficult to believe, but back in those days, it was that bad!

It only took a week before my swim coach asked me to stay behind after training. He was the only one I liked. So, somehow trusting him, I let the coach sit me down in a quiet corner to tell him what was wrong with me, assuring me before that everything would stay between the two of us. The whole story came out, then: The events leading to my being in an orphanage, the worry and fear about my brother and everything else that weighted down my mind. The coach listened compassionately without interrupting me at all and then encouraged me to keep writing letters to my brother, which might help him to ease his mind and get away from bad company. "Not all youngsters are born fighters," he said, "but you certainly are one. You mastered your fear, overcame the spastic cramps in your legs and jumped from a 10-meter tower. That is the attitude of a real champion. And you can learn to live with a situation and accept the things you are not able to change for now. Concentrate on the positive aspects in your life like our swim-team, for instance". The coach smiled then and hugged me.

I do not think I really have to tell you that his speech helped tremendously! I took a deep breath and promised him to try. He gave me an approving nod and then said: "Next time I will tell you my story, how I lost half my family and fled the Soviet Union and the Eastern Block States with only an aunt and a sister left". I was stunned, this sounded like a 'James Bond' movie. Hardly anyone made it through the 'Iron Curtain' alive, at least no one I had heard of! Growing up with the 'Eastern Block' we were all hearing and reading horror stories, heart-breaking reports about people who where shot trying to make it through the 'Iron Curtain', trying to get across the 'Wall' in Berlin, over the high barb wire fences into the West. "And that, also, will be only between you and me, okay?" he added. I promised and went to change, as my bus was about to pull up to take me back to the 'Rock'. All of a sudden that didn't bother me as much as usual anymore. I couldn't wait to hear his story and the following weekend went by faster than normal; even the daily worries seemed less threatening. And perhaps he shared it with me just for that reason.

In fact, I was looking forward to go to school on Monday. There was quite a big gang fight going on that day, though, which wasn't really unusual. Of course, all youngsters from the orphanage were ordered to report to the principal after lessons, being his favorite offenders! I was lucky enough to sneak into the bus beforehand; otherwise, I would have missed the swim training. But it was as sure as anything the principal would pull me into his office at the next occasion, no matter how trivial that might be, just for kicks and for making his point. I belonged to a group of people he would gladly throw out of his school if he was allowed to, just to give an example. My name held the top position on his list of unwanted kids since I was not only from the 'Rock' but also handicapped. The only thing he needed me to do was to look the wrong way in order to stamp me an offender making sure everybody would know! There was a name for people like him in parts of Europe from 1938 on…I am convinced that he was overlooked when the big 'clean up' was going on after the war had ended. Believe me, I do not exaggerate. The way this man behaved is beyond imagination. He terrorized and humiliated children on a daily basis, traumatizing many of them for the rest of their lives just to get his kick. He and the warden of the orphanage could have been brothers; they were surely made of the same disgusting material. It took a lot of strength and determination not to let them get at me, harass me, merely because I was forced to live in the 'Rock' or because of the way I walked.

Surely, we children without loving parents and family never learned to socialize in a healthy way from those two! On the contrary! The only thing we learned was to fight for survival; and these fights were not always altogether legal, which didn't improve our reputation and certainly didn't take away the prejudice we were faced with. So, whenever a more serious crime was committed like heavy theft or assault, two police cars would draw up at the 'Rock' within an hour after school and interrogation would start in the warden's office and last for hours, because the policemen were convinced they would find their criminal among us. And if the offence was theft, all our quarters would be raided and trashed: mattresses and blankets would be sliced, lockers ripped, our belongings thrown to the floor. It did not matter whether anything was found; anyone who might have been involved was grounded for weeks, all privileges taken away and deprived of dinner at least that day. None of us ever had a fair chance and the wrong behavior of perhaps one always reflected on all of us.

However, that particular Monday I was lucky enough to have escaped trouble and the afternoon at the pool turned out to be a real treat: For the first time I trained with the school-competition-team. And what a training that was! 15 lanes Olympic-sized pool and after each lane we had to get out the water and do 5 push-ups, altogether 75 push-ups; and then 15 lanes free-style, with push-ups in between as well, of course. The coach had offered me to skip those, but I was determined to make it, even if it took me as twice as long to get out of the water and back in again as my colleagues. It was a hell of a workout, but I just about made it right to the end. You can imagine, I was actually happy, though very tired.

After training, the coach took me aside and congratulated me to my determination. Then he told me his story that humbles me to this day: His whole family had been thrown into jail and tortured several times because of their different political views opposing the socialist regime and its inhuman treatment of the population. At one point things became a matter of life or death; and he had to leave his family, his life, everything behind, could only take his aunt and sister and flee the country never to be able to return. I was speechless! All of a sudden my personal problems seemed less difficult to bear, for sure a lot easier to tackle. I asked him how they had made it through the 'Iron Curtain', and he continued his story that seemed to me good enough for a Hollywood movie: Through dark night, across minefields and barbwire, against all odds. As soon as they put their feet on West German soil, the guards were not able to follow them or shoot; and shaking and crying they walked down the road to freedom.

After the coach had finished I could only just sit there with open mouth. So, a real hero was sitting there beside me on the bench. I had thought him tough and strong before, but not like this. I felt honored when he said he did not usually talk about this period of his life; and he asked me to keep it to myself as well. Now we had something very special between us, he knowing my story, I knowing his. Exhausted but truly happy about so much trust I made my way to the locker room.

Of course, I could not stop thinking about the story, my imagination ran wild. As soon as our bus drew up at the orphanage, though, reality hit hard: Two police cars were parked on the driveway. At least this time I should be out of trouble. I had not been involved in the gang fight at school that morning, and I hoped the police and the warden would leave me alone. But I couldn't care less, really, because I was still with my coach deceiving border guards, jumping over fences to freedom.

Later I found out the coach had been a member of the Russian national swim-team and had taken part in competitions in former East Germany. Maybe, I thought, through this he had been able to make friends with someone who had later helped him to escape. It was still a mystery, but my coach had promised to tell me more details. But surely, wouldn't he then endanger this possible friend to be found out and sentenced to death? My imagination was working overtime. To honor this exceptional man and the trust he had put on me I trained as hard as I could during the following weeks. Also, to show myself and the other swimmers in the class that I had what it takes to succeed.

*

Let us take a break for a moment and reflect. Quite likely, I had it in me from the beginning to become an athlete despite my handicap. But every talent, big or small, needs stimulation, promotion and support to unfold and turn into a success story. That's where the 'Angels at work' come in: Those wonderful people who help you along the way, enhance the process, give a little push in the right direction to become the winner you always wanted to be and to promote the build-up of a lasting foundation from where you can start to gain confidence, self-esteem, self-love and inner peace.

But the development of a detected talent doesn't seem to be all that easy in our world. Do you know many football or basketball super stars or founders of trade empires who grew up with a silver spoon, tucked away in a million-dollar mansion in Beverly Hills? Hardly. Is hardship needed, poverty, harsh surroundings, violence, in order to become a super star? Or is there only a difference in interests and ideas between a Beverly Hills child and a kid from the slums? I do not think so. For the slum kid it seems the only way out of misery: Work through all barriers, be stronger, cleverer, faster and, above all, be able to take a lot of pain. And the Beverly Hills child? He/she will most likely be groomed for a different life style full of noble education, plenty of opportunities and protected from any challenge too hard to bear.

Every child, any child, should have the right to be put on the path of life that corresponds to their ideas, interests and talents. But reality is totally different, as we all know, because society is still quite locked within a framework of convention, status, racism and prejudgment. One more reason for us adults to watch out for the children in our lives, become one of those 'Angels at work' and encourage, help and support them getting on their way, realizing dreams, ideas, developing their abilities, becoming who they want to be: An athlete, the next CEO of a 'Fortune 500 company' or a famous concert pianist, no matter what their social background is!

So, once again, self-love leads to more inner peace; and inner peace leads to more wisdom. And wisdom enables you to make wiser and healthier decisions on your way through life. I always was a dare devil and great risk taker, and I probably still am. More than once, I came very close to breaking down, to hurting myself, to making a fool out of myself. However, I would not have succeeded without giving all I got and trying as hard as I could, because my efforts were noticed by my special 'Angels at work': My junior high drama and theatre teacher, for instance, or my Grandmaster and his wife, my friends Jo Jacobson and Bill Leone and, for sure, my swim coach! They all and others later in my life saw the fire burning within me, the powerful force of inner strength, raw but pure, that needed direction, and my will power. And they gladly helped me!

Think back and remember your own 'Angels': Perhaps a teacher, your mother, father, grandparents, a mentor, a coach, or just a neighbor who happened to be there at the right moment to say the right words. Walk down memory lane–it is a wonderful thing to do–and think of the positive influence they all, or some of them, had on you growing up, preparing for a career, marriage or life in general. Some of you might come up with quite a long list of people who put you on the right track in one way or the other. Often, we forget them or simply take them for granted. Or we only realize what they have done for us, when they are gone. Most of them do not mind, they simply do what they believe is necessary from the depths of their hearts. Like my swim coach who was one of the first to unlock my true potential; or, not long after, my drama and theatre teacher. Although I remember those two well and honor their mentoring and teaching work, I cannot remember their names. I am not even sure I would recognize them, if I ran into them.

It is a bit sad, really, don't you think? This fits so well our western cultures and democracies. Everybody seems to expect the good deeds: The free education, government welfare and health care, the friendly and prompt response of police and fire brigade, the lights in the streets. After all, we pay our taxes, don't we? And we are responsible citizens, aren't we? So, why do we point an accusing finger at others when something goes wrong, when something shakes our precious little world? Are we responsible? As long as we can write a check for the next disaster relief fund, for a child support organization or a wild life protection scheme, we have done our duty, haven't we? But how much is enough and how little is too little? What is our responsibility and what must a government do? Or is a government not our responsibility as well? Do not get me wrong; writing a check is a generous and kind thing to do! However, can't we do more? Get involved personally? I believe it is the responsibility of human beings in general to take part actively in the shaping of our social and political landscape, to protect it and lend a helping hand where it is needed.

So, do not just provide a bit of money. Donate your time, your expertise, your equipment or your ideas and become part of a movement to improve all our lives. It is so much more rewarding and a wonderful feeling to be able to say: "I have really done something. I have put myself into it!" Now this would be human interaction and responsibility, one of the highlights for us as democratic citizens, for sure! And it would be for free as well. If you do not want to do that, because you are too busy with your own affairs, well, so be it. But don't sit in a bar and complain!

In most of our democracies, you are given certain rights by birth. These should not be abandoned; it would be a sin. And they should never be taken for granted or neglected either! I myself was not aware of some of them until I started to travel around the world as a young man. I met with hunger, poverty, misery and despair not only of individuals but of entire populations. It was a mind-opening experience! It taught me a lot about myself and helped me to build my personality and widen my horizon! But I didn't travel around locked in a tour bus with dozens of tourists taking photographs. And I certainly didn't end up in a hotel room watching TV and emptying the mini bar. No, that would surely be a bad dream for me. Don't get me all wrong. A bus tour can be great, especially for seniors. But what do you learn about a country, about the people, their lives, their culture, their native tongue, if you are taken to one spot of general interest to another just on roads? I never had large sums of money at my disposal. I always traveled light with a few bucks in my pocket and a plain ticket for the destination of my choice. I earned money along the way if needed, stayed with friends, even with strangers. Wonderful people I met that way and came to know things, you do not find in travel agents' brochures.

What I am trying to tell you is: Break away from your beloved boring routine and get out there. Try something new, be adventurous, be an explorer. You will not regret it. The whole world is waiting for you to be discovered. You will come back as a different person. Maybe you do not even want to come back at all, because you found something out there that brings the best of you to the surface and makes you happy! If you wait until you have plenty of money, until it fits in with your career, your family life, you might never do it. You might never follow your dreams, because a new car, a washing machine or a certain period of your life must be dealt with first. It would really be a shame. Life is so short, and you never know when it will end. So, get going. Start to take care of yourself and your dreams right now. You do not really want to sit in your rocking chair one day, perhaps old, lonely, miserable and even ill and ask yourself, "What did I do with my life? Why didn't I do what I always wanted to do? Now, it's too late." Of course, it is never too late to change direction; at least I believe that. But the earlier you build up the healthy foundation I talked about before, the longer you benefit from it and the farther you can go; especially after injury or sickness you will see and feel the difference!

*

That brings me back to my swim coach who helped me to do just that: Build a foundation, which I was able to use as a jump board into a happier future. So, returning to the story, I was working hard to show myself and everybody else what I was able to do. After several months of bone breaking training, I was awarded by my coach who asked me if I would want to join in with the time-training of the relay-teams, just for an additional workout, and he explained what it was all about: "It is real team work. The five members of a team swim 50 meters, one after the other. The timing starts with the first swimmer jumping into the water and is stopped when the last swimmer touches the edge of the pool." I was thrilled: 50 meters free-style against the clock, five lanes, five teams competing. What I have to explain at this point is that I was not able to jump into the water like the others due to my handicap. Therefore, I needed two teammates to hold me upright and then to push me forward into the water at the right moment, a fact that made my partaking in the relay-training the more rewarding.

It was decided that I should be the last swimmer of my team; and I was immensely tense waiting for my turn and cheering my mates in the water on top of my voice. But before second thoughts could settle, I was held up at the edge of the pool and pushed forward. A bit shocked I got some water into my lungs, but could spit it out digging through the water using all the power I got in my arms. It was over in no time, my coach helped me out of the pool; and I was still sitting at the edge, totally exhausted, when the swimmers of the other teams just about arrived to touch the wall of the basin. It only sank in how fast I had been when my coach hugged me and my team members patted my back excitedly. Apparently, I had missed some kind of record by only very little. I was stunned! That was the first milestone put down for me!

The following months I spend more time in the water than on firm ground, I already felt almost like a fish. Of course, I was hoping to become an official member of the team, which would have been a dream come true. I did not know that this was quite unthinkable in the 'outside world' back then. In the 1960's and 1970's, handicapped children were not generally mixed with 'normal' ones, certainly not at sportive activities, let alone at official events! But there I was, training with the school-competition-team as a full member, taking part in the internal contests. I had no idea it was a privilege. Some of the team members had difficulties handling me, though, because they had never learned to deal with someone who wasn't like them. However, since I was proving my worth all the time, they began to accept and like me even. I had not felt better in a long time; and the daily troubles I faced in the orphanage and at school were easier to bear, could even be forgotten altogether at times. Especially in the weekends, when two other swimmers and I were taken to the swimming pool on a special bus for extra training, a privilege to be honored, as far as the orphanage was concerned.

Sometime later, our swim team was invited to a contest by the school in another town further away. I was determined to impress my coach in a way that he would not have a choice but to let me go with the team. I improved my technique and my breathing, became faster and faster; and finally, it paid off: "Well, son, I believe we have a real contender here. Let me see, if I am able to get you in the competition, but no promises, okay?" Now that were the words I wanted my coach to say to me! Little did I know then about the revolution, the disturbances my presence should cause at the event. I was in heaven and my team members were happy, too, to have me with them. After all, I was fast, real fast. One of them even suggested I should be the last in the line as a joker so to speak; nobody would expect me to make up all the time perhaps lost by the other swimmers.

Well, anything for me! As long as I was allowed to jump into the water. But about that I had reason to worry: I was handicapped, wasn't I; and there might be a rule excluding handicapped people from contests. I imagined the worst: A jury voting against me, all kids laughing at me, pushing me aside to take my place. One day before the event, my coach told me such a rule did not exist. But the competition committee was not happy about my taking part; and the officials would get back to him about it. Well, they never did; and I was worried sick the following day, sitting in the team bus that took us all to the competition.

Nothing happened as we arrived at this huge and terrific Olympic indoor pool; so we went to the locker room, changed and got a pep-up talk and our starting positions for the relay-contest from our coach. I was to go into the race as last swimmer, the joker after all. We still did not know whether I was allowed to jump into the water, when all the teams lined up behind the starter blocks on both ends of the pool and the whistle was blown. One after the other went in and my team didn't do badly at all. Then I stood on the starter block held up by two of my mates. Looking over my shoulder, I saw our coach arguing with the officials. My heart stopped beating, hadn't I known! Too late for intervention! It was my turn. Determined as ever I yelled at my mates to let me go. My team had lost time by then, it was going to be a close match; I needed to be fast, very fast. I rushed through the water throwing into the bargain everything I had. When I touched the pool's wall on the other side, I saw my opponents still several feet away. "Yes," I yelled and pushed up my arm. "How was my time, how was my time," I remember shouting quite out of breath, when my coach pulled me out of the pool and hugged me. "Amazing, son, amazing," was all he said.

So, our team had won; we were beside ourselves, patted each other's backs laughing and cheering. Then, however, the officials came over and told us the coach of the team that was second had complained about me and wanted us disqualified. You should have seen our coach: "You show me the national or international rule book, where you can read that someone like him is not allowed to compete, and I accept defeat! Until then we are the winning team," he yelled on top of his voice and then grabbed the trophy and walked off. What a man, standing up for me like that; I was touched deep down, but felt really bad; all that trouble because of me! My teammates turned to me: "It's not your fault," they all said. But the whole business was so wrong. However, it had been a tremendous achievement not only for me but for all of us, a fine example how positive interaction combined with personal effort binds individuals to a close team able to succeed. This for sure reflected on others who would reconsider their attitude towards people different from them!

During the months that followed, we prepared for the next big event: The North German Swim Contest, which was to take place in our swim-hall, an important home-advantage for us. The team grew even closer training hard, improving technique and condition. But something a lot more amazing was happening at the same time: Not just the members of the swim-class began to treat me as one of them; parents and other volunteers watching our training came up to me more and more often taking me in, as it were. "What the hell is he doing here?" had changed to "Great job, kid; keep it up; good to have you, boy!". It was a new and wonderful experience and made up for all those negative feedbacks I received from others all the time.

When the day of the contest finally came, we were all as ready as ever to tackle the task. But, yet again, the question was: Would I be allowed to swim? Our coach, always looking after me, took me aside in the locker room and asked me how I felt and then reassured me: "Don't worry, if the officials had found any rule or regulation prohibiting your participation, they would have informed me". Rather grimly, I told him I was o.k. I was used to this kind of problem.

We all confidently left the locker room and made for the swim hall which was decorated with banners and ribbons for the occasion and packed with spectators: Parents, relatives, teachers from our school and even some people that worked at the orphanage. And, to add to the excitement, even the national anthem was played!

There were 5 teams at the start, which meant two pairs of teams competing against each other; then a drawing of lots to determine which of the winning teams was to race against the remaining fifth team, then the final. I was to be the 'joker' again. Our first run was almost too easy, we won by lengths. In the second run a team from Hamburg, well trained and very fast, did the same with their opponents. Now, a coin was flipped, and it was us who had to go into the race against the fifth team; a definite disadvantage, if we could make it into the final. It was a close affair, but we were able to beat our opponents by a few feet. We were ecstatic. However, it was going to be our third run against an excellent team whose condition had not really been challenged.

It was a thrilling race: The first line went well, our number one could keep close; but the second and third line was clearly lost by arm's lengths. Our number four was a real runner. That is why he was put into this position. He was able to make up a good deal of lost time before I went in. I gave everything I had. But when I reached the other side of the pool, my opponent just touched the wall. I was beaten by a second or two. What a disappointment! I doubted myself right away: Was I not that fast, after all? My coach pulled me out of the water and helped me to sit down. I was completely exhausted, no power left;

and I knew I had reached my limits; I would not become any faster without being able to use my legs. Today, swimming by power of the arms only is a special style; back in those days it was a necessity for me to be able to swim at all!

While I was still sitting at the edge of the pool trying to catch my breath, however, the swimmer who had beaten me came over and congratulated me for my performance. "Don't be disappointed," he said. "You see, I won the North German title many times over and became even second at the German Championships. And this year I am going to try for the national team". I was impressed. So, a superstar had beaten me. Not long after all teams lined up to receive their prizes. A nice second place-ribbon and the smile from a pretty girl made up for the defeat. And yet, it was clear to me then that I would only be satisfied standing in the winner's position and that I would never trade that for anything less. I tried once more at the North German single contest a few weeks later. I was, again, the only handicapped competitor and the officials were quite upset, but couldn't throw me out. I came in third; and without me realizing it fully then, my swimming career had come to an end.

*

Thanks to my swim coach who had promoted my development in such a kind way, I had learned a lot and was ready to move on. It was in those days when the 'Bruce Lee movies' came from Hong Kong. A few years before, I had watched the thriller of Manila: 'Ali vs. Joe Frasier' with my brother; and ever since I had been hooked on any kind of fighting style. So, Bruce Lee rekindled my secret passion. I started to think seriously about learning to box or Martial Arts. But how and where, I had no idea; schools didn't exist around where I lived.

You might as well call it another touch of destiny, when one of my best friends and I caught sight of a flyer pinned to a tree near our school one day, announcing the opening of a Karate Dojo by a high ranking Black Belt Master in our town. Wow, we thought, Bruce Lee and 'Enter the Dragon' right around the corner! Of course, we decided straight away to go and have a look. The place was not far away from the indoor pool. Though I hated to do this to my swim coach, I skipped training on that memorable Monday and went instead to the new dojo. My friend didn't show up. No matter! I gathered all my courage and went through the door.

What I saw looked like a scene from one of these 'Karate-movies' to me: A class was in practice, a very warm and friendly looking man with a black belt around his waist was teaching. I stood in the entrance, stunned and unable to move, when a lovely lady, also with a black belt, came over, welcomed me with a friendly smile and asked me what she could do for me. I was quite overwhelmed by her appearance, and it took me a while before I could tell her that I wanted to learn Karate. Vera Lemmens did not take any notice of my disability and replied that I would need to talk to her husband about it. She kindly asked me to sit down and then went to the man teaching the class; she talked to him pointing her finger in my direction. He only nodded and carried on teaching.

While waiting I watched the students' movements in utter amazement. And when they started sparring I was completely taken in! After the lesson was finished, they all bowed solemnly to each other and the students left for the locker room. Their teacher, Geert Lemmens, waved me over, then; and I humbly followed him into his office where he introduced himself with a friendly smile. "What's wrong with your legs," was the first question he asked me. So, I told him my story and added that I was already training hard at the swim hall, but that I felt this wasn't enough. He agreed and carried on, "Listen, son. Before I will teach you how to hurt people, I will teach you how to heal yourself and others. It is essential in your situation. Besides, hurting someone is easy. There is nothing impossible, so let's see what we can do….welcome to the dojo".

I had the biggest smile on my face when I shook his offered hand. As fast as I could I left and went to the swim hall hoping my coach would understand. I explained to him that I felt I would never make it into any national team, for sure not officially. Moreover, I needed to do something about my legs and Martial Arts might be the answer. He understood and agreed. Well, how could he not. After all, he was a high ranking Jiu Jitsu and Judo Black Belt himself! He even promised to cover for me should I get into a jam with time. What a mentor and a good friend!

*

So, I had started a journey to a much higher level, a new path in my life. I could not be sure where it would lead me; all I knew was that I had to take this chance. And I hoped it would make me strong enough to tackle any rocky road ahead, now that I had to live in this horrible orphanage until my 18th birthday, unless a miracle happened or I decided to run away for good. That was an option always present in the back of my mind. Of course, it had been tried before, but no kid ever managed to stay away longer than a few days before they were caught and taken back in handcuffs by the police.

It is hard to imagine for an outsider how those unfortunate kids suffered emotionally and physically from the torture they were put through by the warden and his assistants after they were locked away again in that 'Rock'. Nobody ever witnessed the beating. They were too smart for that! But the signs of it were clearly to be seen: Bruises all over, black eyes and a personality smashed. In my case, it was even less likely that I would make it to freedom: I was unable to run and could be spotted easily within a crowd because of my handicap. So I would have to conjure up a damn good plan!

However, right now I saw a bright shiny rainbow on the horizon. An incredible chance to get better in many ways: Finding a peaceful way to get my anger and frustration under control, learning positive interaction with the outside world as a result and training my body to work with me instead of against me.

These things hardly anyone taught around here. Martial Arts and especially their ancient healing techniques were comparatively new to our western countries in the 1970's, for sure unknown to the average person on the street. Moreover, handicapped people–children as well as adults–did not have the privilege to be generally included in public sport, apart from short-term rehab with little results. In fact, there was no MD, no book to be consulted for advice, ideas or support. With the help of my feedback Geert and Vera Lemmens, especially Geert Lemmens, created an individual Martial Arts concept, the first of its kind, customized for the special needs of a cerebral palsy patient, for someone like me, which included Yoga as well as strengthening weight training.

Indeed, there is still no guideline to be found today–certainly not for people with cerebral palsy–how to workout or power-train; no guideline for fitness-rehab and surely not how to exercise Martial Arts. I hope, this book will help to close the gap and build a bridge between ideas, dreams and facts. It is meant to show how to minimize physical risks safely helping you on the road to a better and healthier place in life. That is why I dedicated more than one chapter to personal rehab, which will help to guide the beginner all the way to the pro athlete, and the long-term teacher safely to training handicapped people. Along the way, I will remove gossip, wrong ideas and myths that have been growing up around exercising people with CP and other physical and mental disabilities for too long. I have taught and promoted children and teenagers with physical and mental limitations across the globe together with my Master Students for more than twenty years; and I can hardly put into words how wonderful and rewarding this work or, better, way of life, has been. I would not have traded it for anything else. Most of us feel awkward when confronted with handicapped people, especially children, because we have never been told how to deal with them. So let me take away some of the fears as we go along.

*

Art in general is an immense and most amazing subject with a seemingly endless variety of faces and paths. Just think of painting, sculpturing, writing, singing, of opera, theatre and books. It is the same with Martial Arts: There are hundreds of different wonderful ways a Martial Artist can express him-/herself. However, we distinguish between five major categories: 1. Traditional Hard Style; 2. Traditional Soft Style; 3. Pacific Islands and African Arts; 4. Mixed Martial Arts; 5. Meditation/Healing Arts

Hard and soft styles are distinguished by the movements: Soft style means round, soft and flowing movements including wide circles, animal-forms and -movements. This style comes mainly from China, Nepal, India and the Pacific Islands–like the Philippines–and Africa. The hard style is defined by more linear and straight forward movements with short and long hard kicks and punches coming mainly from Japan, Thailand and Korea. Here a few basic examples…

Traditional hard styles:	Hapkido, Tae kwon do, Tang Soo Do, Wing Shung and Karate, Shotokan, Gojo-Ryu, Shin-Ryu, Jiu Jitsu, Wado-Ryu or Thai boxing, Kyokushinkai Karate etc.
Modern hard styles:	Savate, kickboxing, boxing, wrestling or fencing.
More resent modern styles:	Brasilian Jiu Jitsu (and modifications), Kadgamala Do, Hyekatch Do or Shin-Tora-Do
Soft styles:	Judo, Aikido, Sambo, Wu Shu, Chinese boxing, Tai Chi and all varieties, Chi-Gong, Kalarippayat or Capoeira
Pacific Island Arts:	Polynesian Arts, Hawaii Arts, Capoeira
Meditation/Rehab Arts:	Yoga (all forms), Kalarippayat, Chinese boxing, Tai Chi, Chi-Gong, Shin-Tora-Do

I believe, for a start this is more than enough. Besides, there are dozens of varieties from the Philippines, the Pacific Islands and China that mainly concentrate on weapons and hardly on any techniques, apart from foot work: There is Kendo, the Tai Chi Sword, the Japanese BO or the Art of Zen, where the practitioner stands, sometimes for hours, to become one with an arrow before releasing it towards the target, the Philippine knives, the Anis or Escrima training, as well from the Philippines.

Now, how can you find a suitable style? Simply by asking some questions: What type of person are you, and what is it you would like to get out of Martial Arts? Are you the active, even aggressive type or rather the passive? Do you need to release stress and tension? Or do you need to rehab yourself or parts of you? Do you like more to kick or to punch? Let's have some examples: You like sparring and are not afraid to be hit, you need a way to release stress, lose weight and want to learn kicking and punching rather sooner than later? Then kickboxing would be ideal for you. If you are the rather quieter type looking for more mental stability or someone who needs some mental and physical training for health reasons—frankly, in our stressful times, who doesn't?—you should opt for the soft styles and/or the meditation/rehab styles (see above). Many women choose those styles for mental and emotional enhancement as well as for learning self-defense methods.

Now you need to find a good dojo and a good instructor. It is less difficult than you might think. The dojo should meet with certain standards: Cleanliness at all times, decent equipment in sufficient numbers, reasonable fees, insurance. Besides, you should feel comfortable with your fellow students and all should wear suitable sports clothes. The instructor or teacher must have a correct Black Belt diploma and be a member of at least one major association like WAKO, DAKV, IAKSA, ISKA, or WKA, just to name a few; and all students should also be registered with one of these associations. Finally, watch out for children: If there are a lot of them divided into different age groups, if they appear to love and adore their instructor and have plenty of fun training, believe me, you found the right place! Children cannot be fooled for long…

*

It has been a common misconception for a long time that Martial Arts in general are violent or promote violence, which could not be further from the truth. There are several reasons for this myth. For once the movie industry has portrayed the Martial Artist as a fighter without any fear, as an assassin and killer even, for the last sixty years. Furthermore, television has been broadcasting some championships as an act glorifying the events beyond reason. Finally—and I think that is the worst—some mixed-style Martial Arts fighters and their surrounding groups behave disgustingly in public and at tournaments. Too many times, I have witnessed bad behavior, disrespect and violence especially at open competitions and sports events. This is conveyed to the spectators as legitimate, as perfectly all right; and naturally this is brought into private life, into families and schools.

It is a serious problem in need of attention. And I can imagine quite easily you agree with me, when I say violence and disrespect are truly bad examples for our children. Especially for young people today it is hard enough to find their own healthy and safe path. How can a youngster possibly distinguish between right and wrong behavior, if he/she hears about or sees bad sportsmanship? And how can we teach our beginners—especially our children—non-violence, inner peace, self-love and self-respect when we run around acting like maniacs at the same time? Without any respect for ourselves and for others? I strongly believe, we cannot; and the true Martial Artist and Black Belt won't. He follows Bushido all his life, and will, together with his Master Students, set positive examples.

This is, besides safety and health, the major reason why he will never take part in events that promote bad behavior and/or violence. Do not get me wrong, I am not at all against any Mixed Martial Arts. My own style, 'Shin-Tora-Do', includes strong elements of Jiu Jitsu and grappling. But it is of vital importance that every teacher or coach, especially if he/she instructs children and teenagers, promotes a respectful discipline in his/ her dojo or school, and for sure in the ring and at contests!

There was one occasion when I had to face one of those supposed 'super fighters': I was head instructor in self-defense and kickboxing at a dojo at that time, and was standing by the front counter wearing my Gi (uniform) and black belt, when this 'MMA fighter' came in and ran his mouth. After he had taught a private student, he came over to me, showed off a real Clock 45 (gun) and glorified a drug dealer whose body guard he was supposed to be. I asked him to stop this behavior, but he went on provoking me by asking if I didn't think his fighting style was the supreme one, and if I believed I had a chance against him and survive. There were kids all over the dojo and the next class was about to begin! He came closer, asked me if I was ready and then run his head into my stomach. I was pushed backwards, but held on to him with a Monkey-move and breathed the air out of my belly tightening the muscles as we both hit the floor. Then I executed a double hollow-palm-strike to both his ears without hurting him. Had I done the move properly he would have had to be rushed to the nearest ER immediately. To make sure he didn't have second thoughts I then pushed my right thump into one of his eyes, but again without executing the move fully. The man kept going for almost then minutes trying to get me into an arm bar despite my moves. So I told him: "Give up, man. The only reason you do not lie dead on the floor is that I was nice to you. Let me get up!"

But he didn't. He was not only a large bodybuilder type of guy but also a long standing grappling champion. So, I reached for his nuts and asked if he really wanted me to execute this move. For a split second I turned into his left side, and he took the chance to pull my left arm into an arm bar almost breaking it and telling me to tap it up. I didn't move. Eventually he realized he was getting nowhere. I never saw him again afterwards, and I am sure he knew perfectly well who won this unofficial fight! If there had been any doubts, the owner of the dojo was witness.

Some years later, I came across a young Olympic junior champion in Rome-Greek wrestling who went to one of those 'MMA challenges'; the winner was supposed to get $10000. No one told him before that he would have to fight close to 40 (!!!) opponents on the first of the three-day-event. However, that amazing man won all his fights, competing eight to ten hours a day non-stop, before one of these long-time champions finally beat him only because he was weakened by the whole crooked ordeal and made a mistake after about five minutes getting into an arm bar. Although he tapped up, the head grappler broke his arm! The business was settled quietly and swept under the carpet. It was a few years after this event, when I met and wrestled with him non-stop for more than an hour before I was finally able to put him into a head choke. He had to tap up or be choked out. We became good friends afterwards and sometimes worked out together. He actually told me that I was the one of only two people apart from this head grappler who had ever made him tap up and that the first time it had happened was many years before, when he was just a teenager....

So, here we just had a couple of perfect examples of how the attitude of individuals or groups, how bad behavior, lack of respect and violence can cause the development of a negative reputation of an entire community. And since a number of such events are broadcasted and written about for publicity, to catch more viewers and readers for higher quota–which in itself is not part of the point I am making–we should always remember that we are Martial Artists and true teachers first and foremost, teaching and mentoring our children day by day with loving heart!

And today, this is more important than ever. Just think of TV, of video games, adverts, newspapers and the internet! There is hardly a day you do not read or hear about death, murder, assault or rape; and the internet is packed with scams promoting sex, drugs and violence. If parents are truthful to themselves, they will admit they are not really able to leave their children alone with TV and internet without having to worry about them watching inappropriate channels or clicking themselves onto dangerous websites. I certainly would not leave my kids alone at any time using a computer, watching TV or playing violent MMA fight- and other video-games.

So the last thing we need is the promotion of those supposed 'super fighters'. This, again, is not against MMA in general. There should just be no cause for parents to worry about the physical and mental safety of their children training in a dojo or any other sports club–just remember this supposed 'super man' waving around a loaded '45' and committing a violent assault in a public dojo, just because he thought he had the right. I am sure the new, upcoming MMA Assoc. will deal with this problem. There is a lot of potential for great champions to be made–with class!

We have, of course, many fine representatives of the Mixed Arts, true champions and teachers. A number of them are close personal friends of mine I trained and dealt with like; Gene LeBell, Carlos Machado, Chuck Norris, Tony Bader, Geert Lemmens, Benny 'the Jet', Bill 'Super-foot', Mihran Aghvinian, Gokor Chivichyan, Bob Wall, Bas Rutten, George Manoukian, Dan Inosanto and Master student, my former NBL-World Championship partner, Rod Armstrong, just to name a few.

In the first half of the 1990's, I had the honor to train with Carlos Machado on the premises of Chuck Norris' TV show 'Walker TX Ranger' in Dallas, TX. Together with his brother, he has been a great and gentle teacher and became a good friend. Both, Chuck and Carlos were aware of those undesirable behaviors and new developments throughout the Martial Arts world from the start and saw the great potential and need for adjustments. Therefore, they always concentrated on teaching and healing especially youngsters motivating and elevating them daily. Many years before I had the honor to meet and even work with Chuck Norris, he had started this with his youth organization 'Kick-Start Org', former 'Kick Drugs out of America'. For years I was honoured to watch this remarkable program and his amazing results first hand. Through him, I met his second Unit Director, Greg Elam, Golden Glove box champion and Stunt Coordinator at Color Purple & Walker TX Ranger. He became a great friend, always on my side with tremendous readiness to support and help; the whole family is simply wonderful. With always great input Greg also become my mentor for my career as filmmaker.

Whenever I was provoked on the street or challenged to a fight as a grown up, I hardly ever lost. There is always a distance any fighter has to overcome in order to get hold of an opponent. And if you are in tune with yourself, have good reflexes and learned fast and accurate techniques, you will be able to defend yourself and survive when attacked without warning, just like me. Every good instructor can teach you those moves and techniques. However, all your force and power to execute them need to come from deep inside you so that you don't freeze, unable to move, in a situation like that, but walk away, hopefully unhurt. I can assure you, most of my Green Belt students would kick the greater number of those 'bad guys' to the floor without much difficulty! And my friends Mihran and Marwan and I have been known to teach our White Belts in a way that they don't only have the attitude of a Black Belt, but also the power!

It is of vital importance for parents to find the right style and dojo for their children away from an environment of violence, cruelty and disrespect in order to avoid the building of a pattern of emotional instability and negative behavior. That should not be too difficult; there is plenty of information available, especially through the internet (the good side of it!) Most towns have professional websites providing links to a variety of businesses and customer facilities, where you will find useful information about fees, opening hours, and courses on offer, even complaints or claims against a company or business. And you can find out what the dojo you are looking at stands for, the philosophy, the ideal and, of course, you will find its track and success record. So, it is up to us adults, especially parents, to influence our children in a positive way and make sure they are on the road to success and a healthy life.

It is less difficult than you might think: Be part of a simple parents-and-children-day at school; volunteer at a summer-weekend-camp; watch your young ones performing on stage or on the sports ground. It will make all the difference in the world to your son, your daughter! And will make up for all those occasions you weren't available, because you had so much else to do! Believe me; I know that just too well. During my entire career my father never made it to any sports event, never sat in the audience to see me standing on the podium receiving honor and trophy. He sometimes watched me on TV, read about me in newspapers, looked through countless cover stories in magazines and listened to interviews I gave on the radio. But that's not really the same thing, is it? No, it is certainly not.

*

There is a great example that, I believe, rounds up all we have been talking about: It was in February 1993 at the Hamburg (Germany) Full Contact Kickboxing and Thai Boxing qualification tournament for the international Kickboxing and Thai Boxing Championship, the event of the year. For my team, the 'Top Four Hurricanes' (GER) it was the second qualification we were able to reach that year. But this was a Thai-box association event, a completely different competition! The real thing, you might say! We had been training and sparring like never before, even had run through ten inches of snow all winter wearing our uniforms only and not even shoes, just to make us stronger! Needless to say, people who saw us were certainly thinking we had escaped from a 'mental institute' not far away, and it wasn't the first time!

I was the first-ever 100% handicapped person in the history of Martial Arts who had qualified for a full-contact contest which was not, of course, modified for someone with any kind of physical limitation! But there I was, at the top of my career, as physically and emotionally fit as I could be, then. Unfortunately, Geert Lemmens could not support me. He was tied up with broadcasting another Martial Arts event. Neither could my friend Mihran, who was busy as team captain elsewhere. To make matters worse, I had caught a bad cold just two days before the big event with a heavy headache, sore throat, hurting joints and muscles and high fever. And yet, I was sitting in our van ignoring the tiny voice in my head telling me to go back to bed, and the loving advice from my team. Before I passed out and slept all the way to the big city of Hamburg, I remember saying something like: "I haven't trained for over six months for nothing. TV will be there, everybody will be watching. I will not flunk out now!" I came out of fever-dreams when my teammates woke me up in Hamburg….

My most dangerous opponent has never been the man I was facing in the ring. It was the ring doctor! Would he let me fight? Especially that day. Would he notice my cold? I was sure he would not let me step into the ring, if he did! Uwe, Helge, Ingolf and Olaf, my teammates, went to the scales with me. At most Martial Art events you need at least five fighters to make up a team. So it was vital for me to get past the ring doctor. Due to my handicap we had been facing trouble often enough. Therefore, we had worked out a system to get by: My teammates went into the doctor's room first to eliminate the possibility of an early upset of the doctor, which might cause disqualification on my behalf. It often worked, but an unexpected twist was always just around the corner. My boys, of course, all passed without a problem.

When it was my turn, I stepped forward saying hello with a broad smile. The ring doctor was an old-timer, at least 70 years; and I said secretly good-bye to the contest. But while examining me he only said: "Cerebral palsy. Respect, young man". 'Wow!' I thought. Then he noticed my swollen lymph nodes. I told him it was just a little cold and then made the mistake to ask him, if he could give me something for it. He just slapped me in the face, would you believe it, and yelled: "Wake up, kid. That's all you get. Now take off before I change my mind! Who is your ring man?" I told him I did not have one as yet; he only raised his eyebrows and appointed a six foot fighter who happened to be there; and then he wished me good luck… We went out of the room as fast as we could, before he changed his mind…

The arena was packed with people, 2000 fans and spectators, if not more; the air vibrated with excitement and expectation, with shouts and cheers. What an event! Full-contact kick- and Thai-boxing. Just the right atmosphere to punch my opponent's face and climb up my career-ladder, I thought. However, I had to take some aspirin to ease the effects of my cold and fever hoping I would not fall asleep. We found an ideal spot by the ring and watched the fights in progress. At some point, the promoter came up and asked me if I was ready. So, I was recognized a fighter, the highlight of my career so far!

"Anthony, we have a problem." The promoter, Wolfgang G. was his name, had come back to pull me right down again. "Your opponent will not fight you!" Why did I always get this problem? And how could I solve it? "Where is he"; I was really angry to say the least. Helge went to talk to the man. "If he doesn't fight, will I be the winner automatically and qualified?" I wanted to know. Wolfgang nodded. Well, at least something! But I hadn't prepared myself for over six months just to walk away. "Find me another opponent then. I want to fight," I told him. "I like that. And it's better for the timetable, too; we don't have to worry about filling the empty spot," he replied. "Hey champ, you are already qualified, okay? And now let's see if we can find you another fighter."

My team and I continued to watch the competition. Fellow fighters, some of them old friends, stopped by and wished us good luck. This is one of the most wonderful things I have experienced: Lifelong friendship formed at and through competitions and competing, learning to respect one another over the years. Frank Feuer was there and one of my local heroes I always looked up to, Michael Wüebke. He was a world point-karate champion several times over and captain of the WAKO Kickboxing team; a great teacher and wonderful warm person, a good friend. He had staged quite a few fighting seminars in our dojo with a kick to it and always exciting. I was looking forward to seeing him fight that night, even though he didn't compete in our point-karate or kickboxing division. I was sure he would win his match.

And I still needed an opponent. I was frustrated beyond words, but at least I was wide awake now and had forgotten all about my cold. After a while, the promoter was back. He told me there might be an opponent, but would have to clear the matter with the ring doctor and the sports committee. I only shrugged my shoulder: "Whatever, Wolfgang, I just want to fight, that's what I am here for." He nodded and disappeared again....

Helge climbed into the ring for his turn to fight. It was a knockout system: You win, you win; you lose, you go home. One shot for the title. Or in Helge's case that night, three rounds and he was set due to his winnings in full-contact earlier that year and his North German champion title. When the bell sounded, he came out of his ring corner like always: Dominating his opponent with a few quick blows to the head and stomach; so he took an early lead right away and got the respect of the other fighter. At the end of the first round he knocked him about any way he liked and the poor man got a real good old fashioned ass-kicking. Sorry ladies, but there is no other way to describe this massacre! Why his coach did not throw the towel, is still a mystery to me. I tried to signal him to stop this slaughter more than once. Helge was on fire! Hand combinations speedily followed by side- and round-house kicks broke his opponent, destroying him bit by bit. Finally, the bell rang, and the ring doctor arrived, took a good look at him and consequently broke up the fight–another glorious victory by our team captain. And Ingolf had, as always, been a great ring man, irreplaceable for us.

I should have to be in the ring after the next fight. However, Helge's victory made me forget my misery for a moment. We all started to watch the match, when the promoter appeared again: "You still want to fight?" "Yes, of course," I almost shouted. "Okay, it's on. Get ready! After this fight, you're up!" We all went crazy. I made it. I could not believe it! Helge helped me warming up and Ingolf, always my hardest test measure for my readiness to compete, wished me luck. And Uwe–a big happy-to-be-here bear, who can hardly wait for action ("This is going to be brutal, guys"), a heavy weight with lightning speed hand- and leg-techniques kicking and punching like a horse, several times North German and German champion in light as well as full-contact and 2^d at the European Kickboxing Point-Karate Championships that year, gave me a good punch into my belly that almost took my breath away. "Wake up, Sensei," he said. And I could only shake my head.

Of course, we were all more than eager to see who the promoter would come up with. Ingolf put the finishing touches to my bandages, helped me with my boxing gloves and went with my ring man–who I didn't know at all, remember–and me to my ring corner. And there he was on the other side: A 6.2' mountain of a man with long dread locks and built like a brick house. "Where in the world did he find this guy?", I remember thinking. Besides, he looked more like a fighter from Madagascar than from Germany. So, what was he doing here? Qualifying for the Int. German Thai- and Kickboxing title? And how was this exotic creature going to fight...? No matter, I would have taken on anyone!

I was glad to have Ingolf as my cut man. After all, he was one of the most experienced fighters of our dojo, a former light-middle weight box champion, who had his spotless and remarkable career cut short by a tragic medical condition. My worry was about the ring man. Would he understand my unorthodox fighting style? Well, no time for more second guessing, there was the bell. My opponent and I moved fast to the centre of the ring and immediately exchanged combinations, but my arm-techniques and -combinations were too quick and powerful for him. He was not even able to land a single blow. I delivered several hard right and left punches and finished up with my signature technique: A lightning-fast and hard punch to the left side of his head with my right cross-hooked.

He backed off. Unbelievable! I tried to go after him, but my feet felt heavy all of a sudden, dragging across the floor; and I could not move forward fast enough; it was the cold and the fever that got me in their grip. It did not matter, my opponent advanced again with a left-right combination to my head. I blocked both punches, was not hit at all, and delivered a hard and strong same-side-hook to his ribs and one signature hook again to his face, right on the money…he stumbled backwards; and I tried to follow him once more, but my feet didn't let me. And there he came again with a side-kick. I quickly did a 90 degree sideways move, but stayed within range to give him two good combos to the head and ribs, called a doublet. My opponent backed away again, and for the first time I heard the crowd screaming and booing him out.

I was leading for sure by a dozen points without being hit once! But I just couldn't follow him and finish him up. I thought hard, and then it flashed through my mind: 'Doper-rope a la Ali'! So, I needed my opponent at the ropes; and with one or two good blows I could knock him out. "This is the only way," I thought moving sideways to the ring corner. I leaned into the ropes and signaled him to come closer for an in-fight with both my gloved hands–well, we all still smile about this. He waved back likewise signaling a 'No', then pointed towards the ring centre. I just smiled and kept waving. The arena became a melting pot, the crowd went nuts screaming and booing, calling my opponent a pussy.

I tried once more and moved, cursing my feet, towards the centre waving him over. He came out of his corner and attacked with a left jab forward. That was fine with me; my right crossed over his jab and landed on his nose. The cracking noise made him mad and he tried two combos to my body. I blocked both, hit him in the face with a left jab followed by my signature cross-hook to the head. He was hurt and backed off all the way into his corner. And here I was again: Not able to follow him, not able to finish him off, because my fever wouldn't let me. I had enough of this find-me-game and moved back to the ropes giving the 'doper rope Ali' again, waving invitingly to my opponent to meet me half way along the ropes. He declined. The arena boiled.

The round was about to be over, and I was leading by at least two dozen to no points. My opponent's coach, of course, knew this and yelled at him to get back into the fight and knock me out, that being the only chance he got to win. Finally, my opponent pulled all his strength together and came storming out of his corner. That was what I had wanted. I leaned into the ropes, even lowered my arms a little shaking them out for a second, waiting for the ideal moment to punch him out. He was about four feet away from me, when my ring man suddenly threw the towel! It landed right between my opponent and me! He stopped, and we looked at each other, totally shocked. The USPN Europe Sports camera man was right behind my ring corner and did a close-up of both of us (I had not realized he was there at all!). The ring referee picked up the towel and stopped the fight. There are no words for how I felt. I yelled at my ring man: "What did you do that for! What's wrong with you! I was fine! Did you never see the greatest ever fight in the history of boxing! Did you never see 'Ali'!" I don't know, if I was more frustrated or angry. I left the ring and signaled to my team to pack up and leave, NOW! The camera man did another close- up of me ('never got hit once')....

When we came out into the reception hall some time later, we spotted Gunter in the crowd. He was a high ranking Black Belt and once the right hand of our great Geert Lemmens before he showed his real self and got thrown out of our dojo and the association as well. We could not stand this clown. He had harassed me only too often in front of my students making jokes like: 'What the hell are you doing Martial Arts for. It's like someone without arms trying to play tennis. No arms no cookies'. His face showed that he had watched my fight. I was so worked up, I turned towards him ready to punch his nose, but Jan only said: "Let's get out of here, before the fight continues in the lounge!" Of course, he was right; and it would have been bad style! So, we all just started laughing; and that joke of an 'ultimate super fighter' knew exactly what we were thinking....Big time loser! That made my upset a little sweeter. And Ingolf said, "Hey, lighten up, champ. You know you won your fight and so do we and all the 2,000 spectators in the audience." But I only wondered when I would win a match without having to fight ring doctors and other officials. One of our students joined us then to tell me the TV crew was looking for me. "Give them my card. If they really want to talk to me, they will know where to find me," I replied. I was too tired, too upset and just wanted to go home....

Chapter: 4

Arts, Studies – Reflections – Changes from Within

Our team had done well: Eight points out of ten, our usual result, although Uwe's opponent hadn't showed up; so he won his points just the same, and Michael Wuebbke had lost his fight, which rarely happened. The TV reporters never came. And for several weeks the rumor flooded about that my fight was fixed, my ring man having contact to my opponent's dojo. It did not make any difference to me; I was determined to succeed in my division. I was told later the only reason why the fight was stopped was the fact that I would have been the first ever 100% handicapped competitor in the history of Martial Arts to get qualified for the Int. German Full-Contact Thai-Kickboxing Championship. And that wasn't on! Well, I already had come far, being the first competing point-karate fighter with a limitation. Besides, in a sense, I was qualified just the same, if Wolfgang, the promoter, stood to his word.

Although I was looking forward to getting back into daily routine, to my class of gorgeous kids–the joy and pride of my life, the shiny stars of our dojo–I needed a full weekend for reflection and sleep and to get the cold and fever out of my system. Between snoozes, I thought a lot about my family: As little kids my brother and I used to sneak secretly out of bed late at night to watch our great idol 'Ali' fight on TV until our mother kicked us gently back to bed. One night, after we had seen 'The Thriller in Manila' I told her I wanted to be a fighter just like 'Ali'. I was hardly able to walk then, but mother simply said, "You will, son. You will rewrite history and become a champion, an athlete and teacher". She was the last descendant of an ancient Hungarian gypsy family said to have a strong sixth sense. Her and her mother's visions had been legendary. Her conviction and trust in my yet hidden abilities gave me confidence, and she certainly put me on the road there and then!

My grandparents, too, influenced my development crucially. In fact, without their determination and passion I would never have made it out of that horrible institution where I was locked away by the state's Child Services in the first place. They fought mountains of red tape and paperwork until the grinding mills of bureaucracy finally came to a standstill, and I was allowed to live with them and later with my mother and brother. Just imagine: The western society of the 1960's was supposed to be modern and democratic, having risen high above tyrannical leadership of kings. And yet my parents were told their child needed to be put away for his own good; after all, he was crippled, wasn't he? And he didn't belong among normal people! Looking at my boxing gloves and countless trophies, I can almost laugh about it today.

So, life is teamwork! Where would we be without family, friends, supporters and mentors? I was glad to be back at the dojo that following Monday morning finding myself–still half asleep–behind the counter of our little bistro in the dojo preparing coffee for my fellows. What a laugh we all had later, when Ingolf turned up with a whole big cheese cake. For most of us, the dojo was the next best thing to a family. It is a wonderful memory and a shiny example of bonding, inner strength, confidence and will to succeed challenging prejudice, misconception and misjudgment. It shows true friendship and sportsmanship as a result of teamwork on the road to success! No one–big or small, young or old–can say for sure, that he or she was, is or will be able to accomplish whatever the goal may be without the help and support of friends, team members or family.

The teamwork starts in our childhood, with our mother and father, our brother and sister continuing through school, education, job and career, friendship, relationship, marriage. Just think of a basketball or soccer game: No matter how talented and brilliant a single player is, no matter how often he is able to score, the other players must work with him. Exchange passes back and forth, prevent the opponents from scoring and so on. Otherwise, the game will most likely be lost. This applies, of course, to the other way round as well: If this individual mainly works on his own trying to score alone, he will isolate himself within the team, wanted or unwanted. And this will negatively reflect on the overall performance throughout all games and therefore on the position of the team in the region and league.

This makes the work for the coach so much more difficult. It takes away time and attention from other areas, crucial for the team to improve their game and overall performance. And it is so unnecessary and totally wrong. To counteract this happening is, in my humble experience as a team captain, coach and mentor, the most important task for any coach or teacher as soon as he/she starts working with a group of youngsters or pro athletes. A lot more important than any adjustment of drill training sessions and training methods or ideas. It is for sure one of the major ingredients that caused the success of our team, the "Top Four Hurricanes" in Germany as well as in the US. So, unite a group of individuals–no matter how small or how large this group may be–to a team working together as one, and success will come sooner or later! In your professional life as well as in your private.

Even in the world of law enforcement and the army there is hardly a place for a so called 'lone wolf' or 'vigilante'. These characters only exist in the movies. If anyone in those forces of fine men and women ever get that far out and away from their support groups, partners or battalions, may God help us. During my career as mentor and Martial Arts teacher I had the privilege of training and supporting many members of staff of different law enforcement agencies and army departments in my dojos in Germany and Texas, either sent by their superiors or on a private level. I also carried out extensive seminars and motivational workshops within their bases; and many of my finest students and team members overseas came from the army or law enforcement agencies, like Sergeant Nick and his partner from the German Special Forces or Staff Sergeant Anthony Fischer from the US Army base. All these young men had found a second home in our dojo. They were taken into our team, which was more like a big family, and could safely and healthily release stress through the hard training with us. Moreover, there always was someone who would lend a helping hand in all matters of life; there was time for talks and long friendly discussions, exchanges of ideas and relaxation at a game of chess or Bag gammon. And at most weekends we would take part in competitions and have for sure a smashing victory party afterwards.

Of course we took care of all our members, of everyone who joined the dojo, more or less, in one way or the other. I remember a young woman well, who signed on for our fitness and aerobic classes and for light kickboxing one day (Germany). She was really pretty and sweet, and our 'lover boy' Helge had his eyes on her right from the start. She came in about five to six days a week training for hours at the time, although she was in great shape and had no reason to workout that often and hard, except, perhaps, for stress release and fun. Right from the beginning I had a funny feeling about this, but couldn't grasp what her problem was and certainly not why. I was still young and hadn't come into contact with many woman-specific problems. In other words, my experience as far as that was concerned, came close to zero, but soon enough I learned that her problem was quite common among young women.

So, I carefully signaled her I could be her friend and, whenever she needed someone to talk to, the door to my office would always be open. She took it much better than I had expected and soon came to the fitness counter more often, where I was mainly to be found when not teaching. I had noticed that she would only eat an apple or a power bar if anything at all during breaks, and that she would workout like mad afterwards. I had heard about things like that, but really didn't know what to do or how to talk about it. So I decided to consult my longtime friend (let's call her) Lisa Ann. She was a model, very beautiful and a wonderful and loving person to have around. She had gone through rough waters with a gang of 'rockers' that had been after her for years before we told them to get lost. I trained her hard and well to make sure those people never had another chance. Besides, she always ate well and even went to parties with me. So Lisa Ann was the best choice to help me, because all I had ever heard, was gossip.

There is a number of woman-specific problems, fears and worries, a man would find difficult to understand. Pregnancy, for example, a life changing matter, for sure a lifetime commitment at least for the mother! Physical disadvantages, various diseases a female is more exposed to than a man, a variety of mental problems, like eating disorder, caused by expectations, cultural features and fashion 'rules'. Lisa explained well and told me about the typical symptoms to look out for.

Can a man offer help without being misunderstood, or do women even expect from males to be ignorant? In our culture men do not generally talk to their women about female problems; and I think, there is a great need for improvement! Feeling uncomfortable, especially after finding out how deep and complex the problems are, I asked Lisa Ann if she would talk to the girl first. She agreed; and the next time (let's call her) Nicole came to the dojo, Lisa was there, too. Before long, they sat at the counter talking while I was training with my 'little Ninja dragons'. After class we always played The game 'All on Sensei': If the children were able to pin me down onto the matt for ten seconds or made me give up, they would win. Did you ever try to fight off 20 little dragons at once? I would gladly take on a wild lion instead; at least I would have a real chance! So much fun and excellent condition workout for me!

Lisa Ann had done a wonderful job with Nicole; and as I joined them, they were smiling and giggling. Between us, we could convince her to drink my personally created protein shakes and to help herself to the fresh fruit offered at the counter during her breaks, which was a start into the right direction. We also encouraged her to talk to any-one of us whenever she felt like it. Later, Lisa Ann and I went for a hearty meal; it made us feel a little funny after having talked about Bulimia. Nicole began to trust me, and we spent many hours talking, ending up at the counter late at night. My goal was to boast her confidence and make her aware of her great inner and for sure outer beauty as a woman; and I told her that, if the right man came come along, he would surely have no problem to help her tackling her fears.

Did you ever hear the saying that things have to get a lot worse before they become better? Well, in my opinion it is not true. However, I know–through my experience as teacher and coach–there are plenty of people who strongly believe this myth. It sadly is an unproductive and negative way of thinking that more often than not draws negative experience instead of positive. Nicole was no different and a textbook example. Moreover, she kept getting upset about what others might think about her, her looks and appearance. However, being still young and relatively inexperienced, I didn't realize, just how deepset her problems were. Nicole kept coming to the dojo for her workouts, we talked a lot and everything seemed to be fine. But it wasn't.

After a while she stopped turning up and was missing. I received a hint from a friend that she might have run off to Hamburg, and my friends and I were alarmed. The police couldn't really do anything, because she was over 21 and not registered as missing person. So, Uwe, Jan, Helge and I decided to go and look for her around the 'Mile' in Hamburg. This 'Hamburg Mile' is world famous: 4 kilometers long, 5000 bars, nightclubs, restaurants, strip tease clubs, four-star steak houses, hotels, theatres, whorehouses, Pool halls, jazz clubs; all back to back coexisting in harmony. Unless you saw it yourself, you would not believe it! After we had walked the 'Mile' for several hours we went to the famous 'Sankt Pauli Wache' (SPPD) which was the PD station for that area, to seek help, because Nicole could be anywhere; and we only had the weekend to find her. Luckily, we could convince one of the officers that we were not some 'pimps from another town trying to get back our 'horse', something quite common in a city like Hamburg.

He agreed to come with us and we went some of the 'hot-spots' like the 'Green Span', the 'Bistro' and the 'Star Club', where the 'Beatles' had their first break-through, but without any luck. Next came the cheap hotels, and we went to some run-down 'charge-by-the-hour' places that I cannot recommend to anyone showing around a photograph of Nicole we had taken with us. Again nothing finally, we tried one more place, already quite desperate. We all hoped we would find her there. When the rather Sinister looking man behind the counter looked at the photo, he showed signs of recognition. So we demanded the room number. Realizing it was no time for games, especially not with a bunch of muscular athletes, he gave us what we wanted. When Nicole opened the door to us, she started crying and agreed to come with us, leaving all her misery behind. She stayed at my apartment that night; and the following morning I took her to her mother who had been worried sick about her daughter and was glad to see her alive and reasonably well. The last thing I heard about Nicole was that she had joined a rehab group and was rearranging her life with the loving help and support of her mother. One lost soul found gently put back onto the right path, but so many more to go.

*

All these events were still to happen, when my friends and I were sitting comfortably at the counter of our dojo's bistro that sunny morning sipping coffee and eating the enormous cheese cake Ingolf had brought in. It suddenly hit me then how lucky we were and how blind and unaware due to emotional and cultural difficulties at the same time. One more reason for me to intently search for answers and ideas, to counteract negative influence and to detect and hopefully prevent further harm to any of my students and friends….."Remember last year's summer camp?" somebody said. We all smiled and nodded into the circle of friends…..another shining example for team spirit and everything Martial Arts, for sure Bushido, stands for.

The summer camp…. Those camps were legendary; and they run strong to this day changing hundreds of youths' lives, inspiring and motivating them. Initiated and organized by Geert Lemmens and his wife they took place near a small village by the sea every July. Martial Artists from all over Europe came to participate, even legendary Grandmasters from India and the US like Benny 'The Jet', Bill 'Super-foot', Leo Arts, John Blooming, Tony Bader, Emanuel Bettencourt, Dominique Valera, Mike Anderson and the founder of the Kalarippayat Academy in Cannanore, India. They all turned the event into a whirlpool of different cultures, religions, philosophies and ideas, of different training methods, styles and techniques. It was a week filled with pure fun, hardest workouts, condition training, team games, belt tests, long walks across the countryside and competitions that brought all of us to our physical and emotional limits. We learned new techniques and Kata forms, some of which had been invented by Lemmens, and new Yoga and Kalarippayat moves from his wife.

Considering the secrecy, even rivalry among the representatives of different styles during the 1970's and 80's this event took a trailblazer-role, was a barrier breaker for team-spirit and team-work: Joint training, learning, interacting and exchanging of ideas between nations, cultures, styles. And instead of fighting another and throwing hostilities around, we all became friends, in many cases for a lifetime, and took this wonderful experience back with us into our dojos and clubs to communicate it to our students, friends and families. Through these workshops and others on a smaller scale we grew over the years to tolerate and appreciate one another seeing our differences as unlimited source of wisdom and positive influence, which was translated into a much more open view on the world of Martial Arts and, for certain, made us to stronger, more peaceful and loving human beings

The first camp I had the honor to join was the one in 1983. It fascinated me from the start. After the first few months of training in G. Lemmens' dojo, the 'Kadgamala' (Germany). It fascinated me from the start and became the highlight of the year we were all looking forward to. I couldn't pay for it back then, had hardly any money to buy food, but Lemmens let me come just the same. I was able to 'pay' him for his and his wife's kindness when I became the babysitter of the family in 1980. They had two gorgeous children: Mark, a baby of a few months, and two-year-old Jope. I loved the job; and I adored the boys–Today they are both European, even world champions. To this day I have no idea how the Lemmens' managed to put up with my outbursts of anger and frustration and my big mouth in those early months. Well, I guess being called 'Wise Masters' they saw a 'diamond' in the rough in need of gentle shaping and polishing, in the need to be heard and loved, where the untrained eye only saw a lost child with a loud mouth. This first camp mainly did the trick, for sure: In no time I got rid of my anger and frustration….

Remember the last summer camp…How could we ever forget…1984…..My friends and I were instantly transported away from our bistro and the remains of that cheese cake onto the wide lawn that was used as training ground; standing in a circle under the burning sun, kicking and punching the focus mittens of our partners until Vera Lemmens yelled: "Change places". We were about to pass out, then, but surely not, because the training was too hard. No, it was the night before…One of Geert Lemmens' favorite phrases was: "If you can drink and party all night, you can go to school and to work; and you never miss a single workout!" Well, I can count the times I have been drinking alcohol with the fingers of one hand. Therefore, I always played the 'watch dog' for my team mates and gathered them up in the bars and clubs after a big party to get them home and into bed especially before a competition. However, not drinking ever kept me from dancing until sunrise! That particular night was not any different.

There was a large outdoor festival going on in the village not far off our summer campsite. It was the annual event of the area: Two huge connected circus tents, life music, DJ's, enormous dance floor, 4 bars. At least 1000 people wanted to have a good time dancing and especially drinking–the boys, even the girls, up north by the sea were known to drink a lot, and I mean a lot! And the more the youngsters filled themselves up the more they fancied a good 'let's-get-at-someone', and fights broke out by the dozens before sunrise. Our bunch never started one, though; it was a promise to our Master. But when we were drawn into trouble, we made sure we finished it quickly so that we could get back to the fun knowing we better had some, well aware of the consequences we had to face if we were caught on the way back, most of us being drunk like sailors and of course far too loud. Well, more often than not we were caught. Occasionally, however, the Lemmens' gave us a small break and pretended not to have heard us coming back to the camp at sunrise.

So, there we were that night entering the main tent watched over by Marwan and Mihran, just in case: About two dozen Karatekas and kickboxers dressed in our impressing sports wear. Of course, how could we go to such a lovely event without our team jackets! After all, it could be getting cold and a lonely girl might need to be kept warm…So, would we blend in quietly and peacefully? Or would we rather stick out like a sore spot! Well, we were all young, and right from the start it was promised to be remembered. Our friends from Italy were with us. Their Grandmaster Ezio Aragoni, being a friend of long standing to the Lemmens' and great supporter of their sports events and ideas, had become a regular at those summer camps together with his wonderful wife and great students. We youngsters didn't understand each other and had to communicate with hands and arms, which didn't help to keep out of trouble with the local youths…

The dance floor was a melting pot and the DJ's were constantly picking out different dancers with large spot lights. So we decided after a first round of drinks to give the crowd a Martial Arts break dance performance: We formed a wide circle, and one after the other went in to do their bit. Marwan showed his famous 'Robot dance', simply breathtaking! We were yelling and cheering like mad, and before long dozens of pretty girls joined us and the spot lights dashed across our crowd just as we had wanted. Suddenly, Mihran pushed me into the circle, and everyone was screaming: "Go, go, go". I did and finished my performance in Za-zen, which apparently was too much for two locals who, drunk as they were, tried to penetrate our circle. They didn't have to work hard on that: We let them through, pushed them towards the centre and closed up again, which made them go wild, of course. Well, we had not asked for this, had we; just wanted a good old-fashioned night out dancing and so…As I said before, we were still young.

The whole affair was finished quickly: A smooth defend-attack and we already melted into the crowd before the '7 foot gorillas' from the doors could spot us. Not that they were any threat to us, really. It was more the other way around, and at one occasion two of them actually quit on the spot when their employer told them to throw us out. So, the heat was on. Two other large drunken boys emerged and went for Mihran: One attacked with a typical swinger to the head, but found himself on the floor within seconds, though Mihran seemed to have hardly touched him. The other came from behind, and with a sweet haratochi shoulder throw (Seoi-Nage) Mihran sent him to join his companion. The fun didn't end there, of course. Later on Mihran, Marwan, a few others and I were sitting at one of the bar counters, taking a break from dancing and chatting with the girls, when one of those trouble seeking guys came up behind Marwan and pushed him hard demanding space for himself. Marwan didn't move and lifted his glass to take a sip of beer instead. The guy gripped his shoulder and tried to pull him around. Marwan just looked over to us signaling he would do this on his own. He was only about half a foot away from the counter, plenty of space for him! He slowly put his glass down and performed a beautiful spin-hill-kick out of a 190 degree turn. It was one of 'Super-foot's' signature kicks and a favorite of Marwan's. Needless to say, the drunken farm boy was thrown through the air within seconds, and Marwan continued with his drink while the man hit the floor. Or was that before he actually reached the floor? You should have seen the face of the bartender!

It was time to leave, and we finished our drinks. For Mihran and me it had been orange juice. I don't think any of us has ever seen Mihran drink alcohol. A large glass of milk or orange juice has always been his 'signature-drink' in any bar we went. Besides his great sportsmanship and friendship this fact has made him a role model to me and many others. Singing and laughing we headed back to the camp, to the relief of the bouncers and doormen. All the way we were joking about the 'Beer-spin kick' as it would be known from then on for years to come.

*

We had hardly put our heavy heads onto the pillow, it seemed, when we were woken up by Vera Lemmens and Gunter going through the cabins. And at the first glimmer of sunlight we found ourselves–dead tired and without breakfast–on that lawn kicking and punching our focus mittens yet again, spilling our guts out. Someone was quietly saying something about 'beer-spin-kicks' which made us all shake with laughter until Vera Lemmens forced us to kick and punch even harder.....By lunchtime her husband had gotten all the details of the night before; heaven knew who from. This would cause a lot more fun for the rest of our week, if we could survive it....

Not long after, I had my big mouth and boasting ego humbled–by a lady! She was one of the most beautiful Italian girls I have ever met; and she mesmerized me right away. I saw her for the first time, when she was talking to our Grandmaster after class. Dressed in plain jeans and T-shirt, I could not have known what rank she held; not that it would have made any difference to me! I decided there and then to ask her out, well, it least I would try; and when I came across her later, I did my best–having to use hands and feet, because I hardly spoke Italian–to make her like me. She actually smiled.... Encouraged I asked her to be my workout partner at the next training session so that we could, perhaps, become friends?... She smiled again saying: "Randori? You and me? Osu!"

In the afternoon, when we were all lined up again on the lawn and our Grandmaster commanded to get ourselves a training partner I quickly looked around to find my Italian dream, let's call her Carmela. And there she was: Long, dark, curly hair, bronze golden skin and a sweet million-Dollar smile on her beautiful face.....and a second degree black belt around her tiny waist. But it was too late to withdraw now. Needless to say, she smiled at me with sparkling mischievous eyes, and I tried to act the man as much as possible. Geert Lemmens gave the signal to begin: Randori without gear, full control, no accidents, was always the motto; however, to the body or a quick sweep or throw to the floor, he never minded.–The large foot sweep has been Lemmens' signature he always demonstrated with great accuracy and timing.

So there we were; my lady smiled at me and signaled that she was ready to begin. After that, I only remember hitting the grass as often, hard and fast as she wanted me to using any form or technique of her choice...I especially enjoyed landing on my back, catching my breath while she stood over me with this amazing smile lending me a help-ing hand to get back up. Well, I was a good sport. After class she gave me the real crash down: With the help of a friend she told me nicely that she liked me and adored my spirit as athlete (!), but that I was a little too young for her and needed more experience. I kept my face, thanked her and went my way, my pride hurt–and the grin on the faces of my friends didn't help me to feel better. "How could I have known, at least I have tried," I told them off–Carmela was at least 6 years older than me and certainly played in another league, but you never know, unless you try....

*

That brought us back to our dojo; and we were, once again, sitting at the bistro counter, this time without any cheese cake left, but with a bunch of students around listening to our stories. It was good to have all those youngsters and young adults around; I always felt like an enforcer, like a coach, mentor and even a dad towards them, all at the same time. I would not have traded any of these great young athletes for the world! It was quite amazing that every one of the twenty-odd members of our so-called 'A-team' (or original team) had a distinguished difference in character and personality and in the way they fought.

That is one reason why we came up with these nicknames as a character reference. 'Iron Horse' Ingolf, for example: Besides being a wonderful friend and supporter of our dojo he was a great athlete and an important member of our team from the start, we could always count on, which made him so much more special. And believe me, if you stood in front of him, you would never realize that this amazing athlete and loving human being was only able to see with one eye. The other, the left one, was blind due to a tumor behind the eye ball, which the doctors could luckily remove; however, the eyesight was lost for ever and his remarkable career as boxer had come to a sudden end.

When 'Iron-Horse' Ingolf came to us, he was looking for some sportsmanship and a place to workout. Within weeks, he became a regular in our dojo and soon irreplaceable to all of us. The children and young athletes looked up to him; and I had found my stron-gest sparring partner who could always tell me when I was ready to step into the ring. It did not take long before Jan, Helge, Bill and I decided he should become a member of our competing-team. We knew that the boxing commission would not let him fight any more, but we might be able to get him back into the ring as a kickboxer. Of course, he needed to train in a different way so that an opponent would not realize his handicap as a weakness.

He would not only lose his fight then, but could also suffer health-endangering consequences! There was a lot to consider and to take care of before even thinking of a competition.

Rehab, especially for the Martial Artist, was already my passion back then; and so 'Iron-Horse' and I went to work: We had to pay attention to his left as a jab and block at the same time to compensate his dead angle, his blind spot. Also his roll up, main movements and timing needed to be retrained and adjusted to his new radius of vision.

We taped his right hand to his back, so that he was forced to use his left jab throughout the training session; and I put him in front of the heavy sandbag like that as well to improve the strength of his left arm; during the focus mittens training I constantly hit him hard on the left side of his head without warning to improve his reaction, and before long he was able to jab and block with his left arm almost at the same time. I then came up with the idea to bring in a little 'Chi-Sau', also known as 'sticky hands', which was designed to make his shoulders stronger and to improve his reflexes. Ingolf did remarkable, and we all adored him from the start. He trained hard and improved fast, found his own new style more and more. All he needed then was to learn two, three kicks: front-, low- and round-house-kicks, and–to put the icing on the cake–maybe a fast back-fist... and he was ready to go back into the ring. Ingolf never thought this was a realistic possibility. Ask for me, it was just like another day at the office. I only kept doing what the Lemmens' had done for me!

Such an out-of-the-blue medical condition like a tumor behind the eye can, for sure, break down any man, even a born champion like 'Iron-Horse' Ingolf; I knew that only too well. But Ingolf wouldn't give up! He had the spirit of a warrior. Months of hard training, preparation, finding answers by experimenting, changing of fight-style and rhythm, had reawakened his survival-instinct and determination to win. In record time he had assessed the problems, and together we came up with solutions improvising on a daily basis. All this reminded me of the time when my Grandmaster had worked with me as a youngster: No book, no one to ask for advise, no references to similar cases, only him and me and the indestructible will to survive and the need for change accepting pain, injury and fear on the unknown path.

'Iron-Horse' was a lot like me, when I was young; and so were many youngsters and pro athletes I have trained in the course of the years. They all seemed to have this one thing in common: From the need for change and certainly for medical and health reasons, all these great and wonderful young men and women worked enormously hard on a mission at heart. They hardly ever seemed to get tired; they were always willing to run the extra mile, do five more push-ups or reps, when the healthy students next to them were already sitting down. I myself had been no different in the old days; and now I have the privilege to hand down my knowledge and experience to the ones in need for a better place in life. It is a wonderful feeling!

Before the weekend of his first fight as a kickboxer, Ingolf and I sat together at our bistro-counter sipping one of our home made protein-milk-shakes. He told me his story, and I listened with feeling: How hard it was for him to accept his medical condition after he had become the junior box sensation of the year with all the spotlights of northern Germany on him, with news paper and magazine articles, fans and fame, and still so young. And suddenly this had been all over. Old friends hardly dropped in, the members of his box club did not care too much for seeing him around. He was left alone to cope with his handicap and the consequences.

But not any more, now there was a second chance, a moment in time to step back, take a deep breath and jump right into it. After all, what did he have to lose? Not much, not much at all. He was excited like a little child. There and then, I had to promise him not to break up the fight, at least not in the first round. I gave 'Iron-Horse' my word. In return he had to promise me not to drink alcohol. If he did, there would be no more fighting. I wanted to make sure he was on top of the game. Besides, it was going to be his first appearance in the ring again. And I was determined to stand at the ringside taking notes and, above all, a close look if our new concept would work out, if he would see all he needed to see with only one eye.

During the last few days before the fight, we only trained hard once working on strategies and polishing our sparring skills. Apart from that, we took it easy with some Yoga and stretching. The Southern German Open WKA Kickbox Championship was one of three championships where we could gather points in order to qualify for the German Kickbox Championship at the end of the year. Besides these, there was the 'North Sea Cup' and the 'North-Cup Kickbox Championship', which I had founded and promoted for years with large attendance from most styles together, not often seen then.

It was a semi-contact, which made it a lot easier for 'Iron-Horse' Ingolf to pass the health inspection, because there was no ring doctor present. You only needed to show a clean bill of health from your MD at the registration desk, and we got that covered....don't ask how! So, there we were warming up in a quiet place, rapping our hands, stretching out....The first to go into the ring was Andy 'Baby Face'. His techniques were great, but, like his brother, he was not a 'mixer' as we call a fighter with heart. Which is fine as long as you have an opponent who is not a 'mixer'; it does not fit well, because the 'mixer' mostly wins in the long run, especially in the light- and full-contact division. So, in the semi-contact division your success mainly depends on your opponent and your own daily form: Will you be able to keep your opponent at a distance with your techniques, to counterattack and so on, without being overrun by a more aggressive and determined 'mixer-fighter'? So, we all hoped for Andy 'Baby Face' to have the luck of the draw, at least for the first fight. It helped, and he won against another technique-fighter by four points. It was a great display of skills and endurance!

However, it is a disadvantage–winning or not–to go into the ring as first competitor. You display your fighting style, strong points and weaknesses to the following opponents. A good coach will take mental notes of these and will inform his team members accordingly. And that was exactly what happened: Andy's next run was very close, but his opponent fought a little wilder and pushed his win through by a slim margin. Andy was devastated. In the semi-contact division there are no second takings; it is a knockout system: You lose, you go home; you win, you are one round up, nearer to the trophy. 'Lover Boy' Helge came next. He had his go from the start and declassed his opponent beautifully. His reputation probably helped him, because the other seemed somewhat hesitant. And hesitation, even for a heart beat, is the last thing you can afford in a kickbox ring! Heiko and Frank Simon did very well, too, that day; two fine team members and, together with Andrea and Mikosh, always great assets to our 'A-team' from 'Top Four Flensburg'!

Then it was 'Iron-Horse' Ingolf's turn. Our strategy was for him to come out of his corner and hit his opponent hard with lightning-speed techniques to the ribs and stomach. If that stopped the other, he would win. This strategy would make up for the lack of kick experience; besides, most kickboxers are kickers and not heavy punchers, for sure not in the semi-contact division. Well, that was the plan. "Hey, no matter what, you are back!" I gave him a hearty pat on his back; he smiled happily and went up.

Our concept seemed to work: Ingolf's punches were too hard and too fast for his opponent who was–we all need a bit of luck–a Tae kwon do fighter. Many of them have weak box-techniques and mainly use their feet instead of punching. "Close the distance, stay there, do not let him use his feet, stay with him," I was praying all the time. Ingolf did and won his fight! He was flying with happiness, it was wonderful to see. But then he faced a heavy puncher and kicker. This man surely trained mainly kickboxing and boxing. It was a hard fight. Ingolf was able to win most attacks, but let his guard down a few times, and the strong kicks of his opponent wore him down. He finally lost by a few points and was out of the race; a bitter-sweet defeat. But considering what an almost unthinkable task it was to fight off all attacks with only 50% eyesight, especially when you turn the wrong way, it was really Ingolf who won. For us anyway; we were all happy and proud of him. And he, of course, was happy, too.

I was the one to go in next. And I hoped it would be my lucky day; we were two points down and needed this win. I was ready and so was my opponent. I gave my best. However, as so often, the referee was not happy to see me in the ring, and I only got four points from seven I believed I had made during the two minutes fight. So, my opponent won by two points. Jan 'The Viking' came next and succeeded by a margin through his fighter heart. He was a born mixer, like Helge. Then it was 'Big Bear' Uwe's turn, a true fighter, as well a born mixer of the finest sort. He declassed his poor opponent and went on getting all his points like Helge and Jan who won their division as well. So, all in all a good day for the team.

And yet, we knew, we could have done better. However, there were half a dozen or so competitions all over the country to improve and plenty of time to work on strategies, eliminating errors made that day and in the past before the final qualification tournaments

Besides the wonderful moment of victory in the ring, there always was this other one on the Monday or Tuesday after, when we were awarded a trophy and certificate in front of all the students, and pictures were taken for the newspapers. It simply was great and a tremendous motivation especially for the children and youths. At this point I must humbly lower my head in gratitude with a big thank-you for the chief sports editor of the 'Flensburger Tageblatt' who was not only a fan of our work with children and youths, but also a main force within the news world supporting our programs, ideas and sports events! He got us into the headlines almost on a monthly basis. We didn't really have a budget for advertising. In fact, only through hard work, mouth to mouth propaganda and constant build up of our reputation as a team we managed to stay in business for nearly 14 years before I emigrated to the U.S. to continue my studies, seminars and workshops and to promote my ideas and programs for everyone in need to be in a better place in life.

*

So, after all those years I handed over the dojo to my two main Master Students with a heavy heart. No contracts were signed, no agreements written; officially, I stayed owner of the dojo with all its equipment. What a mistake. Within two years, the non-profit business was mismanaged into the ground. My Masters had done their best, but these great athletes were no match for crooked businessmen, greedy landlords, bankers and even criminal forces of the 'underworld' who had apparently opened the hunting season for this old dojo. My friends had listened to the wrong people. Fake sales contracts and rent agreements were (illegally) signed and no money was ever paid to me as compensation. But the worst about this despicable business was the fact that, out of pure greed, all those youths in town had been deprived of a place they had called home for so long. I know the brains behind these highly immoral and illegal transactions. And one day I am going to make sure they will pay the price! Especially bitter for me: As State Sports Advisor of the DAVK (1986 until I left for the U.S.) for handicapped children, working closely together with the DSB (German Sports Association), I had the tools and education to initiate and implement projects and programs for children throughout Germany using my dojo as platform for testing and improving them. And now my legacy had no base any more.

*

When I opened my little business, I had no idea, blue eyed as I was, how hard it was going to be to just keep the doors open, as it unfortunately is—even today—for any organization that wants to help and move things to the better without thinking of the money first, especially in the sports section. It was a constant battle to balance the low earnings with the costs for maintenance and development. Without the active support by volunteers, businesses and sponsors, our organization, certainly our annual kickbox events, would not have been manageable! Our dojo was not profitable, an incredibly important aspect of any business I had to learn the hard way. However, getting professional advice, especially in the sports world, is not easy. There are a lot of charlatans and money scams out there, helped by unregulated laws throughout the sports division in Europe as well as in the U.S. Only a few organizations can be trusted like the German Sport Association, the Olympic Sports Committees in Europe and the U.S., the DAKV, the DSSV, the Kadgamala e.V, the Heart and Sport Association or the Cooper Aerobic Institute of Health in Dallas, Texas. Dr. Kenneth H. Cooper who I had the honor to meet is a celebrated world bestseller-author, a public speaker and researcher in the field of aerobic and cardio health. Nearly all leading authorities in the fitness and health industry see Dr. Cooper as the founder of the aerobic exercises system and therefore a vital contributor to better cardio health.

So, the experienced athlete, the teacher, the committed father or mother who is thinking about initiating a non-profit organization or a health or fitness centre to serve and help our youth should consider carefully. And even people who are about to sign up at a local gym, fitness centre, institution or organization should think hard where they put their money. They should get informed about the financial situation, statements of mission, purpose and program; and they should as well take a close look at the condition of the premises; and know what's up, where the money goes. Old outdated equipment, badly maintained facilities, sloppy paint work, hardly any or no weekly maintenance programs, few, if any, special events; but thousands of dollars throughout the year, and, even worse, money collected at fund raising events. It does not take an Albert Einstein to see the quicksand you are standing in. You better keep your money in your purse!

*

So, coming back to the vital point, raising the money and/or getting a share of the funds available for the initiation, maintenance and development of any kind of organization to help, support and educate especially young people has been a major problem in the sports world. It is not any different in the kickbox sector. In 1977, Geert Lemmens tried to change things by founding the WAKO (World Amateur Kickbox Organization) in Berlin, Germany. Its purpose even back then was to unite all styles and forms under one roof with regulations for education and competitions mandatory for all members. As a consequence, the international Olympic Committee would surely have recognized kickboxing as one style to be added to the catalogue of Olympic disciplines. Large funds from the Olympic committees and governments would have flown into such an international organization, not to mention the money raised by the promotion of national and international kickbox events on an Olympic level! For years, the matter was discussed among the many self-made associations until Geert Lemmens became tired of the fruitless dispute and left the WAKO open only for the truly interested Martial Artists, their teachers and leading personalities. It was a blow to all those small associations when the style of Tae kwon do became an Olympic discipline not too long ago and received all the benefits an honors going with it. The kickbox and Karate organizations blamed each other afterwards for having missed this monumental chance for their thousands of youths to be supported on a large scale and, of course, to profit from tournaments on an Olympic level! But 30 years before, they had discussed away exactly this chance!

For a number of years I had the honor of representing this great organization, the WKA (as well DBO) as chairman of the North German counties. One of my first missions was to unite our Martial Arts fellows in the eastern parts of Germany and to integrate them in the WKA-family. For decades, nearly all Martial Arts styles had been forbidden before the 'Iron Curtain' was finally taken down marking the end of the cold war. It was only in Judo and Jiu Jitsu those athletes were allowed to compete officially and on Olympic level. To practice any other styles, especially in private, was a dangerous thing and punished by jail with all the terrible interrogations, even of family members and friends, going with it. Needless to say, the Martial Arts community was in desperate need for teachers, education, seminars and belt tests. I had realized the shortage, when my team and I had traveled to Dresden (East Germany) not long after the borders had been opened to visit a small group of Martial Artists we had met some months before in Rotterdam, Holland.

*

The occasion was one of the most mind-blowing and strange experiences I have ever had in my whole life with a turn at the end that would change me forever! It was a weekend seminar by the one and only Grandmaster Hirokazu Kanazawa (Mr. Karate), Japanese Karate champion in 1950's. As soon as we heard that this legendary Grandmaster would visit Europe, we registered with all teammates who were able to take that weekend off and go.

I will surely never forget: It was a cold weekend it November 1992, when Bill Leone, a handful of my team members and I arrived at the train station. To pack the sports gear and belt into a gym bag and go off with my teammates has always been an extra pleasure for me. I loved traveling, especially with friends. The atmosphere of a train station alone is worth every effort. Since we were an hour early for the train, we went into the bar inside the station. And, just sitting down we saw the great Benny 'The Jet' on the TV that stood in a corner of the bar. He was getting ready to defend his World Kickbox title at Madison Square Garden. We were thrilled and glued our eyes to the screen. Benny has never lost a single one of his 200 (!) title fights as far as I know; that speaks for itself, and I was sure he would win this one as well. But not that fast...

There he was getting into the ring. A few seconds into the fight two jabs were executed and then, out of the blue–hardly to be detected how it had come about–Benny 'The Jet' placed a jump-back-kick out of a 180 degree turn right on the ribs of his opponent lifting him 6 feet into the air and throwing him against the ropes, almost across. The man dropped and collapsed.... the fight was over and the audience went mad! So did we. Incredible! Had we been in need of motivation to go to Hirokazu Kanazawa's seminar, it was there now! And with rising spirit we boarded our train.

Quite a lot of 'horror' stories we had heard about this legend. Already in his sixties, he was supposed to be still lightning fast in his moves. And it was said that during his entire career he had never given away one single point, had not even been touched! You have to let this roll over your tongue. Well, we did. Nearly the whole journey of half a day. So, we would surely find out in one way or the other what it was all about....!?

On arrival at the place of the event we met the group of East German students. Although we were all about the same age, the differences in behavior, the way we thought and what we believed, were obvious. Just how they looked at our sports gear, designer shoes and brand jeans told us a lot. Not surprising, really, after so many years of isolation from the western world and its goods by a 5 meter wall and barb wire fences, not to mention education and the loss of entire families. So what to do? What to say? The last thing they needed was to be looked at as second-class people. So we decided to be just ourselves and let them come along if they wanted to.

*

However, it didn't take long to realize that most of them found it hard to let go of the old ways, having probably been kind of brainwashed in the youth organizations they had been obliged to join. Most of them kept dropping comments like, "You and your stupid outfits, yeah, really hot. They make you so much better, don't they; it's only propaganda shit." We decided to let these comments slide, to just write them off as work in progress. There was a generation problem that would surely take years to overcome.

But first, of course, we had a whole weekend of fun, learning and, for sure, pain in front of us: The extensive hall was filled with about 1000 Martial Artists from all over Europe and even the U.S. And right before us the legendary 9th degree Black Belt and Grandmaster himself! Normally at an event such as this, a few high-ranking masters would take the lead, for sure in the warm-up phase. But not this time. Grandmaster Kanazawa told us, translated from Japanese into English and German by an assistant "Good to have you. However, you paid to learn from me; you will get me, no one else! On this line only the Grandmaster will stand; even the warm-up will be conducted by me". Well, he was already 62 or so. Up to this point I had been told I was a condition 'buff'; the one who worked out four to six hours a day, five days a week, performing 300 push-ups and somewhere between 2000 and 3000 sit-ups a day! So, naturally I was thinking, "Warm-up; fine, let's get started."

I was top fit, strong as a bull! But not from within. I knew very little about the meaning of 'Inner Chi'; even worse, I was convinced that the good punch comes by the size of the biceps muscle and not the hip thrust. On top of this, I just reasoned, I had received my first-degree black belt after nearly 12 years of long, hard training and never ending misconception; I had finally made it. So, I was found in the first line of Black Belts, facing the Grandmaster head on. It was great being able to watch him from so close by; and I remember him looking over and noticing my slightly different way of standing and moving I had become accustomed to, and I could see him raising his eyebrow. Then, the warm up of a lifetime began. I would probably not have believed this hadn't I been there myself: With his 62 years or there about Kanazawa performed–as a start-up–500 leg-squats, first with his left and then with his right leg followed by a quick front-snap-kick. Then 200 push-ups and 500 sit-ups. And we, of course, were to follow his example! Half way through I was hoping this would be it!

Then five minutes stretching to relax, which saved us from passing out. My legs were on fire, my shoulders felt as if they would explode any second. No time for thought; we had to continue our warm up (!) with 500 leg raises counted in Japanese. After a while, I turned to see how my fellows were coping: Of the 1000 practitioners who had started out, only about half were still 'warming up'! The others had already sat down just watching! And from those who kept going only a handful was able to complete the 500 leg raises. And me? Well, I was standing in the front line. So, there was no way I would sit down, no matter what! Half way through the exercise my left Achilles tendon went on fire; I could feel it swelling up–a symptom, which would haunt me for a few more years and become more psychosomatic than physical. It was the result of an old injury from a few years back caused by the incompetence of a fitness instructor in my town who had let me use a weight machine without proper supervision or explanation. The machine was old and jammed ever so often; the weight was too heavy; and due to the jamming of the machine my left Achilles tendon got ruptured. It should mess with my performance and my mind for a few more years. But this weekend I was determined to take no notice whatsoever!

Over the course of the next four hours we trained in Katas most of us had never even seen before, but through Hirokazu Kanazawa's graceful and brilliant way of teaching, even the lower rank Karatekas got it right. Well, the ones who were still at it. After two hours of power-play workout, there were only Purple to black Belts still standing. All other practitioners were already sitting at the sideline. I must be honest, most of us were waiting for the magic answers, the techniques and enchanted super jump-spin-kicks, which would put anyone out of their misery–some kind of Ninja moves nobody knew any more. After all, he won the K-1 'underground-till-death-or-defeat' six times; never lost; and, even scarier, had never been touched! If he was human, there had to be a secret move, a technique to explain this phenomenon! After all this power workout there was not a single drop of sweat on his forehead. I was strong but not too wise, as you can see…

Grandmaster Kanazawa must have read our minds. At some point, he walked right into our midst and asked us to form a wide circle. His translator, a high ranking Black Belt, was a friend of mine: One of the VP's of Green Peace in Hamburg, Germany, who passed his last test for his next black belt. A great man and supporter of our team. The Grandmaster then explained to us where 'Inner Chi' comes from and how to awaken it within ourselves. He continued, "If you are in this seminar to find some secret technique, you will not find it. You only waste your time. Instead, you should open your hearts and eyes, let go and become through this weekend your true selves by loosing your emotional restrictions and barriers." Until this moment, despite my success as a teacher and athlete, the closest I had ever come to "Inner Chi" was drinking a chi-laté ice tea. Therefore, sitting within inches of this legendary master, I listened to his words as if under a spell, studying his every move, never taking my eyes off him. Kanazawa carried on, "If some of you were hoping to be taught a magic trick, a short cut, you have come to the wrong place. You have wasted your money and might as well go sightseeing. However, if you are willing to open your hearts and minds and listen to your inner spirit, then there is a good chance to find yourselves and maybe even some 'Inner Chi' by the end of the week-end. But first things first: Simplicity and perfection are the major keys besides 100% personal fitness of body and mind to achieve personal greatness. All starts with the 'Za-Zen'. To learn proper meditation and to clear your minds for your new journey are two of the most important foundations for any Martial Artist."

Kanazawa then ordered us all to stand up and go the proper way down into the 'Za-Zen' with him from the start to open our hearts and souls for true meditation, which would be the foundation for everything, for sure the needed base for relaxation to clear mind and soul. I remember thinking, "That sounds strange. Can it be that simple? There must be more to it." So, we all learned first-hand how to properly sit down and meditate. For the first time ever, I felt a strange lightness of my body and a tremendous openness of my mind. It was almost as if I was flooding; my mind had never been so clear. It was amazing; in all these years of Martial Arts training I had never felt like this–or was it just my tiredness that caused this? I should soon find my answer, totally unexpected.

H. Kanazawa knew our questions; they were written over all our faces. He simply picked a high-ranking Black Belt out of the crowd and told him to attack him with all his strength, all his power, not holding back anything; otherwise, he would fight back and he should surely be sorry for it. He made the Black Belt promise and they took up their positions. What followed only took a few seconds and was hardly perceptible for us or even the Black Belt. The man attacked with a roundhouse-kick to Kanazawa's head, lightning fast and with all the power, he was able to gather. Before the kick found its target, Kanazawa who had stood motionless until then parried it and–at the same time–hit his opponent with a back-fist to his nose sweeping him off his feet. Before the Black Belt reached the floor, he placed a strong punch in his Solar Plexus and, as the man was hitting the floor, side-kicked him on the head. There was not a sound to be heard in the hall; we were all floored, couldn't believe our eyes. And Kanazawa just said, "Apart from having chosen one of the easy to spot kicks, he did well!"

We needed another display to at least try to understand. So, the Grandmaster chose another Black Belt and ordered him to attack, but this time with a fast and hard punch. To make it more difficult for himself Kanazawa only stood an arm's length away from his opponent. Now we really paid attention. Again, everything happened within seconds: With all his might the Black Belt aimed a right punch at Kanazawa's face, but just before it reached its destination Kanazawa's hand came up out of nowhere and lightly–so it seemed–touched the Black Belt's lower arm pushing his fist out of its course so that it missed its target by several inches. At the same time he counterattacked with a lightning fast elbow-strike to the Black Belt's shin knocking him out cold. Before reaching the floor the Black Belt was side-kicked into his ribs and he was sent flying backwards several feet. Now we were all truly mesmerized. And I suddenly realized that the techniques we had seen were all well known! So what was the secret? Or did we see it without seeing? Many questions were running through our minds.

And again, the Grandmaster read our thoughts. "My friends; what you just witnessed was a perfect example of 'focus' and through this the realization of 'Inner Chi'. Whether you believe it or not, it is all in you! Has always been. You only need to find the path to yourselves to unlock this natural 'Power from Within', which the true masters call 'Inner Chi'!" He then ordered us to sit and meditate, to let our minds walk to the just witnessed Randori, breaking it down step by step, picturing every bit along the way, every move, every muscle contraction, every reflex down to the moment the opponent was lying on the floor. After that we should start again, this time feeling our way into the position of the opponent and work through the motions from his point of view. It was a surreal experience. It felt like being actually attacked and hit. Even my muscles tightened up, and my reflexes took over. From then on all of us followed the Grandmaster with our eyes and ears without a thought for anything else but the training through the rest of the seminar.

After that memorable meditation exercise, Kanazawa ordered us to put to use what we had just felt and experienced with a partner. We were to forget all our fears and worries, put aside our limitations and inner barriers and only communicate with gestures indicating the technique we wanted to use and who was to be the attacker and who the defender. The stillness that followed his words was so complete you would have heard a piece of paper falling to the floor! I could not compare it with anything I had ever experienced. Through this silence, we found focus and accuracy I believe none of us ever had before. After a while, Kanazawa came over and watched me attacking with all my might and then my defense moves. There he intervened and demonstrated how to unlock my hip and by this free my 'inner power' despite my physical limitation. Then he let me try and walked away with a nod and a smile, pleased about the outcome. It was strange; with every move and through the silence and focus applied my hip felt less and less tense.

My defenses and attacks improved by the minute and so did the ones of my partner; our performance elevated higher and higher. By the end of the second day however, my Achilles tendon burnt like fire; limping badly I dragged myself across the hall, dead tired, because I hardly got any sleep at night through the pain. But I was determined to finish the seminar, no matter the consequences! Looking back at it today, it was very stubborn and stupid and no example for anyone to follow! It was a miracle my tendon did not rupture! At the end of the seminar, I got a bitter-sweet reward, when the Grandmaster told me he was impressed by my performance and iron will to succeed despite my injured foot. He also kindly signed my Karate passport and was impressed once more: The pages were already full and he could not find a spot to write on; so he signed the back cover with a smile. Needless to say, I was happy and proud and thanked him, beaming all over my face.

On our way back home my friends and I hardly spoke. We sat quietly and let the events of the seminar pass through our minds. This 'once in a lifetime' experience changed everything for me and set the foundation and course for my further life journey. Although I knew I always wanted to be a Martial Artist, until this weekend I had not been a hundred percent sure if I also wanted to be a teacher and mentor for the rest of my life. Going home, I found the answer…yes I did. Every teacher and coach should be sure like this! There are far too many around who just like their half days off and the long summer vacations. Do not be another one of those. Sit down and look into yourself; and if you even only come up with as little as an occasional 'sometimes' or 'maybe' as far as extra effort is concerned, get another job quickly! Do not be a mediocre teacher or coach. We need people who are prepared to dedicate their time and effort to form the next generation of leaders and champions, of teachers and mentors, of loving husbands and wives. Sometimes all it takes is one man or one woman, one seminar, a few hours, to change lives forever.

*

Like Hirokazu Kanazawa who changed our lives with one amazing example after another! One of many reasons why: Martial Arts with their countless different paths and dozens of different sides to one and the same idea–handed down through the centuries–hold the answers for a lot of modern problems. As an athlete and teacher, I have never come across anything so complex, versatile and rich as the Martial Arts. I tried other disciplines–soccer (goal keeper), free-style swimming, table tennis, eight ball, mountain biking, motor cross, riding, beach volleyball–with fairly good results once I got the hang of them–it mainly was only a question of time. But I always reached a somewhat dead end eventually, and there was nothing more to learn, nothing more to develop, to gain.

In Martial Arts, I have come far, won many trophies, received honor, reached fame. And yet, there has never been a limit to development, no matter how high I climbed the career ladder. The Arts in themselves are a **constantly evolving, relentlessly moving, self-inventing, redefining, never-ending learning process;** and nothing I ever experienced as athlete or teacher came even close–one of my major reasons to have a loving relationship with Martial Arts.

My fellow athletes and I got humbled every time we visited a different Grandmaster like H. Kanazawa or Gene LeBelle, a different dojo, every time we took part in a seminar, an event, especially when these brought us into contact with a another style, a different country, another culture. It made us feel as if we had just started to study Martial Arts not long ago; we were like children with an unquenchable thirst for knowledge and wisdom sucking in all the information and new ideas presented to us like dry sponges draw water. Energized and electrified we went home afterwards and could hardly wait to share the things we had learned with our students and friends. Many of my old team mates like 'Iron-Horse' Ingolf, many of the Martial Artists from Eastern Europe who had to practice in hiding for so many year like my swim coach, many of my great students, all of them share one and the same experience: **They have been positively influenced, energized and elevated to greater heights allowing their truthful hearts to emerge and even set free** (in some cases) by the **'Power from Within'** unlocked by Martial Arts. They found their true potential, their path through life.

Looking back, it was rather a journey considering my humble beginnings with my swim coach. Followed by Geert J. Lemmens and his wife who had helped me to remove a tremendous mountain, taking quite a personal risk doing so. For most people surely an unthinkable path to go from the wheelchair I partly had to use to a competing Black Belt, even a champion. One more reason for me to dive deeper into the aspects of rehab and healing within the Martial Arts. And over the course of the last 20 years–always my own history and experience in mind–I have combined far eastern healing techniques with western rehab forms and deeply embedded them in my own Art, 'Shin-Tora-Do' Karate, for my Master Students to learn enabling them to help our many wonderful students overseas and in the U.S., especially those with particular needs (our '**Rock-Stars, Black Belts in Live**') to build a bridge of health, love and self-esteem and find a better place in life. To this day they work together side by side making a lasting difference, even changing lives forever in many cases.

Moreover, I documented these techniques and forms step by step–first for my own use, then for my students–to finally integrate them in this book as guideline not only for people with physical or mental limitations but also for the ones with emotional and psychological difficulties, for everyone in need to get more 'fit for life'. Through emotional and physical workout anybody is able to reach their true potential and by that become stronger and more productive, which will lead to more acceptance and consequently to, perhaps, a more satisfying job or career, higher earnings and better lifestyle; and, last but not least, through that to a more positive outlook on life and personal independence.

So let me take you back once more to the beginnings, this time focusing on the actual techniques and healing methods we used in order to succeed.....

Chapter: 5

Arts, Shin-Tora-Do Rehab, Reflections, Global Awareness

It was in the fall of 1979, as I walked with a cane into the dojo of Geert J. Lemmens and his wonderful wife, Vera. I remember it well: After our little meeting in his office, Mr. Lemmens asked me to come back the next afternoon in workout clothes, and I gladly did. The first thing he needed to do, he told me after welcoming me warmly, was to assess the state of my fitness. So we sat down on a matt and I did light stretching to determine my range of motion and my flexibility, which was close to nonexistent. Then he asked me to perform a few simple steps and movements to see how far my balance was developed. Well, there was hardly anything to see: My range of motion was so limited, that I toppled over and fell nearly every time I moved. I remember getting nervous and quite frustrated.

Finally, I had to do ten push-ups, which was no problem, because I could straighten out my legs. But when it came to ten sit-ups my legs cramped up right away. My hip flexors and hamstrings tightened and only allowed me five sit-ups before I had to stop. I was totally frustrated and afraid I would be told to go home; and I would have lost my chance…but as all great Masters, Geert J. Lemmens read my thoughts. He said there was plenty of hope for me to get better; my balance could be improved, my legs strengthened, the cramping lessened. However, to what extent this could be translated into becoming an active Martial Artist and fighter was not for him to determine at the moment. But the chances to become a good boxer were not bad at all. So, I did not mess it up? Even though I was falling over all the time? "No son, I will gladly be your teacher. There is nothing impossible. Let us see what we can do. There are no limits, if you put your mind to it," he told me. My frustration was gone in an instant, and with a smile all over my face I got up and shook his hand. From that day on, I spent four to five days in the dojo every week, after school and whenever I could get away from the orphanage, for years to come.

The first month was one of the most frustrating in my life so far. Every time I moved only a quarter inch too far in any direction, too fast forwards or backwards, I fell over right away. My legs, hip flexors and hamstrings cramped up within minutes limiting me to very small and careful movements. But that didn't keep me from trying the 50 Kilo sandbag hanging from the ceiling, which had mesmerized me from the start. Over and over again. There was a 120 kilo sandbag hanging from the ceiling, which had mesmerized me from the start. Over and over again I tried to use it, but as soon as I hit it hard, I fell on my butt. Swearing like a sailor, I got up and tried again, until Mr. Lemmens intervened. He told me to concentrate on stretching, light steps and my balance instead to find my boundaries in order to overcome them. I was not happy about this, and Lemmens carried on: "Have more patience and leave the sandbag alone for now. Before someone can run, he must learn to walk; and in order to walk, he needs to learn to stand on his feet.

And this applies to you just now more than to anyone else." That was not what I wanted to hear, but I instinctively knew that the Lemmens' ideas of sports rehab were the best chance I had.

But it was anything else but easy to take it with confidence. Not only my body gave me difficulties. There were many youth and young adults who voiced their opinion I didn't belong among them.

The first month was one of the most frustrating in my life so far. Every time I moved only a quarter inch too far in any direction, too fast forwards or backwards, I fell over right away. My legs, hip flexors and hamstring cramped up within minutes limiting me to very small and careful movements. Besides, there were many youths and young adults who voiced their opinion I didn't belong among them. Although Geert and Vera Lemmens made it clear that I had a place in their dojo and was there to stay, it didn't stop those students from commenting on me behind their backs. "No worries, the wimp will quit within the next week," which was extended to 'within the next month,' 'next spring,' 'summer,' 'next year.' To their sorrow they kept finding me around, although I inwardly cried most of the time, and, with tears in my eyes, screamed silently every dirty expression I could think of, while I was working through the pain.

*

One of the difficulties you face as someone with cerebral palsy is finding the right measure while exercising: In order to avoid muscle atrophy throughout your body and heavy tensing and cramping within your tendons and hamstrings you must work out all the time, just to keep mobile and stretched out. But if you overdo and strain your body, especially your tendons, just a little too much, it can result in injury, even death due to the cardiovascular system shutting down etc. It can be compared with walking on the crater verge of an active volcano: One tiny step in the wrong direction, and you had it! However, if you do it right, there is no limit for you.

This difficulty is surely one of the major reasons why hardly anyone wants to be bothered by someone carrying this kind of risk into a conventional gym or fitness institution. Understandable, but the result of little to none education throughout the fitness industry around the world, for sure a shortcoming of the governments and their health department officials. Proper laws and regulations are long overdue in the field of fitness and health! It is a miracle that dozens of senior citizens and de-conditioned baby boomers don't fall off the tread mills and ergo meter cycles with a heart attack or a circulatory collapse on a daily basis around the globe! And it is not just a very dangerous field for them, but really for everyone wanting to improve their condition and health. Even more so, because it is a playground for charlatans, money scams and personal trainers who, having completed a weekend's education without any merit or deepness, are let loose with a worthless piece of paper in hand; without any background of experience and knowledge, not even able to determine as little as a RHR, THR or RCHR, let alone to draw conclusions from the results; or a simple measure of blood pressure and heart rate, to find out whether your client is healthy enough to exercise and which program will fit him.

With this limited to no knowledge, without any continuous education, and I mean a real education of many months, how can you blame the personal trainer next door feeling uncomfortable and declining his/her involvement in such a task, when someone out of the norm and with the need for a special program comes along? However, it is our shortcoming as well; we could all write to our state representatives, our governors. Well, do we? In my lifetime I have been a member of dozens of gyms around the world; and I can truthfully say I have rarely come across a place where I did not witness people exercising in a health endangering way and wrongfully using the machines with the 'personal trainers' sitting, or rather sleeping, on the equipment next to them, only changing the weight stack once in a while, chewing bubble gums, T-shirts sticking out of their pants and the attitude of someone working for a fast foot place that should better be shut; not to mention the illegal use of and dealing with steroids within gyms across the country. Today, I still have the metabolism and toxic level of the time I was 16 according to my blood examination results at my last check up. That only happens when you are drug free! Four times I was witness when a de-conditioned 'baby boomer' fell off a treadmill or Stairmaster in four different gyms. In all cases, those poor people died of a heart attack or a respiration failure. Did that have any consequences for the trainer or gym that did not pay any attention, let alone test their clients' THR (target heart rate) frequently to ensure safety and health?

Do not get me wrong, I do not condemn the hard working personal fitness trainers, especially not the ones with a proper educational background and with a thirst for knowledge who continuously further their experience in order to serve their clients in a healthy and professional way. This is not an attack or bad mouthing on my professional counterparts throughout the fitness world. It is a statement about this unregulated industry with its millions of adults, youths and children who place their health trustingly in our hands, not knowing any better or what to look for. However, it is of highest importance to address this problem on a large scale. Just to name it does not help or make it any better.

Only through continuous education of our fitness professionals, the teachers, instructors and coaches, will we be able to build a well needed awareness in the world of health and fitness. It is my intention to contribute to this education and consequently awareness built up–from the beginner to the pro athlete, from the young teacher to the long-term coach. Together we will be able to change things to the better. Within this and the following chapters you will find details about my research–carried out with the help of my Master Students–and the rehab programs created and first used by Geert Lemmens and myself together with the success stories of some of my finest students from Germany, Texas and California.

Please be advised that everybody, even the ones with the same problems or injuries, needs a different approach and more often than not a completely different rehab plan. And please make sure to **consult your MD before you start exercising, for sure before starting a rehab program**. Also check on the gym of your choice if your teacher or instructor is licensed and insured, and as well if his/her education meets with the requirements to attend to your needs in a safe and healthy way. And for the rehab, fitness and Martial Arts instructor, teacher, mentor and coach–please keep in mind that we all have great responsibility, especially for our youths, guiding and forming day by day. We mould their future, determine their health. In a few months, even only weeks, these kids or de-conditioned people can be physically and emotionally injured for life. So, it is nothing to be taken lightly, we should always give our best. And again, for all hard working and committed teachers and instructors, well, see it as a positive acknowledgement of the importance of our daily work.

And this is the right moment to pay my respects to many fine and wonderful teachers around the globe I had the honor to meet and work with: First the one and only Geert J. Lemmens and team; Gene LeBell and his instructors; Dan Inosanto and his student Rod Armstrong (who trained me and ensured my victory at the 98 NBL World Championships as my partner); Toni Bader (thanks to his efforts I was allowed to study at the sports college) and team; my childhood friends Jo Jacobsen and Bill Leone (GER) who supported and believed in me against all odds; Benny 'The Jet'; Bill 'Super-foot'; Chuck Norris and Carlos Machado (USA); my good friend (and brother) Mihran Aghvinian of Hye katch do; George Manoukian; (the whole Hye-Katch-Do Team) Bas Rutten and Emanuel Bettencourt, his Master Al Dacascus; Michael Wuebke (GER); Sal Comito, Highland Martial Arts, Staten Island NY, USA; Simon Kim who does amazing work with kids in NY together with his twin brother (tigertwins.com); and to Lou, former Mr. USA, body building (CA) who helped me getting ready to defend my World Karate titles in Savannah, Georgia, in December 2000. He is a shining example of a fitness and sports instructor constantly educating himself, keeping his mind in shape and his skills at their best to serve his clients with knowledge and well designed fitness and rehab programs, elevating them safely to their true potential and health–on his own, no matter the regulations -, in my case to the top of the world winning gold three times, setting standards for many generations to come.

*

Returning to 1980, it was not easy for Geert J. Lemmens to train me. There were no reference books to consult and not really anyone to talk to for advice or ideas. In fact, a number of MD's voiced their unfavorable opinion about him working with me. He even received a letter once warning him of the consequences should anything happen to me. And even two years into our workout together the government's Child Services prohibited him to teach me! But Lemmens who believed in our joint journey against all odds continued exercising with me in private or rather in secret against the authorities' orders. I would not like to go into details about this whole business; the times were different back then and can hardly be compared with the situation today. Moreover, the billion-dollar-fitness industry was still a thing of the future and with it the well-equipped gyms and studios, let alone all the useful machines that would have helped us. As a matter of fact, Geert J. Lemmens didn't only open the first dojo in our small town, he also was for sure one of the first throughout Germany to combine fitness workout with Karate, Kickboxing, Yoga and their healing techniques. I remember quite a few fellow instructors and dojo owners voiced their strong disapproval, even laughed at him and ran their mouths behind his back: "And now he even trains a crippled kid; well, he has apparently lost his mind; I wouldn't be surprised if he gives up next week because the boy got badly hurt," were some of the comments my teacher and I heard at a health event in the town we were part of.

So, there was nothing much to go by. Geert J. Lemmens knew we had to build up my leg muscles and decrease the spasms and cramps at the same time. But he was inventive. He constructed the machines we used all by himself before he got this 'Universal Tower-all-in-one '16 stations' of the art gym: There was, for example, this ordinary table, covered in foam material, with a simple joint on both sides where a metal arm was put through going down, with a simple round iron bar sticking out to put the weight plates on.

There were no safety facilities, and for sure no concentric controlled movement was possible; and in order to use this simple thing you needed constant help.

During the first months of training, my leg muscles were so weak I was almost unable to lift the weight bar, and Master Lemmens had to hold it on the way down so that I would not hurt my knees. Overextending my ligaments could even have ripped them. Therefore, he mainly applied the 'negative resistance'-technique, which was long known among Yoga and rehab experts. Lemmens lifted the arm of the 'machine' with only five pounds of weight on it, and I tried to hold it for a few seconds before my muscles started to cramp giving up and I got hurt. Then he told me to hang on and fight against gravity on the way down as long as I could; which, in time, would strengthen my legs and enable me to lift the bar on my own in a 'positive way'.

This training I preferred to the stretching exercises, which–I must admit–I rather hated. But they were necessary and a vital part of my rehab. Without them, my abilities would not have developed they way they did. So, weight training was my favorite in those days, and I could be found in the vacant weight room most afternoons before Karate class began. Having my father's genes and talent for sport helped a lot. He had been Golden Glove Middle-Weight Box Champion throughout the 40's and 50's, even setting some kind of record. Well, like father like son. God bless his heart.

Another machine out of the middle stone ages in fitness, as I always jokingly called them, was the round dumbbell–solid iron; darn, it hurt when it hit your toe; no rubber coating invented yet. Since I was too weak for it and we didn't have the 'smith-machine' (I am not sure if this had even been invented yet) Mr. Lemmens came up with a totally logical idea: He took a simple flat workout bench and placed it between my legs; then he told me to put my feet apart as far as I could and slowly squat down onto the bench in a right angle but without actually sitting down.

Through the first months close to a year, I did exactly that. I was unable to hold myself–not to mention to hold my legs in a squat position–for more than five seconds. I exercised for hours at the time, until I managed to overcome the pain and to control the spasm just for one single proper squat in one afternoon, which had been my goal for a long time. But rather than sitting in the orphanage waiting to get beaten up for nothing or yelled at by the warden, I gladly took the four hour workout for one proper squat and five good sit-ups any day–and some stretching, so that Vera Lemmens was not on my case, in a loving way of course.

At some point, the Child Services wanted to have my knees cut open and operated on. Luckily, however, Lemmens explained to me that the loss of cartilage in my knees was and always would be a continuous problem due to the wrong angle and dragging use of my feet. He also explained that all joints have one thing in common: They work as a close unit. Therefore, it would only disturb the balance and fluids within if a joint is opened and operated on. Besides, you can only take something out, but not replace lost cartilage. So how could an operation make a lasting difference to my health? The answer was clear: Not at all! It was only an excuse to make money off my back, getting the performing MD a little richer, cheating Social Security. Not much has changed since, I believe. Lemmens on the other hand explained to me in detail that if I was able to strengthen and build up my quadriceps, hamstrings and supporting muscle groups, they would lift up my patella and therefore take some pressure off my ligaments underneath. That way there would also be less patella tendonitis and as a result more mobility and little to no pain as long as I kept training and stayed in shape. So there was no reason why anybody should cut open my knees!

I decided to take on the challenge and started to exercise my legs more than before. One of Master Geert J. Lemmen's philosophies always had been: '**On your weaknesses you need to work even harder, and, in time, bring them into line with your strong points instead of only relaying on your talents and abilities**.' This didn't make it any easier for me. But I was determined to turn the table. One evening I was sitting in my favorite solitary spot close to the orphanage. It was my thinking and get-away place: Under a large tree near the forest, not far away from the edge of a natural sand cliff overlooking the valley below. I made a deal with my knees that evening or, rather, told them off: "I do what I want. As much sport as I please. And you can do whatever you want… just don't bother me ever again. After all, I save you from the knife; and you better not forget it!"

Throughout my life so far, especially as an athlete, I must say it has worked like a charm most of the time. And my teacher had been right; as long as I keep doing my leg workout and stay in shape, my knees never bother me. Some occasional aches and pains, perhaps, never anything major. Besides, I had a deal with them, and still have! I am the MASTER of my own destination, for sure the master, the boss of my body and mind.

Back then, however, I remember thinking: "How can it be that a number of MD's, a shrink and the idiots from Child Services who were running my life, make it as difficult as possible for me?" They were all against my training with Geert Lemmens. They even harassed him and tried to take this wonderful mentor and teacher away from me without any sensible reason, without any reason at all. They all swore my knees needed to be cut open. Lemmens was the only one who really cared about me and my health and who took his time to explain so that I understood–a fine moment of truth and a wonderful positive experience differing so much from countless others throughout my childhood…

Another favorite training unit Lemmens was putting me through consisted of a simple mix of ballet, traditional Martial Arts and Yoga. It started out with exercises at the ballet-bar: I held on to it while I stretched out, bent sideways to left and right, stretched my back and hamstrings, moving forward slowly without losing my balance. To attack the weakness in my hip-flexors and adductors he then let me hold on to the ballet-bar with one hand and lift up one leg to a right angle keeping it in that position as long as possible (isometric or also positive resistance training). A few seconds at a time was all I could manage for months. Man, my hip-flexors were on fire! After about a year I had not only to lift my legs, one after the other, but also to stretch them out pointing my feet forward as much as I could. This extended the range of motion of my feet and ankles and improved my mobility. Lemmens then showed me how to lift myself up onto my foot balls and lower down again until my heels touched the ground in a slow motion see-saw move. This exercise strengthened my legs as well and improved the flexibility of my feet even more, which consequently led to an improved walk. We always finished the training with a few short Tai Chi moves and breathing exercises; not that I knew then what they meant, let alone understood them. All I knew was, they were part of the 'package'.

Geert J. Lemmens and his wife never treated me as a child with a handicap. For them I was just another kid in the dojo who only needed a modification of a lot of moves and training techniques. Apart from that, I was simply normal for them–well, with the exception of my overload of energy and my big mouth I could hardly keep closed: Forever joking and boasting that I wasn't born with giant biceps', no, they had become so large, because our teacher let me do push-ups by the hundreds throughout the week…..until I started to listen instead and shut my little mouth! Years later, I saw the philosophy that lay behind his and his wife's way of treating me; and I made it to my own when I began to teach: If parents, guardians and teachers give handicapped children more freedom and more encouragement to develop by themselves, if they let them make their mistakes to learn from, these children will surely gain self-confidence a lot faster and find their own way in life! There are countless possibilities for every single one of our special kids out there.

I had been lucky enough with my parents. They never treated me as handicapped, shielding me from any danger. They never forbade searching and experimenting. I was allowed to go my own way, even when I was heading down a detour path or a road with a dead end. My parents let me find out by myself. Today, I am more than grateful for this sometimes called 'tough love parenting'. It was for sure needed and can be seen–together with the things Geert J. Lemmens and his family did–as a formula for my success. It made me to the one I am today. Everyone is a born winner; sometimes it only needs a little awakening and encouragement. As a result, I developed an unmistakable character. One major element of it was and always has been my never ceasing will to succeed; through that I didn't lose very often. And as a sort of additional insurance I thought up a simple little method: If there was something I wanted to gain in my life, a championship, a place at a school, a degree, even a friendship or a mentor, I thought about it intently and sometimes quite long. And if I came up with a 'yes, I do' afterwards, I gave myself another ten seconds to decide whether it was too much trouble to go after it or not as a last chance to sneak out a backdoor. If this backdoor stayed closed, nothing could stop me any more until I reached my goal, no matter how big it was, no matter how long it would take to get there! I never backed out, ever. As a result, I accomplished or reached almost anything I put my mind to. Even such crazy sounding things like becoming a Black Belt , a Martial Arts champion fighting even able bodied opponents and winning quite often, opening four dojos, becoming a champion-maker and respected teacher–again, the first one of my kind.

Of course, all these are possibilities for every child and definitely for any of our 'Rock Stars' with special needs. From the start, such a child has to face emotional barriers, troubles and nightmares as an individual. Most are traumatic; and if they are not addressed and treated early, there will most likely be lifelong consequences. Just consider a number of things the average person takes for granted: Normal walk, for instance, with normal 'fancy' shoes, instead of orthopedic ones, especially in the case of a girl; normal speech without hesitation or stutter; or speaking at all. And the questions these children ask themselves surely every day like: "How would it be to move about without a wheelchair or a walker; how would it be to see; how would it be to hear what others say?" Try to imagine how it feels like to have a handicap by birth or due to injury that is easily noticed, easily seen: Other kids stare at you every day, tease you, push you around just because you are different; call you names and even beat you up simply because they can do that.

And here we are, complaining about our little troubles on the daily commute, our meaningless daily disagreements at the office; we feel bothered about visiting Aunt Wilma at this place where they had dumped her hoping we will never end up there. We could carry on like this for a long time! And yet, the majority of us are born blessed and don't know it; or some don't care, acting as if it is supposed to be that way! Is it? Or is it the luck of the draw, what parents we have and what privileges or social backround we are born into! You are the judge!

Next time you pass by someone on the street who looks as if he/she could do with a bigger piece of the pie, a helping hand, **you** decide how to react: Ignore again as usual, even being bothered. Or do what you can in the situation: Give a smile and a helping hand to someone who tries to cross the street; to an old lady who has difficulty getting on the bus; give someone the chance to join the traffic on a busy road, not just the hot girl (or boy, for that matter). You will be surprised about the positive and grateful reaction.

And next time a child in the restaurant plays a little too wildly, because the poor single mother did not find a babysitter or couldn't afford one, let it be before running your big mouth pre-judging her. Just smile. It is amazing how many unexpected smiles are returned to you throughout a day! Not to mention how great it is to make someone feel better–just with a friendly smile, a gesture, a little action.

I always keep in mind the first words Geert J. Lemmens said to me when we were sitting in his office in 1980: "Before I will teach you how to hurt someone, how to throw a hard punch at your opponent, you will have to learn how to heal; and in your case to heal yourself first and foremost." Believe me, I needed to repeat this to myself many times in the first year of my training with him, confined to very limited movements and not being able to join Karate lessons on a scale I wanted to. Most of the time I trained alone under his watchful eyes. It was not easy. But he always came up with new ideas that substituted the heavy sandbag and sparring sessions and caused similar effects. Like this brilliant and very simple one: There were these old school-bungee-bands with handles. Lemmens nailed two of them to a wall, shoulder level (later there were four of them) and placed me between them–holding the handles, facing the room–to do punching movements, left arm, right arm and together. It was so simple and yet the effects were great: I did not fall over throwing my punches as I did trying to hit the sandbag; my technique, balance and strength improved; I trained the muscles of my upper body and legs. All at the same time! And after my daily workout and exercises I watched the classes train; and I knew one day I would stand within the ranks because I had promised myself.

Acknowledgment: If I ever paid Master Lemmens five hundred dollars, an amount that I probably never had, it wouldn't be nearly enough. But living in the orphanage, and even after, I hardly ever had any money. I helped around the dojo, but that did not take care of a single private lesson a week, let alone the four to five hours every day, five days a week I spent at the dojo. He and his wife moulded me, protected me and provided me with a safe haven to go to in these difficult times. And through their loving teaching and mentoring they prevented me from getting into big trouble like the majority of my fellow kids at the orphanage. Most of them thought trouble was a constantly recurring, unstoppable event; not to mention drugs, alcohol, crime and violence. These two fine people showed me a path and initiated a journey I never imagined would be possible. And they taught me **that I have a choice–always–which road to take, no matter the odds.** And today, it is my turn to give back!

*

This reminds me of another sad and moving story only life itself can write: In the early 90's a war broke out in Yugoslavia. For a year the UN sat on their behinds and debated about involvement and intervention while an ethnic cleaning went on among people who had been brothers and sisters before. Entire villages were destroyed, their inhabitants murdered cold-blooded, women and children were brutally raped. Thousands of innocent victims were traumatized. No one was really helping. The German government–second largest (behind the USA) exporter of weapons–declared they couldn't get involved because of their role in the 2nd World War, not even together with the UN– however, the same government claimed the credit of uniting East and West Germany! So, the world watched this horror going on from a safe distance; and Yugoslavia was split into dozens of enemy regions.

At about that time, Edo walked into our dojo. He was an amazing Black Belt and former full-contact champion of Yugoslavia. He worked in a restaurant owned by one of his uncles, but most of his family lived in Yugoslavia. He was really strong; and I don't think I have ever had a harder sparring partner. We all liked him from the start. One day he came into the dojo, and I sensed right away that something was wrong. Later on Edo sat at our bistro-counter in tears. I made him a shake and asked if he wanted to talk. It came all out, then: A massive air strike had hit his hometown, and a bomb had destroyed the family's house. In an instant his father, mother, most of his siblings and his Grandmaster who had been visiting the family were killed.

All of us were shocked; and it flashed through my mind how precious and fragile life and health was and that it should never be taken for granted! We tried to find comforting words. But, really, what can you say to someone who had just lost almost his entire family? Seeing Edo later hitting the heavy sandbag we all wished we could help him more. But sometimes you have to accept that there is little you can do–a moment of bitter truth. However, we must never forget, even in a situation like this–lost for words or not– we can make a crucial difference in a person's life by just being there. Being a friend–and in my case being the best sparring partner someone can find–you help ease the pain and stop the aggravation. More might not be done. Wars and senseless violence will continue to happen around the globe, no matter how hard we pray for the madness to stop.

Ask any MD of an ER or trauma centre. For sure, he/she would love to prevent brutal fights, killings, fatal car accidents. Can he? Or is he part of this micro-cosmos we call our little world; and his role is to save as many lives as possible and help, one day at the time, to ease the pain. Frankly, he is better off seeing himself like that. At least he is then able to say once in a while, "I came too late to save that life, but, thank the Lord, I have saved this one here now," knowing he had done much more than was perhaps possible, hoping the little boy would make it safely through the night....

*

And this takes me to a subject within rehab that has been close to my heart for a long time: The abuse of alcohol and drugs. I saw countless tragedies and negative events throughout my childhood and teenage years, which kept reminding me to stay strong and not to give in. Too many friends I helplessly watched wasting their young lives going through hell only to end it in a flash by an overdose. And this is another reason for me to devote several chapters of this book to rehab and my style Shin-Tora-Do. Only if we know the dangers and can read the signs, will we be able to detect and counteract fears and addictions in our loved ones and friends. Only if we have the necessary means can we help and prevent greater harm, so that we do not have to find them wrapped around a tree on a motor cycle or in a run-down motel with a dirty needle in their arm. Like I had to find my older brother on September 11 in 1992…

There is really not much you can say, hardly find any words to describe what you feel. Emptiness and numbness take over your heart and body. You wish you could turn back the time, just this once. You search for answers, ask what went wrong. And finally you start to blame God and the world, and yourself! Had you done enough? Could it have been prevented? And for how long? Could you have done more? A million questions run through your mind like a ghost train. One thing is for sure, the answer lies within your self. Many people do not recognize the signs of addiction, not even in their own children, friends and loved ones, not even when those have been in severe trouble for years. But why not? Maybe they leave them alone too often; maybe they are occupied with their own affairs too much. Just think about it. There are always signs, patterns of behavior; and if you take your time and look closely, you will see and realize there is something wrong. Life and health of our loved ones are the most precious things there are. Do not let yourself find out this after you have lost them! Get into action if needed, because even though prevention is the only effective measure, the process of self-destruction can be held up in nearly every stage of addiction. And treatment and rehab by doctors and counselors provide a good chance for healing and recovery!

Sadly, exceptions write the rules, though: My beloved big brother was one of them and a classical case: Starting from harmless cigarettes, he went to smoking a casual joint (pot). After our mother was kidnapped and the Child Services separated us, he began to consume an increasing amount of alcohol to cope with the unbearable situation. After only two more years, he was heavily on speed and heroin. And to get the money for the daily shot he did anything he could, became a dealer, a thief, a prostitute.

My brother had never been very strong. Highly sensitive and emotionally unstable, he didn't cope well with problems. He used to hide behind my back when trouble was approaching. And when the Child Services took over our lives, it was like a death sentence for him, the beginning of the end. These people claiming they knew what was best for a child showed little to no compassion; they could not care less. They did not even allow us to visit each other after they had separated us. What could we have done? We were only children at the mercy of government social workers. For years, we had no contact. He mainly wrote to my father, who sadly could not cope with the situation. And the woman he lived with couldn't be bothered. She never told me anything about him, where he was or how he was getting on, never even said he kept in contact, when I telephoned. So I had to assume he was o.k. After all, could it be worse for him than it was for me? Being pushed around from one institution to the next, my hands full with daily difficulties, trying to survive the horrors. I didn't know it back then, but the only difference was that I never drank alcohol or took drugs, which provided me with a clear enough mind to stay away from harm, to stay out of trouble as much as was possible–that is for sure one reason why I came out of these difficult times in one piece -. Through all these years, I had an uneasy feeling when I thought about my brother, of danger even, hovering in the shadows; a battery slowly running out. It was scary, and I think it would even have troubled someone living in normal circumstances.

So, it is perhaps not surprising that I decided to go and look for my brother, when I was a few months short of my 18th birthday, not able to stand the tension any longer. However, escape from the orphanage was considered impossible. The chances to get caught by the police, brought back in handcuffs and physically and emotionally abused as punishment were overwhelmingly good. No kid had ever been able to stay away for more than a couple of days. There was a lot to think about: The orphanage was located outside town at the edge of a natural swamp and forest; only one narrow road led to the town and the nearby interstate. Here, the police would look first, of course, and someone like me was easy enough to spot, even if I made it into town. The forest was hard to penetrate, especially at night, and led nowhere. The swamp was too dangerous to get across. For weeks I racked my brain, there must be another way…Then it hit me: A horse would know its way through a swamp by instinct! Nobody would expect me to take this route; and I would have a several hours' head start–before the man hunt was on–to reach an interstate and get a lift down south where I figured I could find my brother. Besides, I had an aunt down there who I wanted to turn to.

An underage youth who runs away from a state institution, rightfully or not, becomes–at least became in those days–an outlaw wanted by the police! By breakfast time at 7.30 a.m. the warden would know I was missing; by 8 a.m. the local police would be searching the grounds and area; by 11.00 a.m. the county police would be alerted, and within 48 hours the national police would hunt me like an escaped convict without any crime committed except wanting to be free and find my brother. So, the right timing was crucial! I sat down and asked myself the famous question, weighing pro and contra, going over the details of my plan. That night I hardly slept, haunted by bad visions about my brother; and I let my 10-seconds-back-out-chance pass…

I asked my roommate for help to get across the swamp on horseback and a female friend to let us out of the building by a window. The girls' quarters were on the first floor; here were the only windows that opened wide enough to get through! The escape night was fixed. And before the night watch made his last round at 12.00 o'clock, my roommate and I were able to sneak up to the girls' room and hide under the beds. After all got quiet, we made a rope from bed sheets and my friend and I let ourselves out the window and down. It was easy enough to get to the stables, saddle the horses and reach the swamp. Slowly, step by step, we went across–it was some experience, I can tell you!–and arrived safely at a spot near an interstate comfortably distant from the orphanage. My friend wished me luck and took the horses back while I hit the road hoping for a hitch-hike. 'The luck is with the brave', they say; and before long I found myself sitting in a large truck heading south. The trucker, of course, asked me what I was doing on the road in the middle of the night. So I told him about my brother. He was amazingly understanding and even offered his help. Just then–and I don't think I will ever forget this–the radio played one of my favorite songs: 'Against the Wind' by Bob Seger.

Since time is money in the transport business the trucker kept going without delay; and by morning we were a few hundred kilometers away from the orphanage. In my pocket there was the petty cash money I had 'found' the night before–sorry warden, payback is a bitch–to get just enough food and drink during my journey.

There is another reason why I tell you about this, my actions and the motivation behind them: Sometimes it is difficult to understand our children, especially our teenagers; the way they behave, how they react to us, why they rebel, take drugs or even run away. The story of my brother and my experiences during this time might help to understand some of the fears and motives behind these drastic measures, which I believe are an outcry for help in a situation that seems impossible to cope with in a healthier way. And if you pick up a few characteristics or behavior patterns as signs of trouble your teenager is in; if only a single youth can be pulled away from drugs and bad influence and brought back home, back to school with and through my book, I'll be the happiest man alive!

It took us two days to reach the capital of Bavaria; and when I finally said good-bye to the friendly trucker, a new sense of freedom and independence flooded through me. I walked around the city, drifted through the hustle and bustle in the market place, sat in one of the many street cafés and watched life go by: Hundreds of people doing their shopping, sightseeing, enjoying the sunny day. A completely new and amazing world opened up to me; and I was determined not to let it slip away again. However, I had to move on. It took me a two-hour ride on an interstate bus to reach my next destination, the town my aunt lived. I was born there, too. It was quite a strange feeling for me, then. A young couple was nice enough to give me a lift to my aunt's house, where I arrived late at night. My aunt was a sweet old lady who had known me all my life and who had always been a close friend to my parents. But she was very religious, quite old fashioned and self-righteous. Of course, she was surprised to see me, though happy, and asked me about my age straight away. I could convince her I was 18, but after two days the orphanage shrink called–I had forgotten to take my aunt's letters out of my locker; and obviously they had been found–and she told him I was with her. I was eating a cherry pie on her balcony when two policemen stood suddenly next to me. They wouldn't let me finish my pie… Rather black humored I tried to joke about it, but without the chance to catch a second breath I was taken to the police station in handcuffs and thrown into a cell for the weekend.

On the following Monday, they let me talk to a social worker. Luckily he was a leftover from the 60's: Long hair, self-made sandals and bag; a 'let's-save-the-trees-and-hemp-plants' kind of man. I could convince him I was just an innocent misunderstood child who needed to be kindly sent home. He took me out for breakfast, bought a train ticket, and within the hour, I was on my way back up north…at least that was what he believed. At the next station, I got off the train and cashed my ticket that was still valid, because I had avoided the conductor. All the way out the station, I was grinning. What a pity, though, I wouldn't be able to see the face of my warden waiting for me to step out the train–sorry man, you deserved this for beating all these kids in your care.

My next destination was Bonn. I thought I had a good chance to find my brother there, because it was his place of birth. I could hitch-hike again and arrived in the evening. Quite exhausted by then I decided to look for a quiet spot in the subway-system first. Next morning I had breakfast in one of these cheap morning diners. Some things just don't change: You can spot a runaway or drug addict, for sure kids in trouble, hanging around the park, at a 'seven-eleven' store, bus, train and subway stations, the local youth club and, of course, in the 3rd rate streets. However, not only undercover police officers and concerned parents look around these places. The predators as well roam the spots to find their prey. I had a few encounters with some of them myself, but being tall and muscular I simply told them to leave me alone, otherwise I would kick them all over the place. But there are many young runaway youths, especially girls, who have very little chance.

The night before I had run into one of those at the train station: She was only sixteen, desperate, confused, and seemed not to know where she was going. I understood her only too well. There were a lot of 'punk kids' around, and it was not too smart of her to be at the station all alone. So, I suggested staying with me if she liked; besides, it would be good to have someone to talk to. The girl did and I heard her story: Feeling misunderstood and constantly controlled by her parents, especially by her father, she had seen no other option but to run away as far as possible. After she had listened to a short rundown of my life so far, she was quite stunned. I asked her if she would not rather like to go back home and talk to her father instead of facing the dangers on the street. After all, she had a home, although her situation was a little difficult. The girl was a bit frightened at first, but I could convince her to call her dad. He came to pick her up; and since he seemed nice enough I told him why his daughter had run away and that he, perhaps, should try a softer approach and give her more freedom. He was quite grateful, and I think, he felt his conscience, because he gave me nearly a hundred dollars. Happy that the girl was safely back home, I treated myself to a double breakfast next morning.

The following two days I spent searching every hangout I was able to find. It seems, the local drug scene can always to be found in the same areas of every big city: First, I went through the parks. It makes me shudder considering the innocent under-aged children who are always there as well! Then I looked around the public bus and train stations, the dives, the "red light"-district bars and the dark side streets. I met many people who knew my brother, but no one had seen him around for a while. One of them suggested he might be in southern France or Morocco. I asked them all to give him a message from me, that I was trying to find him. They promised...

The next night it rained heavily. I was wandering along the empty streets looking for cover, when a police car passed by. After about a hundred feet it stopped and turned around. I knew there was no chance, no use to try and run, especially not for me, anyway. I was thrown into the car and driven to the next police station. "Hey, at least I am going to get some dry cloths and something to eat," I was joking to myself, my black humor kicking in again, this time rather desperate, though. At the station they interrogated me and asked for my passport. I said I didn't have one. No use. They searched me and found it. One of the policemen pushed me to the wall. As he was about to grab me I gave him a good right punch. He tumbled backwards...and that was the moment when the other two joined in. They had just taken out their batons and were about to beat me unconscious as the captain came in and intervened. The policemen let go of me, I was thrown into a cell.

Luckily, it was not a weekend. So I saw a youth counselor the next morning. Of course, this time I could not pretend to be an innocent and harmless run-away. The man knew he couldn't just put me on a northbound train. Also, in two days I would be 18 which meant they would have to let me go then, if they liked it or not. So, they spent thousands of tax payers' dollars to drag me all the way back up north, not to mention the costs for the youth counseling, just for two days! Since they seemed to know I would take the first chance to get away, they put me on a plane to Hamburg, which had the nearest airport to my destination–in handcuffs! This whole ordeal was rather like a scene from a low-budget movie.

I remember talking to a business man during the flight, who happened to sit next to me. He was very nice and understanding. After I told him my story he shook my hand and said he wished there were more youngsters in my generation with my guts and that I would be just fine. When we arrived at the airport, he wished me the best of luck; and I don't think he realized how much he helped me to get through the flight! At the terminal, I was handed over to two policemen who escorted me to the gate, where the warden waited. "Great," I was thinking, "he is going to beat me up as soon as the policemen are out of the way." And sure enough, he pulled over the car just a couple of kilometers short of the orphanage and ordered me to get out. He then asked how I had gotten out of the orphanage and who had helped me. Of course, I told him nothing. We were standing face to face in front of the car, and I could see in his eyes he wanted to hit me. But then he just told me to get back into the car. To my surprise, the warden was rather friendly for the rest of the journey. He even said: "I must give it to you, kid. You have balls. Quite a world traveler, young man. And I am impressed that you have never been in bigger trouble like the other kids; no drugs, no alcohol, no break-ins. I understand that you want to find your brother, but you have to stay in our care until you are 18, if you like it or not. After that you can go wherever you like. I am sure you will be just fine as long as you keep your nose clean." What a speech. I had not expected that!

And I hadn't expected to be treated like a home-coming warrior by the kids of the orphanage either. For them I was a hero: Alone against all odds I had made it longer than anybody else before me. It could not lift my mood. After all, I had not been able to accomplish my mission and find my brother. However, I had two more days to go through; and soon I packed my bags, my uniform and boxing gloves and said farewell to my friends at breakfast. When I finally stepped out of the 'Rock' for good it was an amazing feeling. I was free and could start to build my future, find my own way, and embark on my true journey.

*

I felt strange walking the streets. Only 48 hours earlier, I hadn't been allowed to do that without permission, but it didn't matter any more. Of course, my first destination was the dojo. Geert Lemmens and his wife were surely worried about what might have happened to me. Besides, I couldn't wait to get back into my routine, now without intervention by Child Services and the warden. There was a lot I had to work through, the lost weeks of training; and I hoped the Lemmens' would not be too mad about what I had been up to. They were not; glad to see me again in one piece, they understood. And they helped me to cope with my worries about my brother and my future.

Apart from my financial and emotional situation, it was a perfect time to get going again: Physically I was in the best shape ever, and thirsty like a dry sponge to learn and train. The following weeks I made myself helpful with cleaning and tidying around the dojo and in the remaining time worked out as hard as I could. The place practically became my new home, for sure a safe haven. Some of the students started to call me 'Rocky' referring to where I came from and the way I looked. I liked it a lot. What a fine nickname compared to the ones I was used to: 'Limpy, Spasmo, hunch back'. It felt wonderful, a completely new experience.

One day, Lemmens took me aside and said, "Kohai, remember I told you that you have to learn to stand on your feet first before you can walk or even jump? Now it is time to teach you the next step. It is time for you to learn the cross-over step and the techniques going with it. As you know, they are the most important basic techniques for any fighter". So, I was about to get one of the last bricks for my much needed foundation. But like all my beginnings this was a humble one. Lemmens placed me with my back to a wall and let me practice right and left punches and jabs. He had two reasons for this: First, I could not get carried away with excitement. I had to learn the movements properly, slow to begin with, in order to eliminate what we call 'Chicken wings' in the Martial Arts world. Any reasonably good fighter can spot those wrong beginner-like movements and shoot you down with a strong counter punch before you have a chance to get to him. Second, leaning against the wall I was able to concentrate on learning the techniques without having to fight balance, which improved my confidence. This would not have been gained had we trained on the matt right away. During the following weeks I practiced the cross-over and pass-step, counter punches, right and double punches as well as double-punch and triple-punch techniques. It was a great new form of workout and a tremendous step forward on my way to become a fighter–something I had wanted for a long time.

Though determination and will pushed me forward continuously, sometimes I needed, as anybody else, a little encouragement; especially, when r was tired and couldn't force myself to do another exercise. Next to Geert Lemmens and his wife, Mihran, Marwan and Bohni, it was Peter Beschenbossel who motivated me most within the dojo. This great athlete and kickboxer had deeply impressed me from the start. And for someone who didn't know him it was difficult to imagine that his beginnings had been quite similar to mine. Through a heavy motor cycle accident one of Peter's legs had been almost ripped off. The doctors could save it, but the leg muscles were nearly all gone. Peter had just been released from hospital, when he came to the dojo and told Lemmens he wanted to become a kickboxer, no matter what. Within only six months Lemmens rehabilitated him with a special strengthening workout plan that also included stretching as well as healing elements. And one year later, Peter became German Full-Contact Kickbox Champion....an outstanding example for Lemmens' abilities and knowledge and for Peter's enormous will power! Peter trained incredibly hard and worked with weights, I could only dream of. Whenever there was a chance, I watched him and tried later to copy the way he used the machines and the moves within an exercise. Once in a while he would come over and say hello with a friendly encouraging nod; it always made my day. What a great character and wonderful warm person.

Peter and I had for certain one thing in common: In order to overcome most handicaps or major injuries you need to put yourself through a rigorous workout way beyond your personal 'comfort-zone'. Especially in the case of progressive diseases like cerebral palsy or muscular dystrophy you must push yourself well beyond your personal pain-tolerance-limit to stimulate–day after day, week after week–your muscles and nerve ends, the receptors and their impulses traveling to and from the spinal cord, reactivating the 'pathways' so that positive information is carried to and from your brain through the nerve-system. Only this will counteract the always threatening 'atrophy' and reactivate and coordinate so far unused or misused muscle functions; as a result the motor abilities will improve throughout the body. The training has to be conducted very carefully, though, to prevent injury.

*

I think it is easy to imagine now why a two-week 'personal trainer crash course'–or, even worse, a shorter one–is just worth nothing. The poor boy or girl would not know where to start and what to do, let alone what safety measures he/she would need to apply dealing with a handicapped or injured child or person. But you already know how and where to look for a good personal trainer, who will give you a helping hand during the first weeks of training showing you the proper movements and how to use the equipment safely and to your advantage. You only really need to perform the exercises properly and have a solid foundation of knowledge, the rest will become second nature sooner or later; and for some, especially for those with a handicap or injury in need of a change in lifestyle, a daily exercise. Before you know it, you are on your way to a better place in life!

It has happened not only to Peter Beschenbossel and me but to many of Geert and Vera Lemmens' students. They have rehabilitated, healed and formed numerous people throughout Germany and Europe. Quite a few of them went on to win championships around the globe. But they achieved even more than that: These students passed on the skills and knowledge learnt from them to their own students, who in turn handed them down to the next generation changing countless lives and forming loving families and relationships in the process: A never ceasing, never ending flow of Bushido throughout a life-long journey. Over the past 20 years I researched and documented the remarkable life-paths of a number of those students, who had found answers and cure in many ways within those personalized and specialized training programs Geert Lemmens had initiated, just like me. And so, by hard work and this research and documentation I developed and implemented the '**Get Fit 4 Life–Systems**' with the assistance of my Master Students who are always so delightful to work with.

*

In our humble opinion, rehabilitation goes far beyond the treatment of the injured and disabled. It must also include people who need to overcome addiction and the effects of emotional and physical mistreatment. In fact, it should include anyone in need of a better life. This is a large field and enormously neglected not only in the U.S. but all over the world except, perhaps, in a handful of European and Scandinavian countries. To add to the problem, addiction, physical and especially emotional abuse are not as easy to see and diagnose as, say, an injury. Moreover, therapy in these cases takes time, if a lasting effect is to be gained! With high health care expenses and millions of uninsured citizens, it is clear why those unfortunate people mostly fall through the net. And it is no use to talk about prevention either! Which is a shame for every western country, especially for the ones that call themselves 'leading nations of the free world'; a slap in the face of humanity!

I believe, this is only a matter of greed and indifference towards the individual and his/her value for their country: Expendable and replaceable in an instant; no concern for the hard laboring worker and his/her needs. And certainly not for thousands of homeless living on the street, like in down town Los Angeles on 'Skid row'. They are passed by suffering, even dying, with hardly anyone taking notice. Unless they are so 'bold' to step into our world and ask for money or food, 'dare' to let us see their faces and bother us with their needs: "Why does nobody take them away so that our streets are kept clean and we can walk them undisturbed? Why are they allowed to annoy us, feeling misjudged and mistreated by our behavior?" They even start an argument, how disgusting. "At least then they are taken away and put somewhere out of sight." Many of these poor people are in desperate need of help or medical and psychological treatment. They consume narcotics and alcohol in order to numb their pain and forget their daily nightmares. And to secure their supply they become thieves, dealers and prostitutes. Many are prepared to do anything and therefore turn into easy prey for large criminal networks. And this will go on until proper long-term rehabilitation programs are established, until governments and the public start to really care! Instead of just shouting for the neighborhood clean up, the quick fix!

As an example: It is known, that in the greater Los Angeles area hundreds of homeless and drifters work as so-called 'drug-runners'. Who is watching? No one pays attention in the first place! One of the biggest drug—especially cocaine—dealers in the U.S. has used these people for his deadly enterprise for the last 30something years. And hardly ever is anything done about it by the authorities. There was an occasion some of my students and I had a close encounter with this man who apparently had personal reasons to come after us: I was teaching and helping Jessica who had become my student in Texas in 1997. With deep, true dedication and hard work she removed tremendous obstacles out of her way making me proud like hardly any student before. Jessica became so strong emotionally and physically that she was able to walk away from her nightmares all by herself fighting like a lioness for her son. She became my assistant and we did not do anything wrong, unless teaching, mentoring and healing handicapped children is an offense.

This so-called 'respected business man', however, decided to make our lives a misery out of mere anger and thirsty for revenge, because he had been unable to seduce and drug Jessica. I would not have let this devil in sheepskin take control of her to destroy this amazing young woman. The ordeal that followed was barbaric: The man used quite a number of people for his evil plans who couldn't be brought in connection with him, even our 100% handicapped student and Michelle, two wonderful young women who didn't even know him. He put retired police officers and fake FBI agents on our track to video and audio tape us, he spread lies, cheated and deceived. And for a while, we got a phony head-bounty on us—which he would never have paid, was even not willing to—only to scare us and to fool others into hunting us for free.

All my female students and I were a 24/7 target. And a whole town was watching doing nothing! Except Sensei Bill of the U.S. State Department, former Captain J.T. Butts of Santa Monica PD (current chief of police for all LA airports) and his fine men and women, who were the only officials who acted on our behalf. And so did every Grandmaster with a name and Mihran with his Hye-katch-Do team. They all respected us; and protected us as much as they were able to. And I didn't speak for over a year to keep us all safer and as a silent protest. We were all put through hell. Yet, the more this man tried to break us the more we became determined to prevail. It even made me smile because the almost 10-year-old indestructible bond between us, the compassion, dedication and deep natural respect for on another, grew stronger day by day. Let me quote Bruce Lee: "We teach, we mentor, we like. The decision is ours to make!" Besides, every Marine goes through much worse things and still stands his ground. In the end, this dealer got nowhere. We won, not even blinked, no matter what....

*

Organized crime, especially all types of violence against whole groups of people–conveniently overlooked by the authorities–has always been and will always be an offence against any human culture. Instead, cooperation between government agencies, charity organizations and the Church to take care of problems and find long-term solutions–and I mean real solutions, not just half hearted gestures for us to feel better about ourselves–should be understood. To invade another country, kill their inhabitants and destroy their land in the name of humanity and democracy is just the same kind of crime. Even worse, if done by a nation that claims to be Christian.

Countless atrocities have been committed in the name of God across the centuries: Just think of the 'White Templar Knights' who had burned, plundered, killed and raped their way from England to Madagascar between 800 and 1200 A.D.; only to make themselves, the English Crown and the Archbishop richer! Or the Spanish and Portuguese soldiers: They had come to Middle America as 'reformers' and destroyed civilizations from Mexico to Peru. And let's not forget over 30 million Indians, hundreds of tribes, just erased to give space to invaders who called themselves civilized and Christian. Centuries of slavery in the U.S. and around the globe. Ethnic cleaning in Russia, and in Armenia. Ever heard the saying: 'The winner writes history'? Has anybody ever asked the losers?

Or apologized? Not really in this country! The descendants of those natives who had survived the 'cleaning' still have to ask permission if they want to start an enterprise on the land that really belongs to them to afford a decent home, proper schools and healthcare. And we act as if we do them a personal favor (God bless my old friend Floyd Red Crow, the Western Man, and his **Eyapaha.net** Institute MDR, CA.). What about Central and South America? After we had destroyed a culture thousands of years old, we complained about its children–deprived of their heritage and roots, their honor and pride broken–who come to North America today to find a better way of life, to provide for their families! You judge. Not much has changed since the Middle Ages, only the weapons are a lot more effective.

And there is another kind of assault happening right on our doorstep as it were, on a daily basis: The assault on our environment. Air and water pollution on a large worldwide scale. Destruction of natural habitat and, along with it, the endangering of species, even their extinction; global warming, destruction of the ozone layer. All done for profit. 'Global player' companies have tropical rainforests burned or cut down, as an example; they buy land–used and needed to feed the people–from corrupt governments and local officials of poor countries to increase their profit in one way or the other. Already today we are faced with health problems that might not endanger your or my life directly, but certainly the lives of the next generations. Nobody can say we have not been warned.

Thirty years ago, in the early 1970's, well-respected scientists predicted fatal consequences of the increasing greenhouse effect. The world did not want to know. On the contrary, these scientists were ridiculed and even seen as enemies to the modern economy because drastic changes that would have been necessary, even back then, could not be 'afforded'–they would have lessened the profiit. So please do not judge the survivors of those days too hard.

A brilliant mechanic, working for a French car manufacturer, invented the first converter to drastically reduce the emission of dangerous fumes of cars in the late 1960's (that is right: in the late 60's!). A couple of years later his invention was ready to be patented, but his employer was not interested; he earned too much money with his ordinary cars. Officially, he claimed this 'crazy' idea would jeopardize the car industry, its growths and therefore thousands of jobs–an excuse not to make necessary changes we hear even today in every corner of the world. So the mechanic went to a rival company. This company bought the pending patent together with the proto type….and shelved it. About 15 years later a German car manufacturer introduced one of the first converter equipped cars on a commercial scale. We do not really want to think about the millions of cars that would have run polluting the air a lot less for these 15 years! And did the car market suffer? Certainly not! Instead, thousands of jobs were created–and not lost as predicted in 1972–to produce these converters and to equip the cars with it.

However, let's not make the mistake to think the car industry was finally concerned about our health and our environment. Almost any major manufacturer, any industry around the globe, only complies with the new laws for the reduction of air pollution under the pressure of government watchdogs. Otherwise, they would not be bothered. 'Why, it will not kill me, not even my children. So what, I have a business to run, let the next generations deal with it.' They would get back to the standards of the 70's in a heartbeat. But at least there are laws and regulations established by many governments even though they do not reach far enough and the economy is still ruled by greed for profit and market shares. Thousands of acres of forest are illegally cut down in Indonesia and the Amazon every year, as an example.

So, what can we do? The average person on the street? Well, more than we think! You are the **consumer**, you are the one whose money is wanted. You have the **ultimate power in your wallet**. The (free) **economy is ruled by demand and supply only!** They determine production, distribution, quality, safety standards and price. Profit and market shares of a company depend almost entirely on the **customer's demand**. If he's not 100% satisfied with a product, he will go to the competitor next door. The company must react to stay in business. And if the consumer demands a complete change in production, quality and even company policy, the whole economy will soon follow….

Here are some impressive '**positive**' **examples**: When the concern about nature and environment started to spread on a large scale in the early 70's, a German company that had produced soaps and washing powders for decades introduced a new detergent to the market without chemicals that polluted the rivers or even threatened the drinking-water reservoirs. All other producers in the field laughed about this new product. They even started a dirty campaign against it trying to convince people a washing powder without those chemicals would be less effective and therefore not worth buying. But the consumers (mostly your parents, if you are my generation) decided otherwise. They bought the new detergent; it cleaned their clothes just as well and made them feel better, because they did something for their rivers and lakes. Before long, the market reacted, and today it would be unthinkable to sell detergents with those chemicals. What a victory for the consumer who altered the course of the economy and therefore the quality of our rivers and lakes helping to keep the drinking water reservoirs clean at the same time.

Let us take the cosmetic industry: For decades animals had been abused for testing creams, lotions and make up on an immense scale until the consumers decided it was enough, convinced by activists and animal-protection organizations. Today, you will hardly find a product on the shelves without a label reading: 'Not tested on animals' or 'made without animal products'. And in the 1980's, the public became more and more aware of the greenhouse effect caused by, among other things, octane gas used in spray bottles. The consumers started to demand changes and the industry came out with pump sprays. Today, hardly any teenager or woman buys these old-fashioned spray bottles any more. As a matter of fact, most youths consider it 'un-cool' to use them. And luckily it is just as 'un-cool' and out of fashion in our modern culture to wear the fur of wild animals!

Another great achievement of the customers is the availability of information about nearly every product on the market, may it be the safety standards of children's toys, the components of medicine or the digestibility of certain food. There are magazines, books and TV channels–not to mention the web–where you can find what you are looking for. All these are fine examples of your personal efforts to help save the planet for future generations. And, returning to the largely influential car industry, it is a shame that it took nearly 30 years and a dramatic rise of gas prices due to fast declining oil resources before the manufacturers came out with alternative resolutions–pressed by international organizations and the consumers' demand! Within the next 20 years, I am sure, the good old four-stroke gasoline engine will be history giving way to the electro-hybrid cars or similar inventions. Because we want them, and the industry must follow. Certainly not out of love for our environment and to save the planet, but to keep the customer happy and to stay in business! In the end, however, it works for both sides.

So, we should always remember: We are the ones with the real power; we are the consumers, the fans who buy the tickets for the show. If we do not go to see it, there will be no show! It is that simple. And now we must convince the governments of the so-called 'third-world-countries' not to give in to the pressure and temptations of western industrial nations to buy the trash they have prohibited in their own countries. Just think of refrigerators and spray bottles. In most European countries, in North America and Canada, it is against the law to sell or buy these if they still work with dangerous octane gas. And yet, it is not against the law to export them into the 'third-world countries'. As if the effects of global warming and ozone holes would stop short at the borders of the 'modern world'. Keep in mind: The health and fitness of the individual is connected with the health of our world.

So now we are in politics. Here, the rules of economy can be applied, too. We have the power: If we do not buy, there will be no sale. We have to ask the right questions, carefully listen to and read the statements about missions and intentions before electing any politician into government. And we must nail him/her and the political party he/she represents down to those statements and watch out for the promises to be kept. Otherwise 'Save the Planet' will only be a slogan and a decorative bumper sticker. The importance of the so long overdue 'political clean up' is forgotten too easily and too fast, once a party or a politician is in a leading position. Too easily and too fast, western governments are willing to overlook extensive pollution and to make compromises about health and safety standards in third world countries, in large parts of Asia, Eastern Europe, Africa and South and Central America, in order to keep 'political peace' and to 'improve international economical relationships'–meaning to ensure they can do business with them and increase their profit!

Just think of the tons of toxic waste that are discharged into the rivers without any filter-systems. The 'Rhein', for instance, one of the largest rivers in Europe winding through a number of countries, was nearly completely killed because these countries have used it as 'sewage pipe' for almost 100 years! Large factories blow health-damaging smoke out of their chimneys. Especially in the new industrial countries, in China, Russia or India, it is even worse than in others. And let us not forget the poisonous fumes and particles that emerge from the exhaust pipes of millions of cars in all those countries. Would you like to live in one of their major cities and walk about with a facemask to have some kind of protection against the smog? And the fines their industries may have to pay for polluting the environment can only be considered as 'pocket change' compared with the profit they make.

I believe it is rather a joke to establish laws for higher water quality standards and cleaner air within our borders. It only is a cosmetic cover-up and no more as far as the globe is concerned. If this madness is not stopped, the children of our children at the latest (!) will have to deal with the consequences. They will have to pay the price for our fatal mistakes: The threat of skin cancer if exposed to direct sunlight, asthma, lung and bronchial diseases, diabetes, just to name a few, before they are 25 years old.

It already is '10 minutes before 12' for our planet. And the damages that have been caused by the greed of international manufacturers, land developers and industry moguls, not to forget corrupt politicians, for money, market shares and power, are irreversible and not excusable. Without their active help, an assault on our world of such a magnitude would not have been possible. Had governments not looked the other way while rain forests and fertile land were destroyed, rivers and lakes killed by toxic waste, air polluted.... Had governments not ignored the warning signs, had they not developed a deaf ear for scientists and experts.... you are the judge once again. And you may as well ask: "What's the use of personal fitness if you can't safely enjoy your environment and the air you breathe?" So, let us remind ourselves again that we are the 'consumers', we have the power to turn the wheel. Besides, air pollution does not stop at your home. If you can, grow your own healthy food and have fun at the same time as you save money.

*

Of course, there have been great politicians who stood to their words, kept their promises and moved things: Mahatma Gandhi, Nelson Mandela, J. F. Kennedy, Willy Brand, just to name a few. I actually had the honor of meeting this exceptional German politician in 1979, when I was still a wild kid.....

Being locked up in the orphanage most of the time, my best friend and I took every chance to get away; and since there was no place to go in town, we just hung around the market square. One of those days we noticed something was going on in an old empty house at the square. Curious of course, we went to check and got a real nice surprise: About a dozen kids, youths and young adults were in there just hanging around, doing homework, playing an instrument or reading a book. It looked like a home to us, a youth centre without wardens or Child Services supervisors. Naturally, we joined in; and from that day on we went there as often as we could get away from the orphanage. The word 'squatter' was not that often used in Northern Germany, then certainly not as far as youngsters were concerned. There were the odd drifters or homeless around disused buildings, but not in an organized way with a mission at heart like in that old house. It became a safe haven for us.

The opposing parties, however, were speeding gossip around town that we took drugs, got drunk and did other wild things, a dangerous place for kids and youth. All lies! I never witnessed any drug- or alcohol-abuse, violence or molesting of children. One day, a big fundraising event in the market square was announced with a high-ranking politician as main speaker. Police and town officials wanted us out of the way, once and for all, of course, and gave us an ultimatum. We stayed where we were and even planned a little demonstration to draw attention to our 'youth centre'. On the day of the event, it did not look too good for us, though. The police gave us a hard time, and we had to barricade the windows to keep them out. However, the town major did not dare to have us taken away by force. The public would have noticed. After all, most of us were under age and it was election year... So we found ourselves, this group of harmless kids, youths and young adults, between the police officers and the major's officials who had a finger on the trigger, not knowing what to do. But the only question for us was: Would we be able to make ourselves heard or would we get our heads beaten?

This fund raising campaign was a bigger deal my friends than I had realized–not being interested in politics that much: With the whole town on their feet, the market square was jam-packed. A large stage had been erected by the political party responsible for the event, a live band was playing; there were TV and radio crews, reporters and a lot of security guards. When the main speaker was announced–it was no one less than the German (ex-) chancellor himself, Willy Brand–we decided to sneak out of the house and make ourselves heard. We split into two groups; one went right to the front of the stage and started to shout. The other, with me in the middle, made for the back in order to get on the stage from behind. As we were running along, the security guards came after us straight away. Looking over my shoulder, not seeing where I was going, I bumped right into two huge guys in suits, secret service men you only find in the movies. I fell over, but before they could jump in on me, Willy Brand himself appeared right behind them and stopped the attack. He sat me on a nearby bench and asked why we kids behaved like a bunch of punks. I told him the whole story about our house and us: That the police were about to kick us out because they thought we took drugs and got drunk, which wasn't true; that there were kids who didn't have a place to go and others who needed a safe haven to get away from a terrible home; that we only wanted a chance to prove ourselves and show the town we were able to run a youth centre on our own.

The Chancellor listened attentively and then replied: "I owe you an apology. I will speak to the major about it. And if there are no more disturbances of the citizens' peace, no drugs and no alcohol, I see a good chance for you to keep the house. Most likely a guardian will be appointed to look after your safety." I was impressed but more than skeptical. An official, and a high ranking one at that, who actually stood to his word and you could count on would have been something totally new. But my friends and I were in for a surprise: Our youth house was not closed down; the town appointed a counselor to be there most of the time, but we were allowed to run and manage the place by ourselves. We even received some money later on to fix it up a little more. So, there were politicians and officials around who deserved our trust.

This experience left a deep impression in my memory; and it showed that standing up for oneself and keeping out of trouble and away from drugs and alcohol paid! A while after, at school, I learned that Willy Brand had come up the hard way as well, had lived through the Second World War and had fought for his party to be included in the political landscape. Later allegations about his involvement in secret deals between German weapon manufacturers and the U.S. made him resign from his position. Nothing was ever proved! I remember his speech on TV about this: "If you do not believe I have nothing to do with this affair, if you do not trust me, you are simply not worth for me to be your Chancellor, and I resign." What a great man!

*

There is a connection between all of us in one way or the other, for sure on a deeper and spiritual level as 'one race' on our planet. That is why, in my opinion, hygiene, fitness, self-help and self-awareness are deeply connected with being an active part of our environment–tuned in with nature, as naturally living tribes around the globe call it. After all, we are only a small part of a much larger picture, yet we behave as if we own the world. The only mistake, I believe, our Lord made during evolution was to let us have the awareness of being different and the use of human speech! We all have our share of responsibility towards our Earth, whether you believe it, like it or you don't. And therefore, the actions we take throughout our daily lives make a difference to all of us in the long run. And if it is just as simple as collecting tin cans for recycling, buying an 'environment-friendly' car, using public transport to get to work, taking paper bags instead of plastic ones, keeping our streets, forests, beaches, rivers and the sea free of our litter.

It is us, the individual, the customer, the consumer. That is why self-awareness, health and fitness and self-help are so important on many different levels. We simply cannot afford to wait for governments to do the right thing. We must take as much action as we can to ensure our descendants will have an enjoyable place to live. Especially our children need to be aware of this. After all, they are the ones who will take our world into the next centuries. As an example: You live with your kids in a large city? And they have never seen a wild animal or even a cow? Why not take them to the countryside for a day or, better, for a weekend and let them run around a farm if possible. It will help them to understand that the milk is not produced in a cartoon; that the corn for their daily bread has to be carefully grown and harvested, and the chicken need to be bred. It will not only be a nice outing but a new experience. They will learn to see the connection between ourselves and the food we eat, and it will help them to understand the importance of keeping the environment clean. Our children are the next generation of consumers and therefore responsible for the future. Over 20 years ago, we were told just that; and had we listened, the world would be in a better shape. And let us not forget the growing demand for energy and drinking water by young industrial nations. Rather sooner than later, our resources will not be large enough to satisfy it. So, how will we keep peace in the world then? It is already difficult enough now!

The challenges all nations face today, the pressure mounting up more and more on current and future generations, seem overwhelming and unjust. But, on the other hand, if you walk back through the passage of time: Two ice ages; violent volcano outbreaks that had blackened the Earth for years; the 'Great Plague' the surviving Europeans called the 'black death', cholera and typhus etc.; not to forget all these devastating wars! Millions of men and women died, no matter their age or social standing! And yet, the human kind has always managed to survive somehow–one way or another. People moved across large distances, started again, even re-invented themselves. Therefore, I am confident, that when we finally wake and see the truth, we, as human race, will be able to meet the challenges of the 21st century and overcome war, hunger and world pollution as a whole and succeed. But we must wake up!

That is why I write some harsh words in this book. That is why I tie personal fitness and health together with world health and peace! You might say, "It is too much, too soon. What does all this have to do with me? It's really not that bad, is it?" I believe you have never been to China, India, Africa and the Middle East or to one of these other places where you can feel air pollution first hand so strongly you are not able to breathe. And never seen dozens of dead fish floating in the rivers. This–and a lot more–does not concern you? Global warming and world pollution, again, does not stop at your country, for sure not at your front door. It is time for change. And it is time we speak freely, openly, about our future, and take **'action together as one**'! Just think of our native tribes: There is so much wisdom, there so much harmony between them and the land…

Chapter: 6

Arts, Shin-Tora-Do, Addictions, Illness & Abuse (rehab part two)

Take any tribe that still lives from and with nature like in Africa, Australia, large parts of Asia and right here in America–our native Indians–as positive example. They keep their ancient traditions and ways, and we all can learn from them! For sure, a Martial Artist and Master must live his whole life by the law of the land, in harmony with nature, taking from it with a strong sense of responsibility and prepared to preserve, re-grow and protect.

A thousand years ago, the Indians of the rainforests in Middle- and South America had an extremely effective system to grow the food they needed. Traces of this system can still be seen: Four fields divided by watering channels. One field was sowed in; on another the crop was growing; the third was being harvested, and the last was left to rest. No corrosion of the ground; no over cropped soil like in large parts of Ohio and throughout the Mid West, for example; no fertilizers, let alone chemicals or pesticides, were needed to improve the harvest; the ecosystem was not disturbed, the environment didn't suffer. And yet, this system provided all that was required! In parts of Northern Germany, in Denmark and England, in all northern European sea states there is an effective two-field-system still in use, which is based on the same idea.

Why don't we do the same everywhere instead of using tons of chemicals all year to increase the harvest? We have even started to interfere with the genetics of our plants.We know the answer: It is easier that way to ensure profit and market shares! Those Indians were well ahead of us a thousand years ago. I would even say they were a lot smarter. However, here I must pay credit to the slowly but continuously growing number of eco-farmers in Europe! Many of us have certainly forgotten our inbuilt instincts and lost the connection to our inner self and to nature. It is high time to reactivate those instincts and become aware of who we are and our role on this planet.

You might ask: "How could our farmers stay competitive, how would they be able to survive without these 'modern' methods"? Simply with government incentive schemes encouraging them to combine useful old traditions with new poison-free methods. How could such a scheme be financed? Well, nothing easier than that: In the U.S., for example, we could reduce the expenses for warfare and weapon technology by a quarter of one percent. That would provide us with enough money for all farmers; and there would even still be plenty left for the development and introduction of new energy systems like wind mills and sun-collectors, for free medicine supply for 'every American' and even for better schools and housing! Let us remember this when the next elections come up…

Besides, some countries in Europe already have those incentive schemes on a smaller or larger scale. Well, how do they finance them?

We are all part of the life on our planet. And if we stop taking this life for granted, our nature and the air we breathe; if we realize our responsibility, we will surely re-define ourselves and even find our way back to our inner self. Start trying today, take one day at the time, and remind yourself how lucky you are. Walk along the beach, in the park; say hello to a stranger, a nice old lady, on the way. Become more aware of your personal surroundings; open up to the feelings of your loved ones, family, friends, neighbors. Do not be afraid to try out new things: Join a dance class, a self-defense course at your local gym, a 'friendly neighborhood' initiative (but always be careful and do it with reasonable caution). There is so much to see, so much to discover! Develop a new loving outlook on your life, become an active part of your environment and nature. Live your life out of the fullest every single day. You will feel as if a new person looks out through your eyes. Moreover, through this, you will generate a positive air around you that is conveyed to others, and they will be positively influenced. You will have turned into a fine example for our most precious, our children and youth!

*

Children, specially the ones with particular needs–our 'Rock Stars'–have always been close to my heart. And therefore I will now dive a little deeper into the work of my Master Students, Jessica and Michelle, and me with those wonderful kids and help to create a form of reference, maybe even a guideline, a source of wisdom, where everyone who needs and wishes to research hopefully finds some answers and true encouragement from the heart as we did training with these exceptional and lovely children. This work has been a great experience I would not want to have missed; and I certainly would not want to have missed my 'Angels at work' as I call these two Master Students of mine rightfully because of their loving hearts and selfless efforts!

As in most Arts described, this is what we call 'Jin and Jang' or the 'Circle of Life'. You have surely come across this expression, it is found in various forms and styles. Its symbol even decorates skate- and surf-boards, bumpers and clothes. Therefore, it seems to be just some kind of decoration and the expression just an empty shell. Is it? Or is it simply misplaced? It is certainly taken out of its original context and meaning. Is it only some strange myth from the past? Or does what it stands for still exist, the truth and meaning, within our fast moving and superficial lifestyle? Well, it does. But certainly not taking the form of a slogan, a sales gimmick, the painted symbol of coolness, a work of art expressing the modern way of life!

So, how can we learn to understand the deep meaning of 'Jin and Jang', how can we revive the ancient tradition that lies behind the symbol? Well, the same way we approach 'Inner Chi' and the 'Power from Within'–by courage and inner strength, by the constant search for the truth. Through our action and how we live; through our daily effort to be the most helpful and productive colleague, friend, partner, husband and wife, father and mother in hard and high-pressure times. By elevating, protecting and healing with all energy and all means possible for a human being.

Most people believe this way of thinking and acting only goes for outstanding per-sonalities: Exceptional politicians and statesmen, doctors, scientists, bishops, great thinkers, extraordinary warriors, leading teachers and mentors like Nelson Mandela, John. F. Kennedy, Michail Gorbachev, Mahatma Gandhi, Willy Brand, Albert Einstein, Berthold Brecht, Goethe, Buddha, Jesus Christ, Lao-Tse, Musahi, Budarama, Gogen Yamagushi,

Funakochi, Kanazawa, Bruce Lee, Jene LeBell to name a few. In fact, the centuries have seen hundreds of exceptional leaders, thinkers and barrier-breakers.

How can we as ordinary person ever measure up with these legends and milestone setting humans? Simply don't try. You do not have to. And nobody expects this from you. In fact, if you asked any of those outstanding people today whether they wanted you to, the answer would be: "No, not at all, my friend!" Most of them have walked or walk their path without certain plans or agendas. They have followed or follow simply their inner voice and their heart, their mission in life. Some of these amazing legends I was humbled and honored to meet and was even allowed to train with and learn from. They have made a life lasting impression on me and strongly influenced my path of life and mission at heart ever since I was a child. And that brings me to some of the people–children, youth and adults–with special needs who have been so much part of my life as teacher and mentor.

Beginning in the widespread field of drug abuse: No matter which town, country, continent or culture people come from, in certain cases their stories are almost identical with only small variations as to why and how fast they find themselves in a desperate situation. They all could be roommates, party buddies, even dealers and customers, there is hardly a difference at all. Therefore, their pattern of daily behavior is easy to recognize, their next steps and movements easy to predict, if you know what to look for–but of course, exceptions write the rules as in the case of my brother.

Take these three young men, for example: One of them I met, when I was teaching in Germany, the other two I came across in the U.S. some time later. Although they had totally different backgrounds, all three had fought their addictions during the better part of their youth and young adult life, a fight for health, even life itself, and were desperate for a drastic change. As Olaf came to our dojo in Germany in his last teenage year, he could hardly stand on his feet and was in greater trouble with drugs, the law and vice police officers than he could handle. He was heavily on pot, speed and cocaine mixed with alcohol, a deadly combination and for sure a road through hell with the occasional overdose along the way. Olaf was wild and full of life, but at the same time fearful and desperate, constantly struggling for inner peace and self-love wanting to be accepted. He had no real goal or path in mind; he only knew he needed to get well again and to find out who he was–like so many in our dojo.

I could see the burning fire of energy and desire through his eyes, when we sat down to talk. I told him, if he wanted to become my student, he had to straighten out his lifestyle and become clean. There would be no way to come and train filled up with drugs and alcohol, because that would endanger his own safety and the safety of others. Besides, the other students could easily misjudge him by seeing him under influence of narcotics and would certainly not be able to respect him for who he was, for his character and as an athlete. It would also reflect negatively on our children; that could not be allowed. And my instructors and I would have a hard time to draw the line between him and the other students. I had to make myself very clear about all this, although I knew it put a lot of pressure on him and heightened the danger for him to quit or relapse.

But Olaf did remarkably well. In our dojo he had found a second home and safe haven, friends to turn to and a place to release pressure and frustration in a positive way. In fact, he was so talented that he turned into one of our best fighters in his weight division after only one year of rehab and training. And later he was even awarded 'The New-comer Fighter of the Year' by our German kickbox sport association. Sounds extraordinary? Well, it sure was. The last I heard about him was that he was coping well after his successful rehab and putting himself through school.

His two counterparts in the U.S. were both talented as well: John was, besides a gifted athlete, an excellent writer. His friend, we will call him 'Grasshopper', the son of a well-known Hollywood director, was an actor and had already played some small roles in major movies. Both men also worked as bartenders in several local clubs and hotspots. They seemed to have all they could imagine and to be well on their way to let their American dream come true. Seeing these fine men most people would have thought there wasn't anything wrong in their lives, but if you took a closer look and got to know them, you noticed the imbalance, the deeply rooted unhappiness. And they certainly had partied with the Hollywood crowd a little too often! Of course, there are positive examples within that 'community' like director Michael Preece and Greg Elam–both from 'Walker TX Ranger', old friends, students and supporters of long standing.

So, there was a typical pattern at hand, hard to resist and even harder to break: Too many parties, late nights, too much alcohol–and yet driving home–and unfavorable company in the clubs they worked. Besides, and even worse, in most bars and hotspots in LA, well, let's just say it 'snows' a lot throughout the whole summer. I worked as head of security in two of those places for a while and had to throw out dozens of dealers and pushers during the years. Heavy drugs are constantly passed among guests and colleagues after closing time and at the frequent weekend parties. This environment led to conflicts in John's and Grasshopper's private life. Often, we sat together either before or after our workout and discussed God and the world, but mainly their own and therefore emotional problems: They were trying hard to find the balance between their family life and dreams they had and the work in the clubs. Especially 'Grasshopper' felt pressurized too much by his Hollywood family, particularly by his father who wanted him to make it on his own as an actor. And although he loved his wife and children deeply, the conflicts in his family and the responsibility he felt for them weighed heavily on his young shoulders.

One morning he told me that his wife was getting at him constantly to change his lifestyle and become a better husband and father. Her concern, of course, was well founded, but Grasshopper could not see what had to be done. So I answered him with a simple metaphor–one of my favorite ways of speaking, trying to make my counterpart think and alert: "Let's say you read a dozen books, written by Lao-Tse for example, or another great thinker; and afterwards you believe you are a lot wiser and smarter. Many people do that. They read one book after the other dealing with all sorts of subjects especially in the 'self-help' division. It will make no difference at all, unless they are willing to implement the ideas and positive examples they read about. Besides, it takes a long time for wisdom and knowledge to be firmly established within you, if you are lucky, work hard and are willing to open your heart. To grow and change from within is a process that can take a lifetime, surely a number of years. No book will do the trick over night. If it was that easy, there would be hardly anybody out there in need of changes in their lives. A magic book, a vitamin pill and we are all O.K. That is not the way it works. Good old fashioned–I believe 'earning' is the word, and self-build up is the answer. One day at the time, step by step to the finishing line, where we will meet our Creator. And hopefully we will have been able to gather some plus-points on the way".

Grasshopper and John became dedicated students for about a year and a half. Their training was hard like always when working with me; I never gave anything away for free. They both earned what was in store for them with tremendous effort, and it paid. Eventually, John moved to San Francisco, away from the negative environment, and gotten a fresh start, hopefully a good one. As you know, it is not easy in theses days. And Grasshopper quit his jobs at the clubs and started to work in construction; first at his own house, later at new projects. Before long, he became a full time craftsman. His best decision in life, apart from marrying his sweetheart of his early years.

On thing is for sure, the beginnings of all these stories are almost invariably alike: "I am hot, I am sexy; I am the centre of attention, I am the hit at every party; I am superman/superwoman". And sooner or later, a moment is reached when this turns into: "I am tired, I am broke; I lost my job and lots of friends; I am stranded. What the hell happened? I am alone, please somebody…help me!"

*

However, only too often the roots of negative if not destructive patterns of behavior are found–sadly–in early childhood. When I went through my education and training as teacher in the 1980's they already talked about child abuse a lot; and statistics showed a horrifying course: It was found out that in Europe, especially in eastern and southern countries, four to five men out of ten abused their children and partners physically and sexually and therefore emotionally injured them for life in lots of cases. Similar research in the U.S. showed even worse results: Here it was supposed that 8(!) men out of ten abused their children and women. This is an immensely high number; and I am sure, nothing has changed since. On the contrary! It is more than alarming and impossible to ignore. And if you think about the numbers of unreported cases that go with every statistic and research, the full extent of this nightmare becomes apparent. It is not just a cultural problem; it is a cultural downfall!

As a result–without meaning to give anyone an excuse or free pass for life, certainly not!–it is a not surprising logical explanation, why children brought up in such an environment become abusers themselves, for sure develop a negative pattern of behavior. Their experience leads more often than not to the early taking of drugs, to violence and self-abuse and to the abuse of others in order to numb their fears, to shut away their demons and to release the tension and aggressive feelings caused by their helplessness and despair. At the same time, they draw other children and youngsters into the current who had nothing to do with these things before. What's more, drugs and alcohol are easily obtained: They are sold at every street corner, even at ice cream vans, near schools or on the school grounds themselves. And the daily violence and the crimes that go with them are for free! All these young people come home to face another nightmare of mistreatment and abuse. And if not, thank the Lord! But when was the last time you sat down with your children or teenagers and spent some quality time with them? Do they trust you enough to tell you where they go, whom they hang out with and what it means to them?

If these childhood nightmares are not detected, dealt with and treated in a healthy and productive way, they mark the beginning of a vicious circle that can last a lifetime. A vicious circle of mistreatment, abuse, drugs, crime, jail and mistreatment again, showing itself in an unmistakable and constantly resurfacing pattern of behavior with little chance to see any light at the end of the tunnel. Unless the individual makes a drastic change in his/her lifestyle, choice of friends and, in most cases, their environment; a fresh and honest start that puts the odds on success to be able to break this circle of hell for good.

Society certainly does not make it easy for them in any way! As a result of our 'hash hash' culture these desperate and deeply unhappy kids–addicted, violent and abusive–are dismissed and written off, when they become teenagers and young adults at the latest. They are declared unstable and of no use, no chance for recovery, no chance to break loose from their so often handed down demons–forgotten too easily and too fast. They fall behind and become part of our third class subculture, even if we would never allow ourselves to attest to it, to acknowledge it. Far too often we simply lock them away in jails, put them through years and years of probation, broken only by more jail sentences. And so make it impossible for most of them to come out of this swamp, to get a job, move away to a better neighborhood, to put themselves through school and education.

So, there is a desperate need for rehab, for treatment that deals with the roots as much as the symptoms. (It is estimated that about 30.000-50.000 girls and also boys, many under age, are made slaves in the daily sex-trade and held captive each year in California/ Nevada alone). That is why I dedicated a major part of my work to rehab in this wide and yet often neglected field of abuse and, as a result, counter-abuse–always keeping in mind my own painful experience. In order to stop a destructive process early enough, again, it is vital to recognize the signs. But how can, say, a young mother of two see the signs of abuse on her children, the abuse by her boyfriend or husband, at school or in the play-ground, let alone the abuse of cigarettes, drugs and alcohol, if we as community don't start talking about it more freely and openly? Besides, this young mother most likely suffers from emotional and physical abuse herself, like so many I have come to know during the last 20 years.

There are young girls who were raped by their fathers and even brothers, who were sold to drug dealers or shipped off as a down payment. And yet, instead of these crimes being prosecuted the girls grow up and carry on the way they know best by now. They were never told any different, never learned that there are other means to get what they need and want. With their bodies, they pay for power, drugs, a place to live. It is a simple exchange of goods, no feelings, no heart involved. Many of them go dancing in night-clubs or work the streets as well to ensure the means for their daily habits and addictions that come with the lifestyle. As a result, they become accustomed to a never-ending circle of these habits, violence, deception and–in most cases–drugs. And through their attitude and lifestyle they turn into easy targets for slander, stalking and abuse.

Like in the cases of five of my finest students who shared a heart-breaking, hardly believable experience. Yet they broke the vicious circle, and their love and dedication is a monument of truth. Shinwa at its best, for sure a shining example for what can be achieved. These women rewrote the rules and eventually changed the course of their fate through inner strength and self-love, making me proud and grateful to have been their teacher.

Three of them: Jessica who I have already introduced to you; Bobby Ann and–let's call her–Angelic worked in one of these hotspots in Santa Monica, California for some time, which is so typical an example for exploitation and taking advantage of women with low confidence due to their difficult background. The place itself wasn't any special apart from the fact that a world famous actor had operated it for a while and owned the property. The girls who worked there came and went rather frequently. Not surprising, really, because whenever I was there–being a regular customer for a time–I had to witness emotional abuse of the worst kind at numerous occasions: Rude comments, sexually charged, insults and slander by customers and management alike. And although the girls complained constantly about it, nothing was ever done, and the security in this place looked the other way.

Angelic, a lovely young woman, very beautiful, hard working and always with the most amazing smile, I met when she had just started to work in this restaurant. Due to her looks and behavior, which caused misjudgment and prejudice, she was constantly harassed by men who tried to take advantage of her. It was so bad that she had to have her phone number changed several times. One day, we talked about it; and what she told me still makes me angry. That day she was in a bad state: Exhausted and close to a breakdown because of a heavy accident she had been involved in a few days before, working under strong medication and still in pain. So I went to a beauty spa later and bought her a gift voucher for a massage and a facial just to make her feel better. When I gave it to her, she almost broke out in tears, telling me that I was the first man ever who had given something to her without asking for anything in return! She became my student. Through the intensive training, not only her physical strength improved, but also her confidence and self-esteem. The last thing I heard about her was that she had moved back to her mother and completed her rehab, well on her way, I hope.

Bobby Ann was a long-term student working out with me in Shin-Tora-Do fitness as emotional support and to release stress caused by the terrible working conditions in that hotspot and her own problems. Bobby Ann is one of the last real ladies of the city, old school: Always elegantly and excellently dressed with finest manners. Moreover, she is an exceptional athlete, extremely strong with an immense will power reminding me of the good old days with Joe Gold at 'World's Gym' in Venice, CA. Bobby Ann still trains four to five days a week lifting weights many men can't handle. Before or after she worked out with me she used to run the 'Santa Monica Stairs' for at least an hour. What a weekly training routine! Always a way of life for her.

Over the years, we became good friends, and she told me more and more about her life and her problems. Often, she was depressed and heard her biological clock ticking just too loudly fearing time was running out for her. In other words, she felt old and unattractive. Which was unfortunate, because not true at all and only really caused by the superficial attitude of most men, especially in the big cities and in Southern California in general, who overlooked her great inner beauty and strength. She was caring and sweet and one of those who would walk through fire for the man she loved. So, a great woman. But many of the average men on her age level wouldn't bother to get to know her. They would rather run for the 'quickie' and the young inexperienced girl to feel better about themselves and their approaching midlife crisis.

Bobby Ann's fears and worries were completely unfounded; in my opinion she had never needed a shrink. There was nothing whatsoever wrong with her that a meaningful friendship and caring support could not fix. She needed to give herself time, let life take its course without worrying about age and its signs. She needed to become aware of herself, her beauty and her inner qualities. And she did. Jessica and I could not have been prouder of her. Jessica had helped from the beginning with loving care, teaching and mentoring. Through our joint effort, Bobby Ann became a loving member of our special team of students; and her friendship and positive influence helped us all. So, the special training worked both ways.

Jessica, too, went through the daily tortures as woman and bartender in Venice and Santa Monica. Often looked at and treated as sex toy, an object of desire–an emotional and physical battle that comes with a certain lifestyle and party attitude, hard to break away from. Totally misjudged, because most men never really bothered to get to know her; and the few who did were unable to give her enough space to breathe, jealous of her every move so that she soon walked through a nightmare trying to get away. Eventually she freed herself from the job in that hotspot, after the manager had degraded her to waitress work letting her only do the hard shifts besides harassing her at every occasion. I stopped going there, then. I just could not stand the never-ending slander and emotional abuse any more.

Bobby Ann's case–and many more–is another classic example of over- and mis-diagnose by doctors (and unfortunately by drugstores as well), who just keep their patients happy and themselves in business instead of going to the roots of a problem and curing it from inside. This is so typical for the western 'pop a pill and be happy' culture. And only too often it results in a long-term dependency on medication–with all the possible health endangering side effects–and visits to the doctors.

However, here I must pay my respects to a number of great MD's and therapists who believe in modern and alternative medicine and combine them in a healthy way. Who don't just prescribe a pill and send their patients home. From some of these I have benefited a great deal myself in many different ways (and two actually saved my overall health and even my life): MD C. Konsanis Grapevine, TX Baylor Medical Centre, for instance: Apart from treating patients who fly in from all over the country to see him, he frequently lectures and often speaks in public; I had the joy to teach his son for a year. Furthermore USC Orthopedic assoc. Professor William H. Mouradian and his team; and Richard D. Carson, Dallas, TX, a good friend, a wonderful family therapist, motivational speaker and bestseller author ('Theme Your Grambling'). He helped me during my early days in TX to jump-start my career and bring my ideas to the public.

He even managed to get a TV news crew from CNN to interview me believing in my ideas from the start, long before most did. Thank you, old friend. You made a big difference in my life and helped me to help others even more! Richard was a member of the 'Q', the sports club in Bedford TX where I was head instructor of the Tai Chi and self-defense classes. For sure outstanding MD's are Minas Kochumin and his assistant P.A. C Pinky Mehta, Northridge Medical Plaza, CA, who helped me getting back on my feet (literally) after an UPS truck had knocked me out. After I had been wrongly treated at the ER and the open wound in my foot got infected heavily, they took over and not only saved the foot but also my overall health, perhaps even my life! Thank you both! Moreover, there is Dr. Theo Wegmann (sports medicine) from Flensburg, Germany, who had been my MD for many years. He always encouraged me tremendously and was the first ever MD who believed in me as an athlete opposing most of his colleagues and cleared me so that I could step into the ring and fight. And last but not least, I have to name, of course, MD Kenneth H. Cooper, founder of the Cooper Institute in Dallas, TX who I have already mentioned. So, there are more excellent MD's out there, than it might seem; you only have to find them...–

Many pages could be filled with the names of loving and caring students and patients of my Master Students and me who were cured simply through a build up of confidence, self-esteem and self-love instead of being sent to the next drugstore. Of course, there are a number of serious mental disorders, like schizophrenia for example, that must be tackled with continuous medication. The danger for those patients to worsen their condition and to even become a threat to others if getting off their medicine, must not be taken lightly. What I am talking about are light to medium heavy depressions, little or no confidence and self-esteem, ADD (Attention Deficit Disorder) and similar conditions–nine out of ten times wrongly diagnosed and therefore mistreated–eating and sleeping disorders as well as hyperactivity. These cases have a very good chance to be cured simply by a change of lifestyle; by giving them caring attention and loving support; by making them feel understood and by helping them to find new positive goals in their life. There is no reason for putting these people on a lifelong medication with continuous visits to doctors. Better leave room for the really sick and seriously injured who need our nurses' and doctors' care, and save some of the immense expenses weighing down the whole community. Just think about the thousands of cases a month alone in the U.S.

Moreover, quite a number of so-called 'mental diseases' are not fully researched. In fact, there are disorders we still do not know where they exactly come from, why they occur and what causes this 'chemical imbalance' frequently talked about. So, how is a doctor able to diagnose correctly? Well, it is more or less a guessing game, relying on symptoms and behavior patterns. This leads more often than not to the wrong conclusions, and the patient is put into a category he might not belong. As a result, medication is prescribed that eases the symptoms, keeps the patient manageable and his behavior more under control. Heavy sedation by Methadone, Prozac, Vicadine, Mopfium Hydrocodone and other drugs against pain and depression lessens violence, depression and the desire for suicide, this being the only positive effect, as far as I am concerned. But these drugs certainly do not make the roots of the problem disappear; and therefore long-term medication seems the only treatment possible. So the patient is exposed to severe health risks by–in too many cases–wrong medicine and their possible emotional and physical side effects; not to mention how he must feel: Misplaced, misunderstood and for sure misguided for probably years. Is that the answer, we are all looking for? Is that the best we can do?

Take the so-called 'RLS' (Restless Leg Syndrome; more TV syndrome, really) as an example. It is rather a made-up diagnose without a proper foundation of knowledge about what actually happens in the body. And the people who benefit from this are certainly not the pantients. Everyone who has patients committed to their care should ensure a thorough and accurate examination leaving out nothing that could lead to a wrong diagnose and medication. But sadly, this happens in the field of mental health too often, especially if the condition crosses over and into learning- and behavior-problems like ADD. Again, many of these 'illnesses' are not really researched. All we know is that the heavy medication we apply eases the symptoms and calms down the patient.

So how come that in all these years extensive research has only been carried out in the medicine sector with drugs refined and new ones thrown onto the market almost yearly, whereas origin and development, let alone proper treatment of mental disorders have been greatly left untouched by scientists? Well, look at the billion-dollar pharmaceutical industry in the U.S. and overseas. Who needs scientific research results in that division if all we have to do is prescribe some pills; and millions around the world buy and take them for years. And you think the cigarette industry grooms their consumers! They are bad for sure, but not half as bad as the pharmaceutical industry and their health care providers and HMO's (Health Maintenance Organizations) who would like the MD's to do just that and send the patients on their way with a little pat on their backs... mostly just working on symptoms instead of trying to find the origin of the actual condition of the body or mind and keeping themselves in good business, for sure wealthy, and the customer happy (you can hardly call him patient any longer because he is not really treated).

Talking about research, of course it is important and necessary... if done by independent scientists! There are independent labs, groups, institutes and colleges that do a great job and help the public to find the truth and the right safe product. But only too often you hear about 'research' results and can read about them in magazines and news papers published by pharmacy companies and even by companies selling tobacco, alcohol and food stating the effectiveness and safety of their products. You better read between the lines and take a good look at who had paid the bill for this 'scientific' work. More often than not, it is just another type of advertising to improve sales and to put down negative feedback. So consider hard, be sceptical, get thoroughly informed and read the package-leaflet, before you swallow medicine against sleeplessness or depression, for example. It could save your life, for sure your health; long-term damages like liver cirrhosis and heart diseases are not at all unusual! These drugs will certainly never enter my body.

In hardly any other branch more fatal mistakes have been made over the last 50 years than in the pharmacy and drug industry that pay millions to lobbyists and congresses to influence the public. Not just one 'medicine' was withdrawn from the market, after its side effects had become apparent and people had fallen sick. Just think of the 'Contergan' scandal in the 1950's and 60's: Thousands of innocent children were born disfigured, had no chance to lead a happy and fulfilling life, because their mothers had taken this pill during their pregnancy. And yet, you never seem to see any CEO or producer of products like that going to jail for their crimes. Many 'Contergan' victims still have to fight for at least a nearly adequate compensation, while the company that had produced this medicine is still in business! Why? It is certainly something to think about. Do not believe this so-called 'research' and make sure you know all about a pill before swallowing it. Besides, you do not want to wait for our journalists to uncover yet another scandal. Then, it might be too late for you, too. Nearly always, there are alternative treatments available without any damaging side effects.

*

Coming back to our subject at hand: As long as we do not really know enough about the origins of many mental disorders and have no proper answers, we should be more open to other suggestions and healing ideas. As a matter of fact, there are hundreds of different aspects, forms and methods to be found within the traditional Chinese and Asian medicine that deal with quite a number of these problems; their recovering and healing effects are remarkable. And let us not forget Dr. Sigmund Freud who had researched in this field and classified different mental and emotional problems nearly a hundred years ago. He had also drawn guidelines how to spot these disorders and had found healing techniques and methods. Many shrinks today, however, like to label his findings and the way he worked as crazy and incompetent, which I think is hard to understand.

*

So, there is knowledge available, there are methods to deal with many mental disorders. Caring, loving attention and support with open mind and heart, ancient healing techniques combined with modern methods professionally applied, the wisdom of Martial Arts. All this can be used to help those with particular needs and problems; to help them help themselves and find their place in life.

In Jessica, I had found the ideal assistant and partner to teach our 'Rock Stars'. Right from the start, she recorded all lessons we created individually for the students and their effects on them, the experiences and insights we gained and the methods we applied with great accuracy. So a long overdue base line, a foundation and reference, was built for our further research and studies that I had in mind for a number of years, but had not found the time to put together. Moreover, Jessica had gained considerable knowledge about ADD and similar learning disabilities during years of schooling and training children, which she brought into our work. And while we trained and mentored our special kids, she grew with the task and developed from within, which had been my intention to trigger ever since I met her.

Jessica's personal history was similar to the ones dealt with earlier as I have already mentioned: Exposed to emotional abuse and slander due to her pattern of behavior caused by terrible experiences and her physique, she needed to break the vicious circle and learn to stand up for herself. Just an example: At times, she was thinking about a breast-reduction-operation so that men would not look at her the way they did. I told her she should think hard about it before taking such a drastic step; after all, it was her naturally born body. Nevertheless, it was very disturbing for her not just as a woman but also as a teacher to be seen and treated as a sex-object by fathers of children she taught, for instance. At one point, she said something like 'you learn to live with this'. But I would not! I let these people know that we did not like this kind of behavior at all and that they should be grateful and pay respect to our mostly free service for our young students. Moreover, often enough I had to witness how she dealt with former boyfriends and lovers as well as colleagues and customers from this hotspot she had worked in letting bad behavior slide. Exactly this silence is very often taken as an invitation to move closer overlooking the anguish in the woman's eyes. However, the respectful and strong bond between us, the unconditional affection and admiration we felt for each other and for our 'Rock Stars' and the rewarding training with them worked like a charm! Whose effects were, in return, reflected in her work with the children…And there you have 'Jin and Jang', the circle of life…

*

It was a wonderful group of children and youths: Julia, Monae, our one and only Eden, Case, his brother Max and their friend Calvin. Apart from working with everyone individually, we brought them together as often as possible and let them help each other– often assisted as well by Bobby Ann and our great Michelle. Under my watchful eyes, Jessica led the warm-up taking care of every single student and then worked through the techniques and combinations with them. It was a tremendous positive learning process to understand each other and their special needs, forming deep friendships to last. Jessica showed great compassion, especially for Monae and Eden, and became a close friend and mentor to all of them. She told me once how much she appreciated all I had done for her and that she never had to worry about me. But she had earned every single achievement all by herself: Her degrees, her position as assistant and mentor, the trust and respect of our team; she never got anything for free because of her amazing looks, something she wasn't used to and an important experience on her way to success!

Let me turn to our 'Rock Stars' themselves: Julia was 15 when she joined our group and a sad example for over-diagnosis and, as a result, over-medication. This great young teenager was supposed to suffer from severe ADD and depression, unable to concentrate and pay short-term attention, heavy learning disorder together with severe difficulties to bond and interact within a group. Therefore, her condition was supposed to require heavy medication, continuous monitoring and supervision. But I have for sure learned one thing during the last 20 years of teaching and mentoring these special young students: Listen to what doctors, shrinks, teachers and family members have to say; then talk and listen to the patient/student. Be neutral and objective, take every case individually, do not pre-judge and do not categorize. Deal with one student at the time, open his/her mind and heart. And last but surely not least, never treat these special children and youths as if there was something wrong with them. Just let them become themselves and respect them as human beings. I always keep in mind that this was exactly the way Geert Lemmens and his wife treated me!

So, according to her mother and her therapist, Julia was supposed to be unable and even unwilling to concentrate and to learn as well as incapable to socialize and interact in a group. Yet, she reacted to our class and my especially-designed-for-her emotional and physical workout plan extremely well. The lessons with our special students always began with the same gesture: A warm welcome and a hug! For Julia, it was followed by our warm-up and stretching—with slight modifications to meet her requirements—and the drill techniques that are not only an effective condition training, but also a strong foundation and key for success. They form a major part of our Shin-Tora-Do Karate classes and workouts. And the more they are implemented in the beginner-lessons, the sooner this 'old school' training will bear its fruits—one of the secrets for my achievements.

Jessica took Julia under her angel wings from day one, and they soon became dear friends Julia looked up to her and copied her great foot techniques with remarkable accuracy. She followed our drills, went through the long lines of techniques and condition workouts without ever complaining. Occasionally, she needed a short break to stretch out and relax, but only to return to the group energetically and to try even harder, a true champion at heart from the start! She was always full of life, attentive and curious, never bored or evasive, never sloppy or rude. Was she not supposed to have all these problems and therefore all these symptoms? Certainly not, when she trained with us, ever! The professional application of Martial Arts techniques combined with modern rehab methods, but especially caring attention and emotional support without over-acting and over-complicating worked well and led to success.

Julia developed tremendously, and her parents hardly knew what to say to this phenomenon. It seemed that no one had ever been able to make her do things; she always got bored and simply drifted off and away, again not in our group. We never had to push her, never had to raise our voices to make her work harder. There was no need for that. Moreover, every time she came to the class, she was happy to see us all!

Her yellow belt test turned out to be one of the finest I had seen for a long time, right in line with Jessica's. There were no signs of distress or lack of concentration; and she marched through it as if walking in the park. Her parents could hardly believe it. So, our formula had started to pay off: Old school teaching mixed with care and affection resulted in a tremendous build-up of concentration, self-esteem and confidence. Julia reached a level of inner strength never thought possible. And through Jessica's loving care, her techniques and combinations improved amazingly, which in return inspired and motivated her even more. Over the months, Julia also gained enormous focus improving her performance and causing even greater achievements as Martial Artist, a fact that positively influenced her whole life; and Julia became a strong and loving member of our Shin-Tora-Do family.

A completely different case was our always smiling angel, 14-year-old Monae. she suffered from severe cerebral palsy, epilepsy and emotional as well as learning disorders. One of the major problems with cases like hers and similar is that the patient stays in his/her own world, in his/her 'comfort zone', most of the time cutting out everything and everybody else. And, Monae never spoke. So, it was a real challenge, but Jessica and I were ready for this. As we started the first session Monae turned her head downwards and sideways in a fashion, we soon learned was characteristic for her. She studied us intently and 'read' us emotionally, it seemed. With her eyes, she followed our every moves, especially Jessica's whom she apparently formed a bond with right away. So, it was obvious she did not see us as a threat, as enemies; and there seemed to be no reason for her to retreat, which was an achievement in itself. I decided to take positive advantage of the connection between us in order to catch Monae's attention and see if she would respond to and follow a verbal command. It was of extreme importance. If she was able to do this, her attention-span could be lengthened, and her active reaction to our simple commands would be the vital base to build on; without it we wouldn't have a chance.

To achieve this we played a simple little game: Jessica put Monae on the matt and then sat down at the side of it. I got on all fours and crawled slowly around the room, away from them repeatedly calling the girl's name, inviting her to follow me. Monae just sat quietly and watched me. We repeated the game in the following session, and suddenly she responded. Jessica and I guessed she must have finished 'reading' us emotionally and decided we were her friends she could trust: She started to bob in my direction using her arms and legs to push herself forward. I waited until she nearly reached me and then slowly moved backwards so that she had to keep going, if she wanted to get to me. We carried on like this for almost 15 minutes. Monae enjoyed it tremendously and tried harder and harder to reach me, smiling all the while. It was fantastic to see her like this. Jessica gave her a big hug and a kiss, which made her smile even more; and so it became a lovely custom between them every time the girl completed a task or showed intense concentration.

During the third session, I decided to push it a little further. After all, Monae already did something–despite the fact that she was under heavy medication. Moreover, according to her father, doctors and former therapists she had been neither able nor willing to do anything before. I started our little game as before, crawling around and calling her name. Happily smiling, Monae followed me again. After a short while I stopped and let her reach me. I gave her a big hug and then asked Jessica to call her. Encouragingly I told Monae to go and see Jessica. She struggled with herself for a moment turning her head downwards and sideways like she had done in our first session, looking at Jessica and me, 'reading' us again. "Go and see Jessica," I said once more, and off she went bobbing on her bottom all the way across the room happily smiling. Jessica welcomed her with wide-open arms and then hugged and kissed her. We could see Monae had enough motivation to play this 'go-and-find-game' for the rest of the session. By this alone we had broken so many rules about what she should be able to do and not do because of her severe handicaps, disorders and limitations. She had positively responded to our commands and had interacted with a smile!

But what was it that caused this amazing success? Why were we able to elevate and motivate where others could not? It was CHI, Inner Chi and heart. That was what it took to form a strong connection between Monae's mind and soul, Jessica's and mine: A strong bond of love and trust. And, of course, knowledge about rehab and emotional guidance of such a student. It was quite remarkable to see just how strong and mobile, even totally open and responsive Monae was, when she had an incentive like our verbal or optical commands, our movements or reactions to her. If she lost interest, however, or became tired, losing her incentive, she could even collapse or simply trail off into her rocking motion, her comfort zone. Our goal for the time being was to get her out of this zone and into our world as often and long as possible, providing an incentive like our little game, so far with great results.

We had been able to form the base, the bond between us, the major stepping stone on her road to recovery and success, which we walked together with growing joy. This remarkable young girl continuously surprised us with her emotions and her mental as well as physical strength. It humbled us and let us see our own life in a different light. We simply adored her.

Sadly, Jessica and I received hardly any feedback on how our treatment influenced her life at home. Moreover, it would have been tremendously helpful had we known more about Monae's eating-, drinking- and sleeping habits as well as how often epileptic spells occurred during a day, how long they lasted and of what nature they were. We also needed information on her medication, which was rather complicated–so much we knew–because the doctors constantly changed the medicine and varied the daily dose in order to avoid the immune system getting used to it. It was a shame we were left without this valuable information and had to find our own way. So we managed amazing results without this information.

We already know how difficult it can be for an MD or therapist to diagnose correctly and therefore to determine the right treatment and medication. Especially in a case like Monae's, it would have helped a lot to communicate with the MD in order to find out if the proper dose was hit and if it prevented or only lessened the epileptic spells. There was no way to control these fits. Their occurrence varied from none at all to several during a session and could last between a few seconds to five minutes. Within an instant, Monae would freeze, her entire body tensing up, then shaking, sometimes violently, until the fit eased off on its own. It seemed to help holding and gently comforting her with stroking and soft singing, and Jessica did this with such loving care it was deeply impressing.

*

Epilepsy had been categorized, and treatment started to be developed about 50 years ago. And yet, all we know now is that epileptic spells are mainly caused by a swelling of the brain occurring with considerably varying frequency that results in a build up of pressure in the space between skull and brain. Moreover, it can cause puncturing and penetrating of the inner skull. The degree of penetration depends on the extent of the puncture and its form. As a counter-reaction, the spells occur in varying degrees of intensity and length. The patient is in a coma-like condition, and the body can shake with cramp-like twitches similar to a severe electric shock. Also, in most cases, blood vessels and nerve ends are affected as well, and there is a high risk of blood vessel rupture, which would cause embolism. As you probably know, an embolism results in severe brain damage and even death if not detected and treated very soon. We do not know why the body does not re-route brain functions from the affected areas like it does with speech, vision or hand-eye coordination, for example, when parts of the brain are injured by, say, a heavy car accident or trauma. We also do not know whether this swelling of the brain is caused by a genetic malfunction or a birth defect, and why certain injuries to the head initiate it. But it was found out that it is triggered by stroboscope light used in many nightclubs. Different types of light-shows and for sure a certain level of stress and tension seem to play an important role.

Since we do not know the origins of this illness, we have no proper answer for how to treat it. Therefore, all we do is put the patient on life-long heavy medication to ease the symptoms and lengthen the time between spells exposing him/her to the severe health risk going with it, like liver cirrhosis, heart disease or respiratory shut down. So, yet again, research in the field of epilepsy and as well cerebral palsy (CP) doesn't seem to be of major interest. Once I was even told by the CA special Olympic committee that my findings and accomplishments would overshadow the ones of their own athletes and therapists, and therefore my mentoring and public speeches were no longer needed, although no cure, not even a guideline could be found anywhere!

So, what are all these tens of thousands of dollars raised by foundations and government organizations a year around the world used for? Where does the money go if not into research? And why don't we ask our politicians before we elect them? Why don't we tell them to clean up this jungle of corrupted, so-called non-profit organizations and foundations? In the U.S., you only have to donate six to eight % of the collected money to your cause, depending on the state. With the remainder you can do whatever you like; share it out among the managing directors of your organization, for example, to ensure their huge monthly salary. It is even tax-free! Of course, this big 'pay-off' is well protected by influential lobbyists and interest-groups and hardly ever talked about. And as long as the law is not changed, well, think hard before you open your purse and donate your honestly earned money to one of these large foundations; as we know, there are other possibilities where your help actually reaches the ones who need it!

Some time ago, I had a student for a short while who was the VP of the entire northwest and Texas division of a large and rich CP organization, and born with CP himself. You would have thought him able or at least willing to help with the set up of a seminar for CP-children. It was not supposed to be a costly event. Only a couple of busses to gather the children and a gym would have been needed, I would have done the rest. But the VP declined with hardly any hesitation. He argued, too many rules and regulations would have to be considered, too much paperwork would have to be done in order to organize this. So, nothing ever happened. I really expected a little more fire and compassion. After all, he had verebral palsy himself. But an event like this probably did not fit in with his organization's policy, and he may have been afraid to lose his well-paid job by putting something into motion. Unfortunately, there are a lot more like him around....

But let us return to silent Monae, our 'Rock Star' and champion of life. We had such a great time with her. As soon as she entered the room and saw us, her face lid up like a Christmas tree full of lights, which was a miracle in itself considering her history. Sometimes Jessica and I took Julia with us, and she adored her as well. To be part of Monae's rehab was an important positive experience for her. As it was of course for all of us. The sessions with her were the most amazing and rewarding for me so far. And seeing Jessica's emotional development proved an extra bonus. The girl's response to her was simply fantastic: Sometimes, Jessica was unable to come to the sessions in time. Monae instantly missed her 'Angel at work' looking around the room knowing one important member of her team was not there. When Jessica eventually arrived, she took off to welcome her smiling like a sugar pony at a state fare–again, showing an emotional development nobody had thought possible before. And Jessica showed her extraordinary determination and caring heart by coming to the class, although she was very tired after hardly getting any sleep because of her own personal problems.

However, to create an efficient rehab plan was not an easy task. No reference, no guideline, no overall therapy scheme for patients suffering from epilepsy in combination with cerebral palsy or similar conditions affecting the whole body was in existence. So we gathered information like pieces of a puzzle from the field of rehabilitation in general to combine with our knowledge and experience. A lot of guessing, wishing and even praying was involved, too. I wrote a few poems about it, and one of my favorites has always been this:

Wish
If one truly wishes, the wishes will be answered...
If one truly lives, they will become themselves...
If one's heart (Shinwa) is truly pure, they will be loved for who they are...
If one truly loves, they will be living together forever, within themselves!
Bushido is our way, Sensei, Anthony v. Sager LA, CA 04

But the major ingredient for success we already had: Unconditional love and care for our student as we had for all our special children! And during the weeks that followed our third session, Monae began to respond to a number of different commands, not just her name. Through her experience with children suffering from concentration and learning disorders Jessica was able to implement quite a few helpful possibilities to catch Monae's attention. One of these was the use of our radio/CD player. It fascinated her and she could spend a full session sitting in front of it and just looking at it. You could tell she wondered where the music was coming from. Soon Jessica showed her how to use the switch in order to hear it, and within a week Monae could turn the radio on and off as well. We had a lot of fun just sitting before it encouraging the girl to push the switch into the right direction or simply listening to the music; Rock 'n' Roll and Salsa with their distinct rhythm and bass sounds seemed to interest her most. While she was listening, Monae often fell into this stage of happy absent-mindedness expressed through her face and body, followed by trailing off into her rocking motion—her comfort zone, as we already knew.

As next step, I implemented simple exercises, which I had pieced together from stretching, Yoga and rehab movements. But would Monae be trusting enough to follow our example and copy our style? And if so, how accurate would her performance be and for how long would she be able to carry on? According to her therapist and teachers there was little chance for success. Monae had never responded to sportive activities before and they had given up on her after a few weeks, because she had simply sat in a corner rocking and had not wanted to be bothered at all. At least that was what we were told. It was time to break this barrier, and if Jessica and I were able to do that, if Monae would become active and follow our movements, the whole world would open up to her. I was convinced no one had ever tried hard enough to get her gently out of her nutshell, for sure had never gained enough trust so that she would interact without second guessing.

It was a moment of truth and great importance for our research and rehab with Monae when Jessica placed our silent angel on the matt and we started our little program. It just worked, easy and effortlessly, hard to believe: Monae started to copy Jessica's movements. Slowly at first and with hesitation turning her head in that specific fashion of her, reading our emotions and body language until it became more and more natural to her. I only helped her to keep the balance and ensured she would not topple over; and, of course, I needed to make sure I could catch her in case of an epileptic spell. After a while, Jessica took my place and I did the movements. One of the first exercises was a simple leg raise from a lying position, with the arms close to the body for stabilization, lifting both legs in a right angle first, then up to 180 degrees. Within the hour, Monae performed this accurately to the point.

There were times, however, when she would only lie next to Jessica holding her hand and watch our movement with a happy smile. And then, when we started a different exercise, she would suddenly perform the previous movement in perfect form and timing instead of the new one. Did she do this to please us? After all, both of us were such close friends to her. Or was it due to a kind of time replay, reliving the moment before in order to focus properly and coordinate her movements? It was a completely new territory, apparently no one had bothered to research by means of a long-term study. So this was just as important as it was exciting on a scientific level for me as rehab instructor and teacher. The most amazing fact, however, was that Monae developed so tremendously fast. I had to remind myself repeatedly that we had started to work with her only about two weeks before! If this was just the beginning, what could be achieved within a year!

During the following weeks, we implemented more stretching exercises and Yoga moves like the butterfly-seat: Jessica, sitting before Monae and keeping her feet in place with her own, gently pressing her knees towards the matt. To our surprise she let her do that quite relaxed trusting Jessica completely. And when she got tired or a little tense she gently pushed Jessica away with her hand signaling she didn't want to carry on. Another great interaction and sign of understanding on her part. The butterfly-seat and the leg raise were actually two of her favorites and she always performed them with a big smile understanding that they were part of the session-routine.

To make the training even more interesting, Jessica came up with little games she played with Monae between the exercises–an enrichment to our sessions thought out on her own initiative which showed once more her great heart. One of these games was "Sort the cushions": Jessica put a large pile of cushions in front of Monae and began to sort them after their colors inviting her to help. Seven times out of ten Monae would match the colors correctly. This was a clear sign that she understood. She could not only distinguish the different colors but she was also capable of seeing the logic behind the sorting, making up her mind what was right and what was wrong; another unexpected little miracle.

In fact, this amazing silent girl kept surprising us. Every time we thought we had hit a level to stay on for a while, she surprised us with an unexpected reaction smiling all over, despite her constantly recurring and mainly heavy epileptic spells between and during exercises and activities. You could see how her body was fighting these fits, sometimes heavily shaking; and it was obvious that she struggled emotionally to get out of them. When she did, she went right back to work with a big smile as if nothing had happened.

Nobody knows what a patient actually feels during an epileptic attack. Watching from close by, however, you can see and feel how mind, soul and body, how the entire existence is fighting against it. And since most epilepsy patients do not speak, especially if heavy CP is going with the illness, conventional ways of getting feedback are useless; you can't simply ask them about their opinion and feelings. So, a deeper level of understanding, helping and loving care is required.

Our little 'Go and see Jessica' game became a warm up routine at the beginning of our regular sessions; with great pleasure Monae would follow us all over the room hardly ever stopping unless she had a spell. The daily dose of her heavy medication did not seem to prevent these, only made them, perhaps, less violent. Due to the change of medicine-combination and dose on a nearly monthly basis Monae seemed to be heavily over-medicated at times, certainly less happy, active and rather as if not quite awake yet. Without any feedback from the doctors and therapists, drawing conclusions from Monae's behavior and reactions was reduced to a guessing game. Even more so because we saw her only two to three times a week and had no information about her daily life and events at home to get an overall picture.

Apart from the epileptic fits, Monae's physical condition was of major concern to us. All people with CP have about the same level of hyperactivity of the nervous system and an enormously fast working metabolism. Therefore, they need 3000 to 5000 calories a day. Think of a soccer player in a game that goes on for 24 hours a day, seven days a week nearly without a break, and you can imagine the huge amount of carbohydrates, protein and vitamins a person with CP needs every day. In my teenage years, this was not common knowledge–and sometimes I wonder if it is today -. I had an argument with my Biology teacher about it once. I would have thought as an 'expert' she knew the facts, but she did not and even put me down in front of the whole class calling me a boaster and liar. But I persisted and challenged her to look up some books. After all, I had learned the facts from Geert Lemmens. A couple of days later she apologized. I do not think, it was easy for her....

Monae was alarmingly skinny. Her food intake came not even close to what she needed, 1000 to 1200 calories a day–probably too high an estimate considering her food intake I could witness, and her level of activity. The fact that her father was vegetarian certainly worsened the situation as far as the variety of proteins Monae badly needed was concerned . Besides, like most people with CP, she had no fat reserve to burn at all–her body-skin-fat level reached no more than 3.5 to 4 % which is the bare minimum for anybody to survive. So, Monae was left with a shortage of at least 1500 calories a day, which meant her body had to break down fat and muscle tissue in order to generate energy–most unhealthy especially for a child with needs like Monae. Despite these short-comings, she excelled herself in nearly every session. No matter how she might have felt the day or even hours before, she always gave her best during training with a happy smile–a real trooper, a warrior at heart! And this was a constant reminder for Jessica and me, how small our problems were compared to hers and how well we were able to live.

Due to the rather desperate need for information about Monae's daily life and her instinct as loving mother Jessica, offered kindheartedly and on her own incentive to teach and look after her at home as well, knowing the little girl needed a lot more food and care. And 'free of charge' at that, with only Monae's welfare in mind and the benefits for our studies and research. As we had hoped, Monae's father agreed to the arrangement. Jessica's efforts and work were remarkable and helped tremendously with Monae's rehabilitation and our studies. By now, I think, you can imagine why Jessica became our Sen. Sempei in such a short time like no one before. I would have to look hard and long to find anyone with the same heart and qualities!

She came constantly up with new ideas to keep Monae out of her comfort zone and to develop her learning skills. More and more she made the girl's rehab to her own personal affair. I was proud of her; and considering her history and background a responsibility and task like this was a perfect way of rehab for her personally–and meant to be from the start.

One of Jessica's ideas was as simple as it was effective: She cut large letters of the alphabet out of cardboard and taped them to a huge mirror in her flat. Monae loved to sit in front of it watching her own and Jessica's movements and analyzing them emotionally in her particular fashion. Jessica took advantage of this and repeatedly pointed the letters out telling her how they were called. Slowly Monae began to recognize and memorize them–an important stepping-stone towards simple but nonetheless proper education. Moreover, through this little game Jessica was able to lengthen Monae's attention span like never before! I was deeply impressed and decided straight away to go and look for some good old rehab toys I had been playing with when I was a child.

I found two lovely wooden puzzles: One was a box filled with differently shaped and colored pieces that would fit equally shaped and colored holes cut into the box to fall back in. The other one consisted of a board with hollows in the shape of fishes and seahorses and matching pieces that were cut in half in order to make it a little more difficult to find the right place where they belonged. On my way to Jessica's flat I was wondering if Monae would be able to find the right pieces for the openings and hollows; or would she just try to force them into a place they didn't belong; would she even care at all?

When I arrived at the flat, Monae was sitting on the floor of the living room smiling happily while Jessica was feeding her. And I could see once more how proud and happy it made her to be around Monae, well knowing her work and love made a big difference in the girl's life. My presents turned out to be a great success. Both delighted and made Jessica grateful to get additional equipment that would make her home schooling more interesting and challenging. After the meal and a little rest for Monae, we placed the wooden box before her; and again, she turned her head at first, watching intently as Jessica opened it, took out the different pieces and slowly began to fit them into the matching holes. Eventually she spilled them all out once more and encouraged Monae to try herself: She put a shape into her hand and kept asking her gently where she thought this piece would fit. Monae only needed two attempts before she found the right opening and was rewarded with hugs and kisses–more than enough incentive to keep going and trying hard to complete the puzzle with a beaming face. It was amazing, and I could have spent hours just watching. Later on Jessica told me the girl had also completed the other puzzle. All this might seem only a child's play to you, but in Monae's case, it was an achievement of great importance.

So, Monae developed fantastically despite her epileptic fits and limitations. More and more often, we heard comments like 'we have never seen her smiling so often before she began to workout with you all'; 'Ever since Jessica has started to take care of her at home and school her she seems so much happier and relaxed.' In fact, Monae had grown into a fully accepted member of our group; and it was understood that we would take her with us to our usual 'belt-dinner'–a celebration to honor the hard work we all had done before and during a belt test–among the other students and parents.

It was a wonderful event. And the attending waiter who was apparently quite impressed congratulated Jessica and me to being such great parents to Monae! I thanked him without correcting his little mistake… and there appeared this million-dollar smile on Jessica's face I had seen in the restaurant she worked and the expression on the waiter's face…. It made me realize how important Jessica's rehab was and how much more work we had before us knowing her daily ordeal. Geert and Vera Lemmens had never given up on me, even though I provided them with more than enough reasons to do so. Besides, I knew Jessica's real heart and soul, something most men never even considered to be there! So I promised myself on the spot not to give in or up on her at any time as long as she was willing to try herself, one day at the time! She always was and never stopped working hard and amazing me as a Martial Artist, for sure as an assistant. Even when she came to our classes with a hangover, dead tired and about to pass out, she would try until she collapsed or lost her balance. She would get back up and carry on with tremendous determination.

*

As often as possible I brought all of our 'Rock Stars' together with the other young students for training and interaction. Youths and young adults who have learned early to care for children under these special circumstances develop a natural understanding of themselves and everyone with particular needs. They hardly ever require introduction or explanation when they are faced with a group of children or adults like our 'Rock Stars'. They know the feeling of being prejudged well enough and will join in naturally. Moreover, they will invite others to do the same openly and without a second thought. The bystanders and parents I have come across over the years are the ones with reserve and prejudice; if dealt with the right way, however, they can be positively influenced quite often to let their children just be and experience themselves in the group without fear, even if it means some detours occasionally and special help.

The students of my class never took notice in a negative way, and never felt uncomfortable or argued about anyone in their midst, no matter what type of difficulty these had or how much special attention they required. The same, of course, applied to my assistants and loving helpers. People from 'outside' were the ones who had a problem with these students, a sad fact.

Occasionally, however, we had to deal with quite a different type of student. Once, as an example, a young confused teenage girl attended our classes. She complained constantly about not receiving enough attention, because the special students needed more time and care. She even became rude and cheeky, especially at our belt test. I told her to quiet down, be more polite and concentrate on her techniques instead of behaving badly. But she started to make unfavorable comments about Jessica in order to look better herself and tried to impress me with her body instead of her techniques and performance as athlete. It was time for her to leave our classes. I felt there was little I could do for her before she would come to her senses and start to learn some respect. Unfortunately, she was not able or even prepared to take responsibility for her actions and needed to learn a lesson and find herself first. Moreover, she was taught free of charge apart from a few donations to our petty cash.

Sadly, this behavior was not an exception. Over the years, I had to witness this kind of rudeness and disrespect quite often, not in our special group, though, apart from that particular occasion. I have always been extremely selective when it came to prospective students of mine. Simple misunderstanding, misconception, down to deep-set fears and an extreme need for attention, love and understanding, are at the roots of this bad behavior. It is a logical therapeutic explanation, but certainly neither a free pass nor a reason to tolerate it. If a student gives everything he/she got, then feels he/she cannot go on anymore and needs a well-deserved rest, that is no problem at all. But if he/she is unfriendly and even rude, because he/she feels the need to be pampered and looked at–particularly in the company of students with special needs, or if he/she argues with me in order to get more attention and tries to cheat his/her way through training and into a belt test, well, that is not acceptable. I do not have any compassion whatsoever for such people; and they are not worthy of being my students until they show true respect for the group, for all students and therefore for me as a teacher. There is no room for discussions and negotiations! I will not ignore disrespect, particularly not in front of handicapped children–and certainly not when taught free of charge, either.

A teacher and mentor should not take this behavior personally, but cut it short from the start, not only to avoid unnecessary interruptions and disturbances of the lessons and therefore the learning process of the other class-members, but also to parry negative influence on the whole group and on the individual who could be incensed to copy this conduct. Julia, for example, was highly vulnerable to this kind of bad influence; therefore, it was even more important that I addressed the issue properly. Moreover, it will be difficult to restore respect and order and to keep them, once rudeness and lack of respect was tolerated.

*

Jessica, Magnolia and the other helpful angels understood the idea behind my integrating all children and youngsters into the training as often as possible, and into the following belt test, from the start. With loving care, they helped me, especially with the test, and played a major part in the successful outcome. Some parents and spectators should have taken their work and caring attitude as positive example. But instead, they stood around at the sideline without much interest for their children, ran their mouths and argued with each other about the conduct of the test. Worst of all, they did not take any notice of the fact that their children could hear them and that they might not be able to concentrate on their performance. If we as members of a community, of a culture belonging to the so-called 'free world', can't respectfully coexist during a two-hour class enjoying each other's company and companionship, waiting patiently for our turn without complaint or making a scene, how are we supposed to get along with our fellow citizens, let alone our neighboring countries and different cultures?

This whole subject clearly shows just how much teaching and healing is still required in our cultures around the world, and how much respect has to be learned so that people will be accepted for who they are. All starts and ends with our microcosmic life, with our families, our friends and ourselves. It is like a stone we throw into a lake: Depending on its weight and size, it will generate smaller or larger rings of wavelets traveling slower or faster across the sheet of water, reaching the distant shores sooner or later. In other words, it depends entirely on us how much action and consideration we are prepared to throw into a subject or project in order to produce waves that may or may not travel far. And it is our decision–every single day and night–whether those waves are of positive or negative nature! We are all able to influence our surroundings positively, to move things. It is only a matter of willingness.

*

And this brings me to Eden and her amazing journey. She was, besides Monae, the most challenging young student with the most severe limitations we had ever taught and mentored. And yet, she had a tremendous talent, a kind and caring character and worked incredibly hard. She motivated and elevated all of us every time we saw her. Whenever we didn't feel like giving all we could, whenever we lacked enthusiasm, we only had to look at Eden or think of her; and we found new energy and inner strength to do another twenty push- or sit-ups. There was hardly anybody within her neighborhood and at her school who did not adore her enormous strength, intelligence and manifold knowledge as well as her admirable kindness. In fact, there was no one I knew who could ever resist to be inspired and honored just by meeting her; no one who didn't get a full 360 degree reality check in an instant and long-term motivation at the same time. Eden certainly was–next to Jessica and Marine Clinton who you will meet later–one of my best students within the U.S. by far. She set a loving and positive example for many generations of Shin-Tora-Do students to come.

I met this in every respect remarkable young lady at her school in West L.A., the L.A. Marine Middle School. A local teacher had asked me to talk to two combined classes of students with particular limitations. Naturally, I accepted at once and pro bono looking forward to meeting these special teenagers and already thinking about how to approach them.

Chapter: 7

Arts, Disability & Pro-Sport, Recovery, Reflections, Rehab (part three)

Having spoken to an audience many times, I didn't consider this event a particular problem. On a number of occasions–conducting a class or talking to youths–I had just let things develop naturally, followed my intuition and felt my way towards the young-sters, their dreams and desires by instinct....

Events like this have always been an important part of my work–an excellent chance to help and motivate as much as to learn from and widen my horizon. Often enough, I have had the honor to meet people who should have a major impact on my life and the other way round in one respect or the other; and this particular occasion was no different. I was about to meet one of the finest young personalities I had come across in a long time, and it would be the beginning of an amazing joint journey for nearly three years during which I learned as many lessons as I was honored to teach that young lady.

As soon as I walked into the classroom I felt an enormous positive energy that was not only generated by the quite excited teenagers but also by their two regular teachers, Mrs. Wilson and Mrs. Lopez, who stood out by their kind and considerate behavior to-wards these special children from the start–for sure a reflection of their daily work, two true angels we take for granted so often. The vice principal was also present, a fine man with great positive charisma. He allowed me to speak to this class without having seen or even heard of me before taking a chance on behalf of those amazing pupils sensing, perhaps, it should be important to them. So, paperwork and red tape had been left aside for a change, which showed the vice principal, was a man of action.

After a warm welcome, Mrs. Wilson introduced me to the students who were be-tween 13 and 16 years old. I was taken in by them instantly: Excellently conducted by their teachers, it was impressive to see how these well-behaved youngsters interacted with each other. Standing before them, I decided spontaneously not just to speak about myself but also to talk and interact with them. My aim was to open them up, touch their minds and hearts so that they would tell me about their dreams and desires, their hobbies and ideas about future activities, jobs and careers.

I know, the majority of people would say, "What for? Most of them are severely physically handicapped, and there are retarded (a terrible expression) and mentally as well as emotionally disabled children among them, too. So how do you expect to succeed with this idea?" I believe it is simple: With charm and the heart in the right place! And following the most vital rule: Never behave and for sure talk to any of these special young people as if there was something wrong with them. Even if you think, they cannot under-stand you, most read you emotionally through your body language and demeanor and so understand more than it might seem. Perhaps they will not tell you, but they will certainly let you know by their reactions: Interacting if you can awaken their interest or simply ignoring you or walk away, if not. Be sure, they feel you, and therefore you can find your way into every special youngster's heart. Just be yourself and–even more important– always respectful, kind and open; treat them as normal! This will lead you to great success. But what really matters is that you will make a big difference in their lives. And you will go home afterwards knowing you have won a whole bunch of new great friends!

I began with some information about my life. I told them about the humble beginnings as an athlete and how I had been able to change everything with the help of my wonderful teachers and mentors. Then, initiating the conversation, I addressed the pupils and asked them to introduce themselves with a short description of their intentions, goals, dreams and desires. The response was simply sensational: All youngsters joined in happily and no one, no matter how challenged he/she was, felt left out. I heard the most amazing little stories about themselves and their–in most cases–quite large wishes and dreams.

When it was Eden's turn, she simply left me speechless. She did not only suffer from severe cerebral palsy but also communicated through her so-called 'Dina box', a device to let you form words and sentences like a PC and by the touch of a button these are repeated aloud with help of the machine. When she spoke, it was with a clarity and deepness you would not have expected from a young teenager. Eden told us she wanted to go to college and then become an occupational therapist and teacher. And I had no doubt whatsoever that this would be exactly what she was going to achieve!

One of the boys with Down syndrome was next to share his dreams with us. He wanted to become a professional basketball player. There appeared a somewhat doubtful look on the faces of the teachers, I noticed–not in a bad way, but showing they did not believe this was possible. The other pupils however, did not see any problem at all. So, I asked them to do a little brainstorming with me: "Now what would this boy exactly have to do to ensure he will reach his goal and to accomplish his dream?" The students bubbled over with suggestions and I had to lead them a little. "Training a lot"; "Yes, yes, and play a lot." "Play? Do you mean he needs to practice a lot?" All kids joined in. "Yes, yes, practice, a lot of practice," they shouted. "What about food?" They all started to laugh. "Does he need a lot of candy or fresh fruit?" I got up and paced back and forth sticking out my belly as if it was large and fat. All cheered and laughed even louder. "Well? Candy and burgers or fresh fruit?" They yelled, "Fresh fruit, fresh fruit". Someone shouted: "Candy, candy" "Really, candy?" "Just kidding". It was great to see how much fun they all had.

Finally, I summed up our 'findings' for the boy with Down-syndrome. "Hard work, lots of practice, good food and rest in between, besides being a good student and son, are the main ingredients for success. So why not, you can do it. Go for it," I told him. I moved around the classroom and the pupils carried on telling us about their intentions and dreams. They were all highly attentive, hardly ever drifting off; an incredible fact considering that the attention-span of children with these particular limitations is supposed to be no longer than 10-15 minutes at a time, after which they would need a break or simply wander off. And yet they were enjoying themselves for more than half an hour already. I was delighted! However, to keep them interested I decided to show a sequence of my DVD 'Get fit for Life'. A little demonstration, even just shown by a DVD, very often makes a welcome change, especially, when you deal with teenagers, and the attention is heightened afterwards.

After a short break we carried on with our conversation. A boy, quite disabled, over-weight and shy, told us he wanted to become a race-car driver. "Well," I said, "that's fine, but a race-car driver needs to be in a pretty good shape to concentrate and to be able to make decisions fast, on the spur of the moment. He must be well trained and keep his blood pressure down. You see, most of the school kids today are overweight; and about 25% of all youth between 12 and 21 are on one kind of drug or other, including cigarettes and alcohol." Everyone was listening attentively, and again, I was taken in by their level of concentration. Even if this boy would never become a race-car driver, at least he could perhaps be motivated to watch his diet a little better and to start exercising more. That alone would be a great accomplishment. So I used this moment to ask of the class: "Now, what is good food and what do we know for sure is bad and we need to be careful about?"

Again, this was a double class of handicapped teenagers. And yet the level of activity and the answers these gorgeous youngsters came up with were simply amazing. Even the teachers could not believe this was happening. "Chocolate"; "hamburgers"; "candy"; "fatty chips"; "crisps"; they were all pitching in–the 'ball' was thrown back and forth, a perfect game, a grand-slam homerun, but without the steroids! And I was right in the middle of it loving every moment. A class like this is the place for me to be! I would not want it any other way. It was pure magic. And as the morning drew to a close, all youngsters were cheering and applauding to each other and me, asking me to come back soon. I thanked them for this wonderful time and the pleasure they had given me.

Afterwards, I had the chance to talk to Eden and her caretaker; and once again I was amazed just how much energy and thirst for knowledge shone through her eyes. She had been for sure the most outstanding personality in that classroom. I gave my telephone number to her caretaker and said if Eden would like to learn more, I would be more than happy to come and talk to her family. As it happened, Eden's parents had been looking for a new therapist and trainer for a while, so we promised each other to stay in touch.

Within a week, Eden's mother phoned me and asked to meet and talk about a pos-sible rehab and workout plan for Eden. I gladly agreed. As a footnote: Eden's family hardly paid my work's worth, but that was not the point anyway. I saw her training as an important joint journey, and my payment was the chance to change her life, a chance I got through that morning at her school, which wasn't paid for either, because I had wanted it that way. And this is a great example that you are well paid if you do something positive without always asking what is in there for you.

After I had met her mother, I went to see Eden. She was lying on the floor of the family's private Yoga gym and welcomed me with a bright smile and different tones pulling her head backwards in a fast movement. These tones were amazing and seemed to come from deep inside her. They could be quite loud and long depending on her feelings and deepness of emotion. Soon I should get accustomed to this great way of expressing her feelings, and it became one of my favorite features about her, knowing the pureness of her personality and emotions.

For a while, Eden and I sat and talked about her visions and dreams, what she was looking for, how her present workout and rehab plan was designed, what to watch out for and to be aware of–and all this without a single word spoken! Eden only moved her eyes up or down, and I ran the Alphabet back and forth until I hit the correct letters quickly forming the words and sentences we were looking for. But most of the time we understood each other without words. Over and over again, she proved to me that I had been right about her amazing inner strength and razor-sharp mind back at the event in her school. And this was only the surface of her highly intelligent, compassionate and caring personality; moreover, she was astonishingly open and hungry for wisdom and knowledge.

I set up a timetable for an hour three times a week, and within the first half month, I took my time to evaluate her overall condition with different tests and to build a bond of understanding and trust between us. Training and rehabilitating a child or teenager with special needs is not that different from working with an adult. However, with a young person the responsibility for safety and well being during workout is a lot greater because he/she is still in the process of growing, of building personality and character and therefore more sensitive to influence. Adequate knowledge and continuous education in this field is, therefore, of vital importance for every instructor and teacher, even more so for physiotherapist and sports therapists as well as trainers working in the sector of rehabilitation in general to ensure safe workout and hopefully quick recovery of the patient and student in their care.

*

When I was 16 years old, I learned my first lessons about body-functions from Geert Lemmens and his wife; and at their summer camps we students had to pass a small test about it. Later, Mihran, Marwan, Lothar Vieregge, Peter Beschenbossel, a few more and I were some of the first from the Martial Arts sector to attend special seminars organized by the DSSV and DAKV (major German fitness- and sport organizations) together with the DSB (German Sports Association). And all qualified instructors and teachers of our organisation regularly went to the famous Olympic Sports Education Centre in Malente (North Germany) to further their education and gain certificates. I am more than grateful that Geert and Vera Lemmens had been–once again–trendsetters in this poorly maintained area. They make it mandatory for every high ranking Belt and for sure dojo owner to attend further education if he/she wants to be part of our organisation and certainly if he/she is interested in teaching and testing of our belts. Through that Lemmens has created a highly selective group of extremely strong and well educated Martial Artists. And that has always been his motto: Quality instead of quantity! Right from the start Lemmens had ensured safe training and interaction, and certainly safe and healthy rehab of patients and students by his teachers and instructors.

Many dojos, gyms and even entire organisations today, however, don't seem to care that much about proper education. Only too often, people are not seen as individuals with certain needs, for sure not as patients, but as customers, paying bodies preferably left alone with the machines to keep the costs low. And through the 'low-price-war' raging out there, especially among the large 'fitness chains', these businesses can only survive by a high turnover luring people into their dojos and gyms by dishonourable advertising.

When I was about 21 years old I had an idea about how to enhance existing gym machines with special attachments to enable handicapped and severely injured people to workout and rehab themselves without gym-owners having to buy a room-full of special rehab equipment. I was able to awaken the interest of the VP director of a large European fitness- and sports-equipment manufacturer, and he asked me to meet him for lunch. My friend Helge accompanied me to one of the best and most expensive places in Hamburg, the 'Four Seasons Hotel', where we had an immensely expensive meal with this man dressed in a 500-dollar suit. I am quite sure this all was meant to impress and intimidate me, because it became clear soon enough that he was not particularly interested in working with me; he only wanted to find out about the essential details of my idea, that could be easily realized and with little expenditure. So no contract was offered. He simply was after big business and money for his company and nothing else. I was young, but not stupid. So I told him nothing, and–after finishing our luxury lunch–we just left.

Over the years, the manufacturers began to come out with the 'concentric-move-ments- and negative-resistance' machines. They are useful, but surely not what could have been built and therefore done with them. With any line of the so-called 'rehab-machines' the user can only achieve a fraction of what could be possible; and unfortu-nately, some of them are simply useless. So, this is just another example for the lack of real interest and concern within the fitness industry, certainly in the sector of rehabilita-tion of handicapped and severely injured people and fits into the picture of under- or non-educated gym owners and their staff.

If the drainage pipe of your kitchen sink is blocked, you call a plumber, a well edu-cated and experienced expert, licensed and insured. If your car brakes down, you will surely not let the man down the street mess with it. Again, you would call an expert, a well trained and trustworthy mechanic. So, why should you have to put your health and fitness, even your life, into the hands of an uneducated, uninsured 'trainer'? You want to protect your health and your interests, let alone save your money. It is about time for governments to introduce mandatory education for at least one year in this field. After all, proper qualification is required in other branches to be allowed to work! So, returning to Eden, it is understandable why her parents had found it difficult to get a proper teacher and rehab instructor not only to ensure her safety but also forward moving physical rehab and education without wasting their money and Eden's time; not to mention her trust and hope to get better.

*

Every professional training, every rehab, begins with a truthful and 'down-to-the-detail' assessment of the overall condition of your student. I put Eden through a series of tests to determine her range of motion and flexibility; and at the same time I monitored her pulse to establish her:
THR – Target Heart Rate
RHR – Resting Heart Rate
RCHR – Re-Covering Heart Rate
MP   – Max. Pulse
RP   – Resting Pulse
RCP – Re-Covering Pulse
Blood Pressure
This may sound rather complicated, but it is not difficult after a little training. In the old days, a nurse would have taken the pulse at the wrist or neck, holding on for a minute; but due to the risk of pressing too hard and by that influencing it and even causing lightheadedness, the professional today takes the pulse for only ten seconds and multi-plies the result by six. The heart rate is determined by counting the cardiac (heart) muscle contraction within one minute. The RHR should be between 60 and 80 contractions (heart-

beats) per minute; the RCHR indicates how quickly the cardio vascular system returns to its normal performance and is used as measure for the cardiac fitness (health of the heart and respiratory system).

The blood pressure is measured in two units:

(1) SBP–Systolic Blood Pressure is the pressure on the arterial walls during heart contraction (systole) and is measured on a mercury scale in mm/Hg. The average SBP of a healthy adult should be 120 mm/Hg.

(2) DBP–Diastolic Blood Pressure is the pressure on the arterial walls during non-heart contraction (diastole) Here the average of a healthy adult should be 80-100 mm/Hg.

The blood pumped through the arteries down to the most delicate capillaries carries oxygen and nutrients essential for our heart, respiratory system, for our entire body. Specifically the myocardium (heart muscle) needs constant supply of oxygen and nutrients supplied by the delicate arteries around the heart (coronary arteries) in order to work 24 hours, seven days a week; without oxygen (anaerobic), it does not work properly at all. If the arteries, especially the coronary arteries, are narrowed or even blocked by bad cholesterol and deposits flowing in the blood due to poor nutrition, not only the blood pressure will rise to a dangerous level, but also the supply of oxygen and nutrients will be reduced and can even be interrupted. If this is not treated and the situation continues for longer, parts of the heart muscle die, which results in a heart attack that causes death in most cases.

It is of vital importance to keep your heart and respiratory system healthy by effective and continuous workout, which is called condition training. However, even an injured or damaged heart and respiratory system can be rehabilitated and trained, its strengths and condition improved. If the training is done correctly, the heart muscle will, like any other muscle in the body, become more powerful leading to a stronger contraction and therefore to an increase of the stroke volume (amount of blood pumped with every heartbeat). The heartbeat of a well-trained professional or amateur athlete, especially of an aerobic athlete, is relatively low, because the stroke volume is so high that the heart does not need to contract that often.

Regular checks on heart rate and blood pressure during the entire training of every student are essential. And they are certainly mandatory when rehabilitating children with a handicap. Quite a few conditions–cerebral palsy or Spina Bifida for example–are often accompanied by heart and/or lung problems that can even cause their failure. In many cases, these problems are treated with heavy long-term medication–another feature to be taken into account. That alone is reason enough for every teacher and instructor to have a well rounded-up knowledge in this field. But it is also our own responsibility to look after ourselves; and I do not mean just athletes. We should all know about what happens within our bodies during our daily actions and work.

*

While I was monitoring Eden's pulse and blood pressure, I assessed her range of motion and flexibility, her muscular strength, large- and fine-motor coordination, her movement abilities and, last but not least, her eye-hand coordination in order to design a safe and effective workout and rehab plan with a lot of fun involved. In my opinion, fun is essential, because with fun you work a lot better than without! Therefore, I invented 'exercise'-games just for Eden, which we played throughout the training. Also, I customized several exercise facilities and helpful devices to meet with her requirements.

Again, for everyone who plays with the idea to train and rehab a child with special needs, do not worry; it is not much different from working with anyone else. With the appropriate knowledge, heart and care you will be able to cause a long lasting positive change in the life of your new student and surely new friend; and at the same time, you will gain a long-term client who found a new friend, too. Through that, you can build your reputation as caring teacher and instructor with great skills gradually and ensure the success of your gym or dojo in the long run. You will hardly need to look for clients; they will come and look for you as long as you give your very best every time, with a firm foundation of knowledge, continuous education and always more than willing to learn.

Eden's range of motion was extremely limited and her entire support muscle system underdeveloped, and therefore she was too weak to sit up for long, let alone move about freely. So, the most important aspect of her training was the strengthening of the muscles like the three erector spinae, quadratus lumborum, latissimus dorsi, the rhomboid and levator scapulae, and their counter players, of course, like the pectoralis major and minor, the rectus abdominis and the external as well as internal obliques, just to name the major players. As many of you probably know these are called agonists and antagonists, or more simplified, pro and contra muscles, which means they are the active and counteractive players like biceps and triceps (the first flexes, the other stretches) or quadriceps and hamstrings. You also have to know about the muscles' origin and insertion (beginning and ending) to ensure correct rehab and exercising as well as the safety and health of your patient or client. This brings me to another important aspect of training and the secret of success for any athlete: The achievement of the full range of motion, in the case of rehab and therefore in Eden's case, as much as possible with the prospect of more and stronger movements later on.

The muscles form a natural brace around the joints and bones, supporting and moving them, creating 'static' for the body like for a house. Imagine you break away a major part of an outside wall to build some great French doors, but without taking care of the house's static. It will not be too long before the other supporting walls will crack, break or even collapse depending on the size of the part that has been taken out. So you will have to pay the price for disturbing the static. The same applies to the body, even to the whole nature itself. We will have to pay; it is only a matter of time. This in mind, let us take Eden as a study example to deal with the different muscle groups and their function as well as their build up and strengthening.

All cerebral palsy patients are in extensive need of muscle build-up, stretching and daily improvement of flexibility at the same time, which is no contradiction if you know what you are doing. This misconception is a tale in the world of body builders! Eden's hamstrings were extremely tight, and the deltoids of both shoulders were underdeveloped and weak, which limited the use of her arms so that they, in return, never had a chance to develop. Moreover, due to her sitting in a chair all day the hip and ilium crest, gluteus maximus, all three erector spinae muscles, which run up and down the spine from head to hip for support, and the rhomboid and levator scapulae were also underdeveloped and weak. As a result, Eden became tired too quickly and all these muscles tensed up easily to spasm-like cramps. A vicious circle: The underdeveloped muscles caused Eden's weakness, the weakness caused her tiredness consequently resulting in even less ability to sit up for long, let alone to move; so the muscles would not develop, causing constant pain.

It may sound rather complicated, but if you know the muscles' origin and insertion and the function of the muscle groups, training is not very different from the workout of a 'normal' person. However, if you would like to go deeper into the subject, there are a number of excellent books about Kinesiology, anatomy and physiology available. I cannot point out the importance of base-knowledge about the human body and its functions strongly enough to ensure the patient's safety and successful training.

Another major problem with CP is the always underdeveloped calf muscle (soleus) as well as the tibialis posterior as a result of wrong use of hip and knees and wrong hip-foot movements that can cause even a shutdown of some areas in the calf muscle. In return, again, the lower legs, especially the calf muscles, are hardly in use at all and therefore extremely vulnerable to injury. Besides, standing up, let alone moving, is hardly possible. If you know how to deal with this properly, again, there will be no difficulty. I almost ripped my Achilles tendon in a gym; a perfect example of completely wrong training due to the lack of sufficient knowledge. Had the dojo owner known anything about it and helped me, nothing would have happened.

Of course, there is a safe way to build up the calf muscles of a CP patient; you only need to follow a few guidelines and safety measures: Use your body weight to start with, it is more than enough. Do not work with heavy lower-leg-machines to begin with, for sure not with a calf-machine. Instead, take machines that train the entire legs like a squat-leg-press in a lying position, or a roller. It is a great way to safely work out all major muscles. Another possibility is to stand on a small step or wooden block holding safely on to the ballet bar. Lift yourself up on your toes and stretch your feet to the highest point contracting the calf muscles, and then lower yourself slowly down again. Try to stand on the step with the front part of your feet only and do three to five raises. Then repeat the exercise with one foot letting the other hang down relaxed. Do again three to five raises, then change feet. Finish your exercise with some stretches for each calf with your hands against the wall. Eden's calf muscles were extremely weak, and we worked hard on them from the start.

The upper leg muscles of a CP patient also require particular attention. Hip flexors, quadriceps and hamstrings are profoundly underdeveloped, especially in cases like Eden's or Monae's. Due to their weakness they tens up easily, and movements are extremely limited and uncoordinated. The knees are hardly supported which causes a limited range of motion and pain in the joints, even their complete lock-up at times; patella tendonitis is the consequence. To strengthen this group of muscles and eliminate the misbalance for a better overall performance of the entire lower body during the daily activities, regular exercises with conventional workout machines like the quadriceps and hamstring machine for leg extension or leg curls are not possible; the muscles are simply too weak, the range of motion too limited. Therefore, I used the negative resistance technique Geert Lemmens applied when he worked with me some 20 years before to ensure Eden's tiny muscles would not be overstrained.

It is quite a simple exercise: Eden lay on her belly and with one hand I applied light pressure to the upper part of her knee to keep it on the floor. Holding on to her foot with my other hand I gently lifted her lower leg asking Eden to resist the movement until she almost reached her gluts. Then she had to push her lower leg back down against the light pressure I applied to it. We started out with two to three units per leg, but Eden, being a real fighter and born champion from the start, managed five units within two months. Extremely important is the stretching out of the hamstrings after such an exercise. Eden would gladly leave out the stretching just like me when I was young.

To strengthen the hip flexors I let Eden perform leg raises that would also take care of the obliques and lower abdominal muscles. Normally you do this in a sitting position lifting your legs in a scissor-like motion, for example. In Eden's case I modified the exercise in order to avoid overstraining, improve her balance and to protect her lower back: Stretched out she lay on her side and lifted one leg, then rolled over and did the same with the other leg. At the beginning, she performed two to three raises with one leg before changing, repeating the exercise 15-20 times depending on her level of energy and strength. However, as I already said, Eden was a fighter and therefore improved a lot faster than I or anyone else had expected. Within only two months, she was able to raise each leg three to five times with 20-50 (!) repetitions. It was an outstanding achievement!

In order to keep her balance during this exercise Eden had to use her hands, which is another difficulty for people with CP and for the ones suffering from injuries of the spinal cord. The coordination of hands and fingers is badly developed as well their strength. In the beginning Eden could hardly make use of her hands at all, she had great difficulty to close them; and moving her fingers separately was nearly impossible. For us just another challenge; we were determined to improve her abilities by at least 60-70% before the end of the year. In order to accomplish this I made Eden exercise her fingers by kneading and forming a lump of patty whenever there was a moment to spare. We also played two little games with a lot of fun involved. Here the first: Every time she needed her hands, she would naturally use the back of them flipping them over, often with a kind of dragging motion to it. So I was politely on her case continuously reminding her to use her palms instead and stretch her fingers at the same time. This was meant to heighten the awareness of her movements and to imprint the more useful motions into her daily activities.

The other game was equally simple yet most effective, not just improving the strength and flexibility of her hands and fingers but also of her entire arms. Moreover, in a playful way I made her move and stretch dozens of other muscle groups at the same time: Lying in front of each other I asked Eden to stretch out her arms, hands and fingers as much as she possibly could to reach my fingers. When she came too close I simply moved them away a little so that she had to try with even greater effort. This little game also was a fine warm-up we did at the beginning of almost every session. Eden was a great sport. No matter how hard I pushed her, she tried until she even collapsed sometimes, a real Black Belt in life! And I came up with this slogan just for her: 'The impossible we do every day, miracles need a little longer'.

When creating a rehab and workout plan, especially for one of these special students like Eden, I think my favorite stage has always been the invention of little games to wrap up exercises that are necessary to overcome certain limitations. Naturally, children have a lot more fun playing than just training in a regular way. And concentrating on a game they and even adults tend to forget about their limitations and are able to overcome them a lot faster in many cases. Moreover, a game played with pleasure always elevates and influences the patient emotionally in a most positive way.

With Eden, there were several problems to overcome. Though born an athlete, she had never been challenged and had surely never come even close to her full potential. I needed to find a way to motivate her, elevate her and to make her move as many muscles as possible at the same time together, improving her condition and coordination abilities. So, playful exercises were required between regular training units that would let her forget about her physical limitations; that would motivate and push her to widen her range of motion to full extent and use as many muscle groups as possible, working together as one without even realizing it to avoid worries and fears and therefore restraint. The coordinated teamwork of all muscles was of great importance not only for Eden's overall performance but also for the command over her movements. The latter would give her greater independence and surely more fun during her daily life.

The majority of us take it for granted that we can sit on a chair without having to worry about falling off or toppling over; that we can eat and drink, get dressed, have a shower or use the toilet by ourselves. But for Eden all this–and a lot more–was only possible with the help of others. Quite frustrating, especially for a teenager, and for sure causing emotional problems. With that in mind, I put even more energy into creating additional fun workouts and games with competitive background to enhance and speed up Eden's progress of recovery so that she would gain more freedom by improving her motor-skills and range of motion.

The games I thought out were really quite simple and yet had great effects. Like this one we played a lot as warm-up and condition training: I drew a wide circle into the soft carpet of the room we worked in and marked a spot as starting- and one, opposite, as finishing-point. Eden was positioned in the centre of the circle while I waited, on all fours, at the start. Once the signal was given, I began to crawl as fast as I could along the circle line towards the finishing-point; and Eden's task was to prevent me from reaching it. She was allowed to move in any way and direction she thought best to cut me off and therefore beat me to the finishing-point. She would also win the game, when able to touch me with a hand or foot. Eden was a great opponent from the start, highly competitive and inventive. As long as we worked out together, she beat me at least two out of three times, and it became a standing joke between us, when we started the game, that this time I would break her record and become the champion of the day. Eden would only smile and roll her eyes: "Not in my lifetime, get going, let's play". It was great fun and caused an incredible enhancement of her overall performance and condition as well as her confidence. She would roll over and around, move her arms, hands and legs, pulling and pushing with increasing speed–and work all her major muscle groups at the same time to beat me. It was wonderful to see her joy and improvement.

Soon I was able to introduce another game, also meant to increase her condition and sense of competition. It was a simplified version of my 'alligator condition training' that had been part of Shin-Tora-Do Karate for years: Under normal circumstances the students would be on their hands and toes, then lift themselves up and use their arms and legs in alligator-fashion to move forward. For Eden, however, this would not have been possible then. Due to a very limited range of motion, most CP patients find it extremely difficult to lift their arms above their heads; they would only reach shoulder level at best and become exhausted in the process rather fast. The same applies to the legs: With the hip flexors extremely weak, raising a leg is nearly impossible–a few inches, perhaps, before losing balance and falling over. Therefore I had to trick the CP trapped in her body by eliminating the force of gravity and so prevent early exhaustion:

Eden lay on her belly and I put my hands on her soles to keep her feet from slipping backwards. This is quite like using a stair master, only in a lying position. Eden pushed herself forward bending and lifting one leg after the other as high up as possible, rolling her body from one side to the other, and using her arms in a similar fashion like an alligator moves. I helped her a little so that she worked all her leg-, arm- and major back-muscles at the same time. And I encouraged Eden to particularly use her hips and to bend her knees, moving them up to her belly or even beyond as much as possible before push-ing herself forward to improve the range of motion and the use of her hip flexors. Work-ing as many muscle groups as possible–and as often as possible, together in harmony–again, was of vital importance to Eden. Sitting in a chair without moving much more or less all day, she was hardly able to use those muscles at all, and some of them were even shut down at the beginning of our training.

As a CP- and MS (muscular dystrophy) -patient you need to exercise constantly dur-ing your whole life! If you don't, muscle atrophy will kick in within 72 hours after you stopped to train; the time-span depends on your overall condition, health and age. So, no matter how well you have built up a group of muscles, it will recede once you stop exer-cising it. And this is no exaggeration! You can imagine now just how essential Eden's overall training was. Every teacher and instructor must keep this in mind when he/she trains someone with CP or MS. And the more exciting and fun loving he/she designs the workout plan, the better is the chance that the student or patient will keep training.

The 'alligator' game had tremendous effects and Eden played it with great joy. It also made her body ache, a fact she simply loved (every athlete knows how I mean this!), feeling her muscles like that sitting in her chair for the rest of the day, knowing she had worked well! This exercise combined with the other regular training units soon led to a considerable improvement of her muscle groups' interaction and strength; especially her leg- and hip muscles profited a lot, causing greater mobility. As a result, Eden became so strong and well coordinated that she was able to play 'the alligator' on her own, without my help, in no time. Within months, she actually raced against me all across the floor from one end of the room to the other with great joy. I had hoped for this development, but I did certainly not expect it so soon. Neither did Jessica who was, of course, involved in Eden's rehab as well. I always loved to watch her taking care of her after class the way she looked after all our special students; and I have hardly ever seen anyone else treating them so sweetly, apart from Michelle and Magnolia, Eden's nurse. We all need these people in our lives from time to time–no matter who we are and what we want from life or not–who just do their magic, always so effortlessly and never complaining. Whenever I come across one of these angels, it saves my day and makes up for all other times I do not feel so motivated. They put a smile on my face and fill up the batteries for me to move forward again. It is simply great to see I am not alone, and there are others out there who dedicate their life and daily work to our special children, never asking for much in return. Magnolia, one of Eden's nurses, definitely was an angel at work and became a great friend not only to all the students and me but to Jessica as well, doing her bit of magic to help her along her journey.

Michelle, too, helped with Eden's rehab as much as she could. Sadly, did not reach the same level of education in Shin-Tora-Do rehab as Jessica did with her work, especially with Monae. But this was only due to the fact that she fell down a stone stairway supposedly at work and got hurt badly. So, she had to end our joint journey with our special students prematurely for the time being; especially sad because this wonderful woman had much to go through in her private life before she was emotionally strong enough eventually to leave her nightmares behind and every abusive man. Apart from teaching and mentoring, I couldn't do more for her. Michelle had to learn to stand up for herself on her own in about the same emotional areas as Jessica. Nevertheless, I made it clear to her that she could turn to me any time of day or night and that she was under my personal protection like all my students.

Eden's remarkable journey was definitely helped along by Jessica's, Magnolia's and Michelle's support and care. When it comes to rehab and recovery efforts, particularly for children and youth with special needs, the importance of emotional support and overall care must not be underestimated. They will intensify the feeling of well-being and speed up the process of recovery a great deal. So, besides plenty of healthy food and adequate resting breaks the loving treatment of these three women, with lots of hugs and kisses, elevated and positively influenced Eden more than any 'professional' treatment could have done.

Another fun-exercise was the 'snow angel' to tackle Eden's arm- and shoulder-problems in particular. As mentioned before, lifting up the arms above shoulder level is difficult if not impossible for every person with CP. And in Eden's case, the situation was worsened by her extremely small and weak shoulder muscles caused–again–by lack of proper and sufficient use. Moreover, up until then all caretakers had picked her up from the floor by pulling on her arms. By this her shoulder joints were overstretched, so that the heads came almost out of their sockets. Repeated injury of her tiny shoulders were the result, which could, of course, have been avoided by simply picking her up in a proper way. So I kept reminding Eden to flex her biceps muscle every time she was pulled up or around. It would take most of the pressure off her shoulders and so protect her joints. To ensure their recovery I gave her Glucosimine with vitamin E and C in liquid form right from the start. This product is absolutely safe to take and works miracles; it helps a lot to rebuild the cartilage in the joints. Together with the exercises, nutritious food and loving care, it did an excellent job!

I am sure you all know the 'snow angel'. I think all children who have the chance to play in freshly fallen snow love to 'draw' one lying on their backs or bellies, moving away the fluffy snow with their arms and legs and leaving an angel-like imprint on the ground. I remembered this fun from my own childhood, when I was thinking about how to exercise Eden's arms and shoulders without having to fight gravity. It was ideal: To begin with, I let Eden stretch her arms down close to her body as much as she could. Then I asked her to move them slowly sideways and upwards in a semicircle across the floor as high as possible, extending them all the time but with a light bend to protect the elbow joints. During the first weeks she was not able to bring her hands together above her head; there always was a barrier at some point. But with great inner strength and will power, she eventually overcame this obstacle, pushing the barrier-point further and further up until her hands reached each other.

The 'snow angel' also was a good breathing exercise. As you surely know, proper breathing helps to improve the muscle performance and overall health. So far, Eden's respiration had been more or less too shallow and inconsistent as it is with most CP and MS patients, due to problems with–and often underdevelopment of–the lungs and the whole respiration system as well as difficulties with swallowing, caused by complications at birth. So, there was yet another feature I needed to focus on from the beginning. To improve inhaling and exhaling at command and free will I introduced a fine little exercise with meditative background for Eden to do before going to sleep every night. And this is something for you, too. So why not **start tonight:**

Lie down and relax for a moment letting your day pass by. Then start to consciously inhale and exhale, but slowly and without concentrating too hard on it. It does not matter, if you 'miss' a breath at times. Just carry on with the next one. Let this new energy you are taking in with every breath slowly sink in. Then close your eyes and start to concentrate on your inner eye (located between your brows) until you see a light shining. Slowly inhale and exhale, relax more and more, and then slowly strengthen this light, your inner eye (your Chi) and let it flow through your body without any pressure, warming and healing. Start in the head and, with every breath, let it slowly wander down to your shoulders, to your chest into your belly, to the hips, down your left leg, back up again and down your right leg; then back up through your hips, your belly to your chest and into your left arm, to the hand, then back to your chest and into your right arm, to your hand; back to your chest and once more down to your belly into what most Budokas in Japan call the 'Centre of the Sun' or Harra, the centre of Inner Chi, the source of strength and inner peace. On its way through your body let the light rest in tired or injured parts until YOU decide to carry on.

Eden was an excellent student and religiously did her breathing and meditation 15 minutes every night before going to sleep. It helped her tremendously. When she performed the 'snow angel' and, moving her arms upwards, reached a barrier-point, she started to consciously breathe more deeply gathering force and commanding her arms to move on and break the barrier. The success was all hers! This exercise was as well one of her favorites she always did with grace and great pleasure. And one day, perhaps, we would do it together at 'Big Bear' in fresh fluffy show, we kept joking. Within a couple of months Eden was able to bring the palms of her hands together above her head every time; and after a moment's rest breathing in deeply she brought her arms back down in a perfect movement, slowly exhaling. After she had reached that level, I told her to rotate her hands, palms facing downward, thumps facing upward like in the Tai Chi movement 'Sun Greeting'; and so, as a byproduct, I set the foundation for her own specialized Tai Chi movements to be exercised later.

After about three months Eden performed the 'snow angel' in perfection, and it was time for a more challenging version of this exercise: Lying on her back again with arms stretched out close to her body I asked her to inhale deeply and then, while slowly exhaling, to lift her fully extended arms straight up into the air to a vertical position with her shoulders, then further up and backwards past her head down to the floor. After deeply inhaling again, Eden had to lift her arms once more and move them back to their original position by her hips, palms facing downwards, thumbs upwards, slowly exhaling. She managed better than I had expected, and so we combined both exercises to a unit executing three to five sets with six to eight repetitions, which filled just over 15 minutes with shoulder-arm workout and breathing exercise improving her hand-eye motor skills and coordination abilities at the same time.

After Eden's arm- and shoulder-strength had improved, it was time to concentrate on the overall teamwork of all muscle groups in harmony and to build up their support-functions. Two Yoga positions–the 'Child Position' and the 'Phoenix'–came to my mind that would, combined, form an excellent exercise to heighten her overall health, condition, strength and flexibility. I only had to modify the beginning- and ending-position of these Yoga moves to pay tribute to Eden's still limited motion- and balance-abilities.

To use all her muscle groups together at the same time always was the hardest task for Eden. In order to succeed, she needed her entire strength and concentration–the 'fight or flight' principle. Eden's will power, however, seemed to be without limits; and the way she executed the new exercise simply was amazing: She started out lying on her belly. At first she had to slowly move her arms–palms facing upwards–backwards until the elbows were nearly fully bent. Then Eden's legs, one after the other, had to be moved sideways and her knees pulled up until these, too, were fully bent underneath her body. After that she dropped herself down into the complete 'Child Position', relaxed and breathed deeply a couple of times gathering energy for the next Yoga move...

The transfer from 'Child Position' into the 'Phoenix', or also known as upper facing dog position, was extremely exhausting for her, and if she wasn't on top of her game and concentrated hard, watching her balance and her hand- and foot-positions, she would topple over or break down, unable to complete the move. But, as we already know, Eden was a real fighter and extraordinary character. She just saw this exercise as a welcome new challenge, putting all her energy into it; and every time she completed the moves, she was incredibly exhausted and happy at the same time. She would never give up, no matter how hard I pushed her, motivating all of us and making me grateful to be her teacher and friend. And I realized that, if we could make this work regularly, there would be no limit we could go anywhere from there.

Eden became stronger almost on a weekly basis. It didn't take long before I only needed to intervene–holding her sides, for example–when she was about to fall; and I helped her just enough so that she could complete her movements. Both positions she did with variations: Starting out lying on her belly she stretched out her arms and hands as far as possible and from there moved into the 'Phoenix' position–Eden style, which meant she would not come up all the way and would rest her elbows on the floor before transferring into 'Child Position'. It was a remarkable achievement. And as a well-deserved reward, Jessica cooked an extra special meal for her. Eden was always hungry after class; not surprising, as we have already talked about how much energy a person with cerebral palsy, muscular distrophy or also paraplegia needs a day; even more so if he/she is an athlete in a weekly workout/rehab routine, let alone a teenager still growing! So, again, healthy and wholesome meals throughout the day are essential.

There was one day Eden felt particularly well and full of energy. So, after she had transferred from the 'Phoenix' position a la Eden into the 'Child Position'–lying down as best she could–and had rested for a moment breathing deeply, I asked her to push herself even more and transfer into the 'Four-Feet-Stand', which is, as we all know, the starting position for every crawling move and therefore the beginning of real independence! She transferred! With hardly any assistance! And held the position even on her very own for a moment, because I let go of her for a few seconds! That after only six months into the workout. Time for celebration with hugs and kisses from Jessica.

These Yoga exercises–with special modifications–were some of Eden's greatest challenges to her balance and strength during the following 6 months. Therefore, we concentrated on them and on smoother transitions into the different Yoga positions, constantly building up her muscles and improving her abilities to command her body. Working through the movements with fantastic will power and inner strength, she seemed to get stronger by the day; yet we never trained with grim determination, just with a lot of fun and joy. And Jessica and I made sure she got plenty of reward and emotional support.

Once Eden's condition, muscle power and especially her ability to keep her balance had reached a higher level, I decided to try the next step, which was a leg- and arm-raise from the 'Four-Feet-Stand'. So, she first moved smoothly into this position and then I let her lift one arm and the opposite leg, at the same time holding her sides only with two fingers so that she would experience the movement of her muscles and the balance to the full. Eden's performance was an almost perfect example of powerful body control: Gracefully she lifted her arm and leg, stretching them high into the air nearly reaching the ideal position. For the ordinary person this exercise may seem easy enough, but for someone with severe CP and all the difficulties coming with it, again, is an achievement almost beyond description. Jessica and I were speechless! Time once more for celebration. It always was an additional pleasure for me to see the loving friendship growing and intensifying between Eden and Jessica, which formed a strong part of the foundation for both their ways to success.

Eden's abilities developed so fast during her first year of training that I had to adjust, modify and even invent new exercises to ensure her body and nervous system did not become too used to the movements forming her rehab plan, but would be challenged over and over again and kept on edge all the time. Every athlete needs to challenge his/her muscles continuously and change the workout routine at least every three months to build up his/her overall physical condition and the muscular system. And this applies even more to people with cerebral palsy, muscular dystrophy and paraplegia due to the fact that their nervous system and muscle fibers are in need of a lot higher physical pressure to counteract spasm and atrophy as well as to rebuild and strengthen the muscles. This means students or patients suffering from one of these 'progressing' conditions need to reach their personal pain-tolerance-limit as often as they possibly can–and push themselves beyond to find the next limit, simply to ensure their muscles are stimulated enough to develop. And here lies the reason why so many patients cannot reach their full potential, if they are not in the care of a well-educated and highly knowledgeable teacher or therapist. They never get pushed safely beyond this particular point. So how could they possibly find their pain-tolerance-limits? If never experienced first hand, they will not be able to get across. Which is a shame; there are so many born champions out there, waiting to be awakened.

As Eden's overall strength and flexibility improved, it was time for the next level. Although the range of motion and use of her arms and hands, as well their power, were a lot better, it could happen any moment that her still tiny and injured rotor-cuffs (shoulder muscles) would give up causing her to fall and collapse on the floor. So I needed to find a safe method to improve her fitness and to take away her fear to fall–a mental barrier–at the same time, a method that would eliminate gravity as much as possible for her to work out more freely and so build her confidence. I came up with something quite simple: I measured Eden's training room and went to the next home-store to buy two lengths of strong steel cable. These I fastened next to each other on two opposite walls of the training room just below the ceiling so that they would run across the whole length of the room. I also put spacers on both ends to be able to adjust the tension of the cables and prevent them to sag when put under pressure. Then I went to a store selling hiking equipment and bought a climbing harness and tow support straps with safety hooks on either ends. With these hooks, I connected the harness with the secured steel cables. I put Eden into the harness and made sure her hands and knees had contact with the floor by adjusting the length of the support straps accordingly. Now Eden could move forward, crawling bit by bit on all fours across the room safely supported so that she did not have to worry about losing her balance. She felt as if she was space-walking and completely lost her fears; and her abilities, strength and range of motion improved considerably. She liked this exercise so much that it soon became her favorite. In fact, it didn't take long before she raced me across the room with a huge smile on her face!

It simply was mind blowing: With the modified Yoga moves, the 'alligator'-game, the 'snow angel' in two variations, the breathing exercises, the stretching and leg-workouts Eden had the training plan–and therefore the inner strength–of a pro athlete. After one single year of rehab!

With our great new device that hardly took up any space–just two steel cables running from one side of the room to the other–I was able to introduce two more exercises. For these I bought two handles a rock climber uses, which laid themselves softly into the hands so that they were not too hard for Eden to hold. Even though the strength in her hands and the ability to use them had improved a lot, she still found it difficult to close them or release their grip at her own command all the time. I lowered the straps just enough for Eden, sitting on the floor, to take hold of them with fully extended arms to ensure she would work all target muscles, which were the rhomboid (middle upper back), the latissimus dorsi (largest back muscle), the trapezius (upper back and neck) and, of course, the deltoids (shoulders). These muscles were not used at all while sitting in a chair most of the day. The first exercise was a slightly modified version of the back-pull-up. Eden pulled the handles contracting her back muscles as much as possible until her hands reached rib-level. As a second exercise, Eden pulled the handles sideways to left and right, stretching out her arms as far as she could, working especially her shoulders. She did three sets with 10-12 repetitions of both training units; and so we were able to add two more strengthening exercises to her weekly program that also improved the use of her hands.

Within weeks Eden's incredible progress challenged my inventiveness yet again; and this time I went to a fitness shop and bought a set of three rubber bands, used for workout, with different tension-levels. I fastened a safety hook on a wall close to the floor and hooked a rubber band to it by its centre. I sat Eden before it and put a wooden block (a plastic one would also do the job) at the wall for her to press her feet against. This provided her with more space so that she was able to work the band with full range of motion.

To challenge especially her biceps, even more the steel cables with their equipment became handy again: I lowered the support straps to about her shoulder level. Eden–in a sitting position again–gripped the handles, palms facing her body, and pulled herself in by flexing the biceps. For another workout of her back muscles I asked her to stretch herself forward, again as far as she could holding the handles, and then to pull herself backwards in a smooth but powerful motion contracting the latissimus dorsi and rhomboid. All three exercises were as well integrated into her weekly training plan (twice a week, three sets each, 10-12 reps).

Rubber bands and steel cable devices provided excellent means to develop Eden's back-, shoulder- and arm-muscles, together with the use of her hands and so took care of quite a variety of body areas. And yet this equipment was quite simple. It is all a matter of taking your time and thoroughly thinking about your patient's or student's abilities and limitations, and then using your inventive powers to modify known fitness and rehab exercises and create new ones with the help of existing facilities in order to draw up an individual workout plan. And by now you have surely realized the importance of a well founded knowledge about Kinesiology, physiology, anatomy and body mechanics if you take on the task of training people, not just the ones with special needs.

Footnote-Disclaimer: Feel free to use any of my ideas and workout equipment to help people who need to be in a better place in life. However, always take care of safety. The steel cables must be at least a quarter of an inch thick and the fastening devices extra strong to hold the pressure the cables will be put under. I used two for each just to be on the safe side, if one should come loose. You should check the bolts and spacers at least once a week as well as the hooks that hold the cables and the rubber bands on the walls. Make sure they are firmly fastened; otherwise, the devices may become dangerous catapults breaking loose and injuring your patient and/or you. If you do not have adequate knowledge, ask a professional to install them for you. Moreover, when buying harness and safety hooks, ask the sales assistant to inform you about their strength so that you will know they can hold your patient's weight and ensure his/her safety.

Due to Eden's amazing recovery, her inner strength and abilities as athlete and student she was ready to be invited to her first belt test sooner than Jessica and I had expected. This test was not just a reflection of her condition that particular day, but cast a light on her relentless and courageous efforts on a daily basis and her future path of recovery and life in general. Eden never gave up, never complained, always gave her very best with all the power she could generate, no matter how hard she had to work for her achievements; and so she motivated everybody who saw her training. The belt test we designed for her was a compilation of her weekly routines. There was not much difference from a normal one, only modified to meet her personal abilities.

Within two years of our training, Eden rose from white to green belt. We conducted the last test at Venice Beach opposite the LAPD sub-station; and many people were watching. It was a great event: Little Monae got her yellow belt and Julia her orange. Many people applauded when Eden received her green belt and was awarded the title of Jun. Sempei for her outstanding performance and for setting an example by her daily efforts for all of us. And last but not least, our Jessica was awarded the honorable (for the time being) purple belt in Shin-Tora-Do Karate and the title of Sen. Sempei for her exceptional achievements in her personal life and in her outstanding work with our special children, our 'Rock Stars'. It was a great event and the highlight of the year!

*

Around that time, our team of selected students and friends was expanded by three more great children: Case, his brother Max and their friend Calvin. I had met Gina Mc Kinley, mother of Case and Max, in one of the gyms around town a few years earlier, when Case had been three or four years old. He suffered from cerebral palsy and I had told her I would be more than happy to start teaching him once he would turn five. Now Gina had come back to me about it; and I went to pay the Mc Kinleys a visit. I have always found it quite helpful for the evaluation of a new case to take a look at the family background, if I had the opportunity. After all, with your training, especially when rehab is required, you always address the whole person. Gina Mc Kinley and her husband Jason were wonderful loving parents who cared well for their two sons Case and Max–two adorable boys. All of us bonded right from the start. After a brief evaluation, we agreed to give it a try. As a starter I asked Gina to come along with Case and watch Eden's training session for a while to get a picture of what can be done. Eden, as always, gave her best, inspiring and motivating the boy and his mother and charging them with so much hope and expectations that we started on a twice weekly workout the following week with Max as well. It didn't take long before both boys were a great part of our special group.

Eden could not have been more pleased to hear that it had mainly been her performance and attitude that had caused Case's, Max's and, later, Calvin's training with us. And she kept asking about their progress, showing great interest in the boys–and showing us her big caring heart and wonderful character once more, the true Black Belt in life she was.

From the very beginning, Case reminded me a great deal of myself, when I was a child, but although he was severely handicapped, his abilities, especially his balance, were developed more than mine had been. However, there was plenty of room for improvement, of course. So I started, as always, with a careful evaluation of his overall condition and fitness. Every single case of people in need of special care is highly individual. Even though there may be superficial similarities to others, the background with family, education and close environment, the personal limitations, difficulties and emotional situation as well as medication and nutrition are always different. So every patient or student must be taken on his/her own without exception. Case was a great little child with a caring and open personality. It was a joy to work with him, always full of life and the broadest smile on his face, even when he lost his balance and fell. Do you see the positive pattern? Our children and youths with the most severe difficulties always had the biggest smile on their faces; not to mention their positive attitude towards life and people, their family and friends; a characteristic for everyone to learn from!

Case's abilities to stretch were extremely limited. Especially his hamstrings and calf muscles were profoundly tight and needed loosening and build up. But stretching was not the boy's favorite. He could happily live without, like most of us. That was not an option, of course. So he had to lean against a wall stretching one calf muscle after the other as a warm-up every session; and then we often sat down and tackled his tiny feet in a playful way: Case had to try and push my hands away, stretching them as much as he could, one at the time. After that I asked him politely, if he allowed me to stretch his feet the other way round, toes pointing upwards and towards his body, again one at the time, knowing he could well do without. We were joking a lot about it, and I told him that I had just been the same long ago and that Geert Lemmens and his wife had always nicely been on my case so that I had hardly been able to skip stretching quietly and unobserved; but that I was glad in retrospect to have done my exercises. After that, Case became a dedicated 'stretcher'. He was such a trooper and gave his best, well, most of the time.

The experiences of my early days also helped his big brother, Max. He was a great boy and one of those natural born athletes who would succeed in every kind of sport they chose. However, due to the fact that Case needed special care and a lot of help, he seemed to be hard up at times. I realized the tension between the brothers and Max's need for more attention he thought he was not getting. Sometimes he would push Case during class; so it was time for me to sit down with him in a quiet corner. I asked him why he behaved like this and what he was thinking about it. Max didn't really have an answer to that; and I told him about my older brother and the fierce fights we had when we were kids, but loving each other dearly just the same; how hard it was for him to see our mother caring more for me than for him, it seemed, but only to ensure I had all I needed, knowing he was o.k.; therefore his behavior at times was more or less an outcry for more love and attention than disrespect.

With Max and Case, it was just the same. The fact that their parents went through little ups and downs in their marriage, of course, did not help. But it was just something all young couples go through. And having a handicapped child and an extremely strong and active older son can put a lot of pressure on parents, with all the worries, visits to doctors and appointments for therapy. I had seen my mother in tears often enough, so I knew only too well. I think Max understood. After all, he was a great child with a big heart. But to take the pressure off him and to be able to concentrate more on Case's needs, I decided to put him into another class where I could challenge him better and give him the attention he needed. His mother agreed, and it turned out to be just the right decision. At about the same time their friend Calvin joined us. He, too, needed a bit of guidance, emotional support and caring. He fitted in well and showed great interaction with Case and all the other kids who occasionally took part in our classes.

Little Case could never wait for the next session; full of life and energy he was ready to take on every challenge. He had some difficulties keeping his balance, especially when he didn't pay enough attention to his walk, moved forward too fast or lifted his arms too high. To help him with this and also his stretching and muscle build up—you should always tackle a variety of problems at the same time, if possible, to improve the overall condition as well—I used one of Geert Lemmens' training philosophies once again: Keep your student's mind busy with lots of fun-exercises and games, so that he/she simply forgets about his/her difficulties and weak spots, moves naturally and learns without concentrating too hard. So I came up with an old game we used to play at the dojo a lot. It was called 'fire ball' and involved the whole class.

To keep it easy to start with, however, I cut out the running around and let all children form a wide circle instead. Now the ball was to be thrown to the neighboring kid on the right; and it should be passed from one to the next with gathering speed to make it even more fun. Besides, whoever—including me, of course—couldn't catch the ball or let it drop had to step out of the circle and perform five to ten push-ups, depending on strength, condition and age! We always had a great time. Although Case lost the ball a lot at the beginning, in fact he hardly ever caught it, he had so much fun and was so excited about competing in a team and trying to catch the ball, no matter how high he had to lift his arms, that he was able to forget the fear of losing his balance and fall, so tricking his CP. And he didn't mind at all to perform his 'penalty' push-ups, even ten at the time without a problem, almost giving his older brother the run for his money.

Case's overall strength, his balance and hand-eye coordination improved fast, and within weeks he caught the ball quite often. And every time he did, he yelled on top of his voice over to his mother who was watching close to tears: "Mum, did you see that! I caught it! I caught it!" You should have seen his beaming little face; wonderful moments that paid for my efforts ten times over.

We also played a variation of the 'fire ball' game: With us sitting, again in a wide circle, the ball had to be passed on to the right-hand neighbor by a throw or push, but with an unexpected twist to it, so that everyone had to watch their 'opponent' closely, upper body fully turned towards him, in order to get the ball. And, of course, the one who didn't had to move over and perform five push-ups immediately. Full focus and concentration was required; and so Case moved his upper body and arms in different directions without thinking and therefore hardly ever lost his balance. The exercise strengthened his arm- and shoulder-muscles and improved his motor-skills and hand-eye coordination even more with lots of fun involved. I even saw him dropping the ball on purpose sometimes so that he could do the push-ups…with his face beaming all over; what a trooper!

It did not take long before he became a great soccer and football player as well. The latter proved to be quite a challenge to his balance, though. In order to throw the ball accurately he had to lift his arms above his head. But at first, he did not dare to move them beyond his 'comfort-zone', which was round about chest level, being afraid to topple over. So I told him to take a beat, breathe deeply and concentrate on his balance before throwing the ball. It worked well. He did not only catch the football more and more frequently, but also threw it with increasing accuracy lifting his arms up high. Often we got all our young students together in the weekends as well, just to play these games. It always was great fun and intensified the team spirit, interaction and friendship between them, which made me even prouder to be their teacher!

Case, Max and Calvin were developing well, and as an additional treat we took them to Mihran's dojo Hye-Katch-Do in the Valley (City of Reseda, at White Oak and Satercoy Blvd.) to take part in a seminar with Geert Lemmens and his sons Mark and Jope who were on a surprise visit to the U.S. We were all excited to meet them, especially me, because I hadn't seen them for over 12 years; and I would step onto the matt and face my old Grandmaster as a 4th degree Black Belt for the first time. I was anxious like a child to see his and his sons' reaction to it. But, of course, all went well; and the whole event turned out to be a great and wonderful experience for all of us. My Grandmaster closely watched my work with Case and Max on the matt. And especially Case was so motivated that he excelled himself hitting the focus mittens with the biggest smile on his face. He was even able to duck and move to the left and right a little without falling down! My Grandmaster was very impressed by his performance, and at the end of the class, he awarded me by saying, "Your work with kids has always been extraordinary and wonder-ful to watch." It was the greatest compliment I ever received from him and for sure the finest reward for me as teacher and mentor.

The seminar was an extraordinary and uplifting event for all of us. Later on, Max, Calvin and Case proved their skills once more in a great ball game with dozens of other kids enjoying themselves tremendously; and Monae just had the biggest smile on her face all the time! In the end Lemmens put the icing on the cake for me when he said Case reminded him a lot of me back in the old days. Especially nice, because I exercised with Case just the same way he had trained with me. And I used the same concept that had worked for me as well as for Eden and the other special children: Exercises, techniques and equipment modified to meet with Case's special needs, a lot of fun and loving support.

When it came to teaching Case the various techniques, we simply broke the moves into different stages, so that he was not pushed him too hard. It helped his body and motor-skills to adapt first and ensured the position of his feet and hips were correct. This way he learned his punches and blocks improving his strength and endurance tremendously. After a while, he even managed double punches and left-right combinations really well. So, Case went to his first belt test together with his brother and Calvin; and all three passed without any difficulties. One problem we had to deal with, however, could not be trained away. Like most people with CP and QP Case did not sweat like a 'normal' person. If this cooling mechanism does not work efficiently, the body can overheat very fast. The majority would probably think hardly sweating is quite a blessing, but it is not at all. This condition usually comes with health problems not to be underestimated. In California, the sun can be quite hot at midday and during the afternoon; and while I needed to ensure Case's rehab and fitness and push him to higher levels I had to watch him closely to prevent overheating. Therefore, it was extremely important for him to rest and drink a lot during workout, especially in the summer. So long as he attended the classes I could keep an eye on him, but at home, when he trained on his family's front lawn in the hot afternoon sun, his parents needed to do that which surely was not always easy.

*

To summarize, I think it has become quite obvious by now just how much knowledge and even wisdom is required when mentoring, training and for sure rehabilitating anyone with special needs. For the ones who do not know much about people with certain limitations many features may appear complicated, even alarming. But I hope I could give you a positive insight into the daily life and needs of our 'Rock Stars' and their families.

Too often and too fast we are misunderstood and prejudged out of ignorance or particular fears. And most people simply do not have a clue how to react and behave when they come across someone with special needs, physical limitations or emotional difficulties. One of the goals of my work is to build a bridge of kindness and understanding between all of us and so help to further the integration of people with these special needs and their families.

I strongly feel it is more than overdue to close the gap between our worlds caused by misconception, misunderstanding and prejudice. After all, there is not that much of a difference between a 'normal' person and someone with a limitation. Certainly not in the world of sport, it only seems as if there was. An athlete always is an athlete; and for sure a pro athlete always is a pro athlete, no matter how big or small the difficulties and limitations are he/she needed or needs to conquer. It all comes down to inner strength and will power. I have been able to prove that, and so have others...

Chapter: 8

Arts, Rehab (part four) Disability–Pro-Sport, Recovering & Success

It has not been made easy by the public and for sure not by officials to become part of the world of sport, let alone pro-sport as a handicapped person. At tournaments, my greatest competitors were the ring doctors–why a person with a handicap should be considered 'too ill' to fight is beyond me!–and the judges who would or would not– depending on their attitude towards handicapped people–award me with the points I deserved. And it is not made easy enough today to become accepted and recognized. However, if I can help to heighten awareness and take away misconception and preju- dice towards my people; and if I am able to motivate and inspire anyone–child, youth or adult–with special needs or heavy injuries out there to take up sport, even in a professional way, and so perhaps find a better place in life, my mission will be accom- plished. And this achievement will be greater even, if I get positive feedback from some of my readers telling their stories of personal success!

There is no such thing as a hopeless case. Improvement is always possible, without exception! So, now let me introduce you to an outstanding athlete whose journey to suc- cess has been extraordinary for sure. And yet his achievements clearly show that anyone, no matter the odds, is able to walk a similar path with the 'Power from Within'.

However, and this applies particularly to the athlete, fitness client and most certainly to the rehab patient and de-conditioned person, who work hard to better themselves: Please do not overdo it! Especially in the first three to six months of your new adventure. Think of it as a lifetime 'path', no need to rush! Particularly, if you have not worked out for a number of years! The risk of injury is tremendous otherwise. Even more so if you have just overcome an older injury or recover from a trauma your body sustained, espe- cially a car accident.

As you probably know, our nervous system forms a close net of highways, roads, streets and side lanes that connects every part of our body with the control centre, our brain. Information and commands are transported back and forth to ensure we 'function' twenty-four hours a day, seven days a week. The spinal cord, our widest highway, is the major player within this amazing net. And if the flow of traffic, especially in that section, is disturbed, reduced, blocked or even cut, the effects can be fatal and far reaching de- pending on the heaviness, extension and location of the problem, because the impulses carrying the necessary commands and information to and from the brain aren't able to just jump across an injured or defective area.

However, Eden's, Monae's, Case's and also my own examples show that the body is able to counteract when properly stimulated; even if the spine is severely injured through a heavy car accident, for example, as it was the case with Marine Clinton Cloudle from

Bedford TX: Driving home after boot camp he lost control of his car and crashed into a tree. He just about survived, but was left paralyzed from his waist down due to severe injury of his spine at one of the upper chest vertebrae (thoratic). This resulted in extreme atrophy of all major muscle groups affecting his legs, arms, chest, his lower abdominals and back. The fine-motor skills of his hands and fingers were almost gone so that he had to mainly use his palms instead, like most people with paraplegia and similar conditions.

I was working in different gyms and conducted private classes and personal rehab in my house, where also our team met for training, when I was introduced to Clinton. He had still not quite come to terms with his situation, which was, of course, more than understandable. So it was particularly important to sit down with him first and talk about issues of his life, his emotions, fears, dreams and expectations, before evaluating his physical condition. Clinton told me about his life before that fatal accident: He had been a celebrated high school quarterback and proudly showed me a picture of himself from those times, stuck to the keys on his key-chain. After school, he had wanted to become a Marine and he sure did, living his dream until it was cut short. So, he was very frustrated and angry. Again, every training should invariably start with a conversation like this; and the more time is spent on personal details the more success is guaranteed later.

The effects of cerebral palsy and paraplegia are quite similar as far as abilities and limitations are concerned. Also, the need for plenty of nutritious food during hard work with wholesome calories, protein and vitamins and the danger of overheating the body are features that apply to both conditions. But generalizing and categorizing always is a mistake. It does not only put a limit to the general approach and your client's path and therefore rehab, but can also endanger his/her health. So, once more, every single person must be taken on his/her own without prejudgment. Even if it seems you know the answer to his/her problems already, there is no way you can see what you both have to do to accomplish successful rehab before you conduct a thorough examination. Besides, you do not want your new student or patient to feel like 'just another case', especially not after a life-changing traumatic experience with its strong emotional aspects. It would most certainly add to his/her frustration at a time he/she needs your help not just with the physical injuries but also to come to terms with them. Every good therapist knows this; and the more intensive the emotional support the better the chances for recovery.

Right from the start, I could see Clinton's strong personality and inner power, although he was still quite shaken up. In fact, he had so much charisma that anyone who met him during the following years, not only when we went to events and competitions but also at a lot of different private occasions, was impressed by him. He inspired many youngsters and adults who just came up to him to talk and compliment him to his great work and achievements as an athlete. And great they were, indeed. Once a marine, always a marine, regardless if injured or not: Clinton became a pro athlete and fighter all the way to world champion in self-defense with me as his partner, and an active member of our success-team, the 'Top Four USA Hurricanes'. And once a student, always a student. I had to learn this from our old friend Marine Bill Chatfield, from the U.S. State Department, who came to watch our belt test in TX with J. Pat Burleson and Jim Harrison, Channel 8 broadcasting this wonderful event. It was my 3rd degree black belt and Marine Clinton's yellow belt test, which he passed in impressive fashion. Marine Chatfield had been Clinton's fan from the start and a great supporter of us and our work. You won't find many people like him: A great man and one of the few working in such a high position in politics and homeland security, who has not only inspired me with his integrity and honesty but many of us by helping those in need wherever he can. A true friend, you can entrust with your life. And should I ever have to go to war, it would be him I would like beside me at all times, knowing I would be save. One of America's finest!

At Clinton's house, where our first get-together took place, he had a fully equipped rehab gym that had been designed for an ex-soldier and veteran who had also been paralyzed by a car accident. It was reasonably well equipped, although I missed the 'real ideas' as nearly always when looking at so called 'rehab machines'. Among the facilities, there were a back-pull-down station (latissimus dorsi), a biceps-curl and a triceps-curl station, and different attachments for additional workout. To get a picture of his overall condition and to see how far the workout on his own had brought him, I asked him to show me his daily routine. There were quite a few aspects missing, and it was obvious Clinton had only received a basic introduction and a 'demonstration' tape about the use of the machines and then had been left to fend for himself. He was hardly getting anywhere; and, watching him struggle with the machines and their attachments, it became obvious why he was so frustrated and needed help.

So, I went home that day to design a rehab plan with exercises directly aimed at Clinton's muscle groups, especially weakened by heavy atrophy, to restore the well-needed balance within the muscle support system as well as training units to improve his overall condition, strength and movement coordination abilities. Although, as said before, there are quite a few parallels between cerebral palsy and paraplegia, and a common denominator may be found in some of the rehab exercises, it is the specific details that make a vital difference; and if you pay close attention, you will realize them and take them into account while creating the workout plan. And exactly that makes you a champion trainer and -therapist, and for sure distinguishes you from the crowd.

The first training routine was put together for a three-month test trail and, after that, meant to be changed and adjusted for the following 12 weeks. As you know by now, this change and adjustment is necessary to keep the body challenged and muscle growth stimulated—especially important for amateur and pro athletes. Moreover, your body's biological rhythm follows the rhythm of nature and its seasons. And if you consciously adjust your training, even your whole life, to this rhythm you create a harmony that will help you to succeed, working with your body instead of against it. This may sound a negligible detail, but it is the 'little things', the slight differences, that cause you to gain this extra point, making you the winner.

Do not be tempted to use steroids as a shortcut. You will pay the price for this eventually. Besides, what for? My own example and that of many others clearly shows you can accomplish anything you want with inner strength, will power and without negative side effects. Only then, you can truly and honestly say you succeeded. It is a great feeling!

*

One of the biggest challenges Clinton and I were facing was his inability to make use of his stomach- and lower back-muscles, which caused imbalance and severely limited range of motion. At the beginning of our training, Clinton would topple over nearly every time he left his safety- and therefore 'comfort-zone'. None of his support muscles responded, or just with a fraction of their normal abilities and Clinton's needs. So at first we concentrated on stimulating them to gain response and as a result enable them to interact with the rest of his body. And if you build up agonists and antagonists equally they will not just work together as one enabling you to move, but form a natural brace around your bones and joints protecting you from injuries, muscle pain and strain, and create a perfect support system. And that was exactly what I wanted to do: Build a natural shield around Clinton's torso for safety and as foundation to increase his range of motion and flexibility for more mobility.

I began with a combination of 'Inner Eye' (mediation- and energy-movements) and negative-resistance strengthening rehab and fitness training Geert Lemmens had used with me, because I had been too weak for positive resistance workout just like Clinton now. To tackle his abdominal muscles I unfastened the back of his chair, lowered it down to horizontal level and secured it. Holding Clinton safely I lowered his torso backwards and asked him to 'resist' the movement as much and long as possible until he lay flat on his back. Although the abdominal muscles did not yet respond within the first days, they would in time, being continuously forced to work and, therefore, being stimulated. Through that, receptors and motor-units would be reactivated and the so-called 'muscle memory' would cause build up of muscle fiber to meet the 'demand'. Natural and full response would be the result. Like water finds the 'least way of resistance', we re-use old nerve pathways!

Especially during the first days of our abdominal workout, Clinton was not very happy. On our journey together he became quite angry at times and even threw the odd tantrum which always made me smile, reminding me of someone I knew a long time ago who had quite similar outbreaks before he began to see a light in the tunnel. To help Clinton across these spells I told him about my early days and the angry frustration I had felt when my disability kept me from improving as fast as I wanted to or I had setbacks. At those moments Geert and Vera Lemmens always lifted me up and encouraged me to ignore the barriers that seemed to bar my path, be more patient and concentrate on the things I was already able to do.

My English was quite insufficient still, so it was not easy for Clinton and me to understand each other, yet he followed my lead and kept going just the same–a great sign of trust and confidence in my judgment and abilities taking my personal accomplishments as an answer to his questions.

With the negative-resistance workout, we also tackled the latissimus dorsi, erector spinae, pectoralis major and minor, seratus anterior, rhomboids, trapezius, brachio radialis, rectus abdominis, as well as the external and internal obliques, just to name the major players that were in a state of severe atrophy. Especially all forearm and chest muscles were as heavily affected as the back and stomach muscles. For the latissimus dorsi, the rhomboids and the trapezius, we mainly used the back-pull-down rehab-station with the handle bar before the face or at the back of his neck: Using the two lightest weight plates, I carefully pushed the handle bar down for Clinton to resist the movement until especially his latissimus dorsi was fully contracted. And while I was pulling the bar back up, he had to hold against the movement as much as possible. We did three sets each, with eight to twelve reps. Clinton used special gloves with built-in hooks he put on the handles to keep hold of them, because he was still unable to do it with his hands alone.

We worked on the rhomboids and trapezius in similar fashion. To train these in a normal way, you would lift yourself up into a 45-50 degree angle from a lying position, arms fully extended, stretching all back muscles, and then pull yourself up and the handle bar to your chest, fully contracting rhomboids, trapezius and upper latissimus. But I did the 'positive' movements for Clinton and asked him again to resist them as much as possible.

From the beginning, I kept a close watch on Clinton's breathing. As a rule, you exhale while contracting and inhale while relaxing a muscle or muscle groups. So, as an example, inhale first and then exhale while pushing or pulling the bar of a workout machine, or throwing a punch at the heavy sandbag. That way you provide your muscles with as much oxygen as possible.

*

This simple rule is not the only one that applies to sportive activities of anyone, regardless of their physical situation. And there are many more that often only need slight modifications to meet the requirements of a person with limitations. However, many instructors feel uncomfortable and are hesitant, if not having a rejecting attitude towards handicapped athletes in rehab finding it difficult, even impossible to accept and recognize them as such.

And sadly, even today, you do not find handicapped people–be it by birth or as a result of heavy injury–in mainstream sports. It seems, you only hear about and see highly specialized individuals with the right background and education. And only specific rehab-institutions and foundations organize sports events for handicapped athletes on a regular basis, but these are mainly many miles out of the range of most disabled people. Moreover, hardly any gym or fitness studios, especially the ones belonging to large chains, provide facilities for cerebral palsy or paraplegia clients.

And yet it is a billion-dollar industry. However, improvements have happened. In the 1990's, for example when a large company running fitness clubs introduced a special scheme including Martial Arts with self-defense and Yoga classes. But the company hadn't come up with this on their own initiative: A while before I had offered to install and supervise just that to their CEO and GM, having conducted–for free–a number of months-long seminars to benefit the 'Susan B. Anthony Breast Cancer Foundation' in one of their clubs and as a test run for the whole TX and mid-western region. My offer was declined. It was supposed to be too dangerous and impossible to realize! A certificate and a thank-you from the company's mid-western Texas headquarters representative, was all I received back then. This company was not the only one that took advantage of my background. Almost every club I signed up with, especially the ones owned by large chains or foundations, used me as advertisement to get more clients or to raise tens of thousands of dollars. I had never been compensated. There is a limit to everything; I simply began to work mainly from home, conducting special classes and training students individually at my house, helping their special needs. This was much more rewarding!

*

Let us return to Clinton and our joint journey from extreme rehab to team member and world champion in the Arts. He was improving well. And to enhance the process he started to take a food supplement called 'The Missing Link', a power source of proteins, vitamins and minerals. It helped him to recover quicker, he was less sore, and he got more Carbohydrates and vitamins that were so important for his by now power workout. It helped him as well to regain weight and muscle mass and to reprogram his PNS (spinal nerve system). And that was what we constantly did with our training: We stimulated the muscles, reactivating their response and rebuilt the information-path to and from the brain; and so worked our way slowly but surely beyond the injured part of the spine, extending and improving Clinton's abilities. His muscle support system started to regain its original shape more and more as a result.

For a good therapist and instructor it is understood to keep a close eye on your student's or patient's progress within his/her daily routine to ensure the exercises and methods applied cause continuous improvement and, of course, well being. Six months into the rehab it became obvious our workout plan and the existing equipment would not meet with the requirements much longer. So it was time for the next step. I sat down to do some research and soon found a company selling professional fitness equipment for a reasonable price. I had the 'Smith' machine, and a flat bench with a facility to incline, on my mind and explained my ideas to Clinton. Especially from the 'Smith' machine he could only benefit. It was engineered to enable the user to stop the handle bar any time by simply turning it, which made it so much safer to work with. Besides, his rehab station was not equipped for proper chest-workout, something highly important because Clinton's pectoralis minor and major (large and small chest muscles) were extremely weakened by atrophy.

Since Clinton had received some money from his insurance company, he was able to buy the well-needed new facilities, and so we ordered the 'Smith' machine, the bench, a medium heavy sandbag, a double-end speedball, a set of weights and special gloves. The equipment was well engineered and had a life-long warranty, all in all costing $800 plus– an excellent choice, thanks to the 'Body Builder Discount Outlet Store'. Within weeks, the equipment was delivered, and after another day Clinton had a great little gym ready to be used for extending his workout. Before we started, I explained the importance of simultaneous build up of his antagonist and agonist muscle groups to form a firm brace around his torso for safety and to smooth out his still quite prominent imbalance within his muscle support system.

Clinton always was as eager to learn as he was prepared to work hard, and he understood the importance of our task ahead. So we added one more day to his weekly routine, splitting it into three units: On Mondays we concentrated on back and shoulders, Wednesdays were for chest and triceps, and Fridays we worked on his biceps and abdominal muscles using sandbag and speedball as well. As a light warm-up routine for all units we did three sets of 'abdominals', with eight to twelve reps of course for maximum muscle growth.

With the 'Smith' machine Clinton was a little too eager for starters, though. Reminded of his days as high school athlete, when he had worked his muscles with a bench-press, he was quite excited to try the Smith machine in the same way and asked me to put a 10 pound weight on each end of the handle bar, underestimating the weight of the bar itself with its special facilities which added up to about 45 pounds; besides, there was the friction of the bar running in a pre-set movement. I let him try knowing, of course, that I could stop the bar any time simply by turning it! As expected, the weight went straight down, and he was not able to push the 65 pounds back up. Perhaps this may seem a little unfair, but Clinton needed to realize that too much eagerness can easily lead to unnecessary frustration, especially in a situation like his, where patience is required. Eventually, he took it with a laugh, good sport that he was. And with less weight, he then lifted the bar all by himself and only needed a little assistance with the negative movement. In fact, he was already able to perform 80% of the back pull-downs without assistance; I just corrected his direction and the angle of the bar if needed. The same went for the bi- and triceps exercises. Only when he became tired or a little dehydrated did I help him to complete the exercise, which shows that plenty of fluid throughout the training is vital. Therefore, Clinton had a spray water bottle handy all the time.

Through the continuous stimulation, Clinton's muscles were growing well, his balance and overall strength improved, and he was less exhausted after exercising. Eight months into the workout, he had put on a respectable 15 pounds of weight. Full of new energy and enthusiasm he soon asked me to start with the Arts and self-defense as well. No problem. He was already practicing these. Rehab and Tai Chi are major aspects of Shin-Tora-Do Karate and always will be. I explained to Clinton that someone who needs rehab at first to get to a higher level already is an active member of our community of selected men and women in our Art. To extend the variety of exercises we included the double-end speedball and heavy bag in our training routine. For maximum safety and flexibility I had bought the excellent 'Chuck Norris gloves' that minimize the risks and enable you to use your fingers and hands at the same time.

We started with the speedball. I showed Clinton how to use it properly and explained its benefits: He would train his shoulders, abdominal muscles and obliques, improve his balance, range of motion, hand-eye coordination and techniques, and he would be able to find out how much he could move around in his chair without toppling over. After an amazingly short time, Clinton managed the speedball. He could even move from side to side like a real boxer and throw double-combo punches without losing his balance. That he was a natural with great talent for the Arts was obvious from the start! Only occasionally, the ball would mess with him and make him sore, too.

The 50-pound heavy bag was nothing to laugh about, but Clinton conquered that in no time as well. He hit it with great determination and rather well considering his humble beginnings not even a year ago. At first, we worked mainly on his shoulders and keeping his arms up as much and long as possible. Through this, he improved his overall condition and general strength, his motor-skills and coordination abilities, trained deltoids, biceps, triceps and both brachioradialis all at the same time! Clinton was unstoppable. Within a month his already accurate left jabs and right punches sent the bag flying, and in no time he did double and triple combinations as well–time to get out the focus-mittens. Soon he performed crossover and double punches with great accuracy and timing. And only when he became too tired and dehydrated after a–by now–double session he occasionally dropped his arms. Then I reminded him by gently hitting his forehead with the mittens, the way I treated everybody else, which always made him swear like a sailor and try harder, like a true champion, a born winner. With immense determination Clinton worked himself all the way up to ten minutes focus-mitten and another five to ten minutes heavy-bag-training; it was remarkable by any standards, but especially for someone with paraplegia and that–again just for the records–after less than a year of rehab.

Clinton was a born athlete; he had proved that before his accident and it showed throughout his rehab: His muscle memory was working overtime, an aspect I had been counting on from the beginning. It did the trick: He constantly gained strength and improved his abilities–and his confidence grew, his self-esteem prospered. Especially the condition of Clinton's hands was something we could really be proud of: Their strength and grip had improved by at least 40%.With cerebral palsy and paraplegia these cases are rated in numbers! So, it was time for me to design a testing protocol customized for Clinton's abilities, but–like for anyone else–with all aspects of Shin-Tora-Do: Techniques, timing, condition, self-defense, sparring: All modified to meet with Clinton's abilities and needs. In no time his muscle memory went on overdrive, taking over, despite his injury

*

At about that time our selected little group was extended by Jonathon Wells, a fine and talented young man with a lovely family and great background. I had met him at a dojo in Forth Worth TX, where he trained and I occasionally taught. His big dream was to become national champion one day. Although his techniques, especially his foot techniques, were very good, he had never been able to win first place so far. So, already good friends, we sat down together and I asked him why he thought that was. He did not have an answer apart from "bad judges, maybe?" "Surely not, my friend," I answered. "The judges are hardly the problem." And I told him what my Grandmaster had once said to me: "If you only score five to six points during your fight and are deprived of two or even more and so lose, don't even think of blaming the judges. You, and you alone, are responsible. You have only given the bare minimum to get through your fight; therefore, you do not deserve a lucky break! You need to fight as if it were your last time in every competition! Any competition! Always! Scoring 20 points and more! Then it makes no difference, if a judge does not give you the five or ten points you think you scored, you will still win! Moreover, your appearance and personal Bushido will be so powerful that the judges will surely notice and see you in a favorable light." As said in the beginning, only if you give 100%, no matter the odds, will you receive 100% in return!

Jonathon looked at me in amazement, the next question written on his face. And yes, I would have another look at his techniques and gladly give him some tips as well. When things come together, it is often for a good reason. Not long after our conversation, Jonathon's teacher closed down the dojo to concentrate on another one far out of town. So the boy became an active member of our group and a great asset to our team, the 'Top Four Hurricanes USA' as well as my partner for the self-defense w/p division. But before that, I had to change his quite common fighting routine. A hundred times, I have seen these 'standard' attacks, especially in the Korean style; and I wonder, why they have been around for so long: Jumping forward with leg in the air, knee bent, trying to land a high round house-kick to the head preceded by a back-fist. Most predictable and therefore not too difficult to beat, yet often seen at Point-Karate events. Jonathon needed a crisp and hard attack-routine with razor sharp moves of a large variety, and I was helped with this by Tony Hatcher, many times world Karate champion, whose father was a high-ranking Black Belt and former national champion, and Master Unaz. Both had joined the group shortly before.

For Clinton, these were exciting and greatly uplifting times. As active member of our little community, he was involved in all our activities. Our weekly routine, weekend trips and sports events, had become a new way of life for him, second nature. Just like it had become second nature to me and as well to Eden, who we all considered a fully-grown athlete with the strength of a lion and the heart of a tiger, although she had never competed. These two amazing students are an excellent example and show that handicapped children, youths and for sure adults, can become great pro athletes, and that it is possible to cross over from rehab into pro sport without major difficulty!

We had put together a fine self-defense routine with partly invented moves that excellently met with Clinton's requirements, and he exercised enthusiastically with Jonathon and me as partner. It was not only a great physical workout but also an emotional one that contributed to his self-esteem a great deal. His balance was improving to over a 100%, and so was his range of motion. This new routine with blocks high above his head, moving about in his chair launching counter-attacks when I got him from all directions, pulling, pushing and holding on–needless to say, he used many of his major muscle groups strengthening them enormously, and his nerve-paths recovered fast. He also improved his motor skills and hand-eye coordination remarkably at the same time. So, for Clinton the training worked wonderfully through the combination of rehab and Arts. And, finally, yet importantly, by becoming a valued member of our team Clinton was able to forget his handicap most of the time, and his outlook on life was once again a positive one.

It had become spring, and the first invitations for state and national championships were arriving. We all tightened our workouts to be ready for the challenges. And the chance of a state, even national title kept Clinton going with even high spirits. Jonathon, too, developed well. I taught him an old successful fighting style I had learned from 'Iron Horse' Ingolf, Grandmaster Kanazawa and, of course, from Geert Lemmens, including a single right hand power punch straight to the head as an opening with a kick to it, no hesitation, no warning signs, deadly if you execute it well–Ingolf's signature move. Also, a full force straight front-kick to the stomach, followed up by a straight right punch to the head, one of Kanazawa's favorite attacks; and one of Lemmens' favorites: Wide side stand and, therefore, little target for the attacker, a fast back-fist-'bluff' and instead a fine side-kick to the ribs followed by a lightning-fast back fist or right punch to the head. So there was quite a variety of attack- and defense-moves in Jonathon's routine, which he practiced with Hatcher and Unaz as his sparring partners getting many helpful tips at the same time. Equipped like that, Jonathon would not only fight off his opponent, but could also surprise the following competitors who would not be able to predict his fighting style.

For Clinton we created a champion routine with a punch to it: At first, I would launch an attack from the side, and Clinton would block it, pull me down punching me with a back-fist, or palm-strike to the head depending on the distance. My second attack, this time with a cane, would come from behind; Clinton would block it with a high cross-block, elegantly re-directing the cane which would bring me to his side, where I would receive an elbow- or palm-strike, again, depending on distance and angle. In my last attack, I would try and grab his shoulders. Clinton would re-direct the move, then palm-strike downwards into my groin and then flip me over the side of his chair. The whole routine was timed for two minutes, including walking into the ring and greeting the judges. Clinton trained with great enthusiasm; it was wonderful to see him in such spirits.

The TX State Championship was his first big test and also his first Martial Arts event. Needless to say, it impressed him. And I just loved the wonderful energy and magic that filled the whole place: All these great competitors; children and youths running around excitedly and fighting their guts out; dozens of divisions at the same time; all these forms and styles, Katas with weapons and music, traditional and modern fighting–simply fantastic. For us, all went well: In Clinton's division there were three pairs at the start and Clinton reached second place, showing good form and accuracy. Jonathon came in second as well. And I won both my divisions. So we qualified for the upcoming US National which was the one and only 'Legends' founded by Bruce Lee and J. Pat Burleson and watched over by no one less than Grandmaster Joon Ree, as I have already mentioned.

Back home again, there was no time to be idle. I trained hard under the watchful eyes of J. Pat Burleson–honored and proud. Clinton's routine needed adjustments, and so did Jonathon's. He was not too happy with his performance at the TX event, finding it more difficult than he had thought to keep out of his old fighting routine. Once a certain style is established and practiced over a number of years, it is not an easy task for an athlete as well as his/her teacher or coach to change unfavorable methods and techniques. In Jonathon's case, it was more than worth the extra efforts. I told him to open his mind for different forms of exercising that would help to re-program his style. One of them was focus-mitten training, which does not only increase overall endurance and condition but also hand-eye coordination.

Another excellent method is the so called 'Mix it up'. It boosts the fighter's reactions when attacked and under pressure as well as the accuracy of his moves. Moreover, it tightens the bond between student and teacher, an aspect of great importance to me as it has been for Geert Lemmens. I have never been the one who would stand on the sideline instructing from a distance; there always was a strong emotional connection between my good students, fighters and me. At the ring, there was no need to yell and run around, I only had to close my hand to a fist and drop it for them to realize it was time to turn up the heat and finish the deal. I was sure Jonathon and I would be able to form a close bond like this, too; and so I put him through an extreme physical and emotional workout that carried him to the borders of his abilities and back. He did well, great character he was.

(My little stepdaughter Jenae got a big crush on him, and Jonathon handled it really nicely; it only was an innocent dream, with Jenae being so much younger than he was. We took her with us to another State event to compete as well. She did fine until her opponent turned up the heat. She started to lose her concentration and drive, and I could feel she became scared. So, I broke up the fight. I knew she was not really into competing. Her training was more for her 'Inner Chi' and her safety later in life. She would not become frightened and would fight back should she ever be attacked.)

Clinton exercised like never before; it was amazing to watch. We could delete some minor faults mainly caused by his balance during pull-downs, worked on different angles and positions and tightened up his routine. The 'Legends' would be our first big National in the U.S. by the NBL and SKI; and if we could all make it among the first four places, we would automatically qualify for the next National and hopefully get a ticket to the World Championships at the end of the year. Time passed fast, and I hoped I could keep Clinton and Jonathon elevated and motivated enough so that they would forget their limitations and barriers altogether, and their performance lead to success. Well, the proof lies in the pudding, so it seems. All you can do is giving your very best until it is time to step into the ring.

However, Jonathon fell ill with a heavy flu just a couple of days before the event, which was unfortunate for him, having prepared himself so well. And it left me without a partner for the self-defense w./p. category. So, I phoned my old friend Renshi Mihran in L.A. and asked him if he would take Jonathon's place. You already know he did, and the success was all ours in the traditional self-defense w/p division, getting 3 x 10, 1 x 9 / 4 x 10 points–a 'dream-result'. The success was made even greater by the fact that Mihran and I had gone out behind the building to put together our routine, which we had not been able to do before due to Mihran's last minute arrival. There was just enough time for me to show him what I had practiced with Jonathon and for Mihran to spice the performance up a bit.

In the handicapped-category, Clinton excelled himself and came in second after me. The last division–self-defense w/p choreographed with music–simply was fantastic. I always remember, Prof. Dan Baker, one of my greatest idols and strongest opponents, was still competing in the next ring over, when the head referee was about to start the competition. So we asked him to wait, and one of Prof. Baker's USA-team members bailed in for him until Prof. Baker came rushing over. And although time was pressing he thanked us first before starting–a wonderful gesture of a great personality! We felt honored that we had been able to help him. He became a good friend, too.

Over the past 25 years, I have had the honor to meet many outstanding Grandmasters. They all stood out not only through their exceptional achievements, but also through their kindheartedness–Shinwa at its very best. One of the first who deeply impressed me–apart from Geert Lemmens–was Bill 'Super-foot'. I was about 14 years old when I saw him for the first time. Some years later, my friend Bill Leone and I managed to get into the World Kickboxing Championship 1986 that took place in Munich, Germany. We saw kickboxing and box superstar Troy Dorsey 'destroy' or rather 'pulverize' his opponent, J. Joong. Hard Kata! Incredible! Bill 'Super-foot' was also there and I, bold as I always was, decided to go and ask him for advice. In those days, I was hardly able to stay on my feet for long and still used a cane most of the time. But Bill 'Super-foot' just smiled at me and said: "If you work hard, maybe one day I will come and see you fight! Maybe at a World Kickboxing event?!" And he even gave me his home address in the U.S. and told me to visit him whenever I came to the States–the beginning of a wonderful friendship.

And 15 years later, in Savannah, GA, 'Super-foot' and his wonderful wife Kim sat for four and a half hours waiting for me to come up onto the main stage and defend my world title from the year before! I asked him to bless my gloves with tears in my eyes. And they even waited until I returned later to perform a 'Fantasy Hard Kata'- demo (blind folded) right next to my strongest competitor, Prof. Dan Baker. However, the greatest gift I received that night was a respectful and happy nod from my childhood idol 'Super-foot' who had honored me by staying and waiting for me so long!

*

After the 'Legends' we all kept training hard and went to various competitions on different levels, qualified within both major associations, the NBL and AOK (TX State Championships, Dallas National-AOK) and got our ticket to the World Karate Championships in Colorado Springs. Jonathon had learned his lessons well. He won the TX State and Dallas National in his division, declassing his opponents with 20-1, 12-0 and 14-0– he even had the time between moves to look my way, and I could signal him it was time to close the deal. One of the judges came over to us afterwards and congratulated him to his amazing fights and overall performance–and me to such a great son! Delighted, I thanked him and said I really did feel like a father to Jonathon, and a very proud one....

Clinton and Jonathon were motivated beyond imagination and we all prepared for the ultimate crown, World Champion 97, with great determination. However, it was not meant for us to win the title at that championship. Clinton came in third place. But it did not matter in the end. He already was a champion before he went up onto that world-stage. A champion in life, for sure, showing to himself and everybody else what can be achieved with inner strength and will power–even after a fatal accident that had left him paralyzed not too long before! And one year later, we were back for revenge–and succeeded!

*

John, a great young man of about 19, had difficulties to overcome, similar to Clinton's. He, too, was paralyzed through an almost-deadly car accident a few years before. When we met, he was quite depressed and in search of answers for himself. He needed someone who really cared, someone who would give him some tools to build up a more solid foundation of self-reliance and confidence. Rehab was required to get him going again and to help him re-define himself. He showed tremendous determination and will power. Three times a week he put his wheelchair into his car at five o'clock in the morning and fought his way through the traffic from Castaic (Disney Land) to a private gym near Santa Monica, where I conducted self-defense and fitness classes, to be in time for his training sessions at seven o'clock. This is surely something to think about for all those overweight 'I am too tired to go to the gym down the road' who instead try to take shortcuts with dangerous diet pills or operations. Please do not, unless there is no other way for health, safety, and orders by your own trainer or a licensed MD.

Within a month, he lightened up tremendously and became a great and dedicated student reminding me just how much I loved my work, how important it was and how much could be achieved, if you put your mind to it. John's training program consisted of a combination of western rehab and eastern healing techniques like Tai Chi as well as breathing and relaxation exercises, similar to Clinton's during his beginnings. Moreover, the rubber bands I used with Eden proved to be an excellent device for him as well.

The most important aspect of John's rehab was the reactivation of his sense of balance and feeling of safety, which would result in heightened confidence and therefore self-esteem, besides the build-up of his overall condition, muscle coordination and strength. To begin with, I applied isometric techniques I used with Clinton; they work miraculously, and in cases of cerebral palsy, paraplegia and muscular dystrophy they are some of my favorites. The first exercise we did was mainly aimed at the shoulder- and forearm-muscles as well as biceps and triceps: Sitting upright (not bending forward!) in front of each other we fully extended our arms horizontally; John brought his palms together, and I put my own palms to the back of his hands, enclosing them. Then we both pressed our hands together starting on a moderate level to be increased, keeping our upright position, not leaning into the pressure and without using our shoulders too much. It has to be kept in mind that this is not a kind of competition, and the pressure must be reduced as soon as your partner is getting tired. We then changed the position of our hands–mine inside, his outside–and started pressing again, repeating the procedure three to five times. Our goal was, of course, to increase the level and duration of pressure safely and–essential–in the correct body position.

The following exercises were two modified variations of the 'Sun Greeting'–a Yoga move that took a great part in my workout–and John liked them a lot: Inhale and press your palms together in front of your chest; then move them slowly away from your body horizontally, exhaling. In the other variation, you move your arms straight over your head and down before your hip. Apart from being excellent breathing and relaxation exercises, you work all major muscle groups as mentioned before as well as the pectoralis major and minor. Just do not rush or push your arms and make sure you breathe correctly.

John recovered in record time: His muscles grew and strengthened, and his balance improved almost on a weekly basis. Moreover, his attitude and outlook on life changed with the same speed, too. He became much happier, contented and confident and looked forward to our next training sessions. We were all proud of him, and he inspired us with his great inner strength and determination. Although he never competed, his workout program and spirit were of an amateur athlete.

Some time into his rehab, John and I sat together one morning and, talking about his amazing progress and the methods we used, he asked me why my approach was not found in mainstream rehab. I am quite sure it has a lot, if not all, to do with money: Life-long medication and equipment like wheelchairs etc., and short-term rehab with little results, all worth ten thousands of dollars. Who profits? I only charge–and more than once I have not charged anything at all–say $45 for my classes so that people can afford to stick with a long-term rehab plan and get real results. Three classes a week/ 12 in a month / 144 in one year add up to $6480 +/- 10-15% depending on class and fees.

And this makes the fact so much sadder that John and Clinton were eventually tempted to submit themselves to highly questionable and risky surgery costing around one hundred thousand dollars! Instead of believing in their already barrier-breaking recovery and trusting the results they were getting, they took a shortcut. We would have been able to stimulate their nervous system more and more, to rebuild the information-highway further and further down until it would have reached their legs once again, carrying the necessary impulses to reactivate the muscles, within one or two years.

This 'miracle' operation is performed in Mexico: The spinal cord is cut open from head to hip and the PNS 'cleaned' of injured or defected areas. The risk of infection and even death is unbelievably high, not to mention the growth of scar tissue. In fact, the operation is so dangerous and questionable that it is prohibited in Europe and even the U.S. There were no recognizable results to be found. Neither John's nor Clinton's abilities improved in any way. On the contrary. And now, they have lost most of their money and probably brought an action for damages against these people. And yet, MD's and therapists are allowed to hand out pamphlets advertising this operation to these young, vulnerable adults when they come to their 6-monthly check up, not considering their emotional distress and the will to take a shortcut if they have the money to burn. In all these years, I have never heard of a single case of complete recovery, not even a partial one. It is almost criminal, for sure highly immoral. So, the old saying seems to be proved: If something sounds too good to be true, and plenty of money is involved, well, then it is mostly not true!

Although this is a rather dramatic example, it shows–once more–there is no such thing as a 'magic pill', a 'wonder-treatment' or 'miracle-method' with long lasting positive effects as a shortcut, neither in rehab nor in pro sport. It all comes down to hard work, determination and the power from within. Through that **you will succeed**! It has been proved by many of my students and me. Just be patient and do not let time, heaviness of injury or disability and therefore necessary effort, discourage you.

*

Useless, even wrong treatment also occurs, unfortunately, in the widespread field of damaged or defected inter-vertebral discs only too often. Statistics show that an increasing number of people suffer from these problems, such as slipped or even herniated discs, especially in the area of the loins (lumbar vertebrae), causing considerable pain in many cases. Partly, mobility and performance can be extremely restricted resulting in inability to work and therefore early retirement, let alone the lack of joy and happiness in life. The MD's and Chiropractor's answer to that are more or less heavy painkillers, treatment with warmth, ultrasound, low laser or spinal cord-correcting, although they know after looking at a simple MRI (Roentgen tomography) -, that with discs, slipped more than 3,5 millimeter, any of these treatments are useless, a waste of time and the patient's money.

One of these cases I came across in CA: Peter Kasper–an inspiring actor and filmmaker–was a colleague and friend of 'Grashopper' and John, who I mentioned before. All three worked out in the same class with me for some time. Peter suffered from a profound connective tissue-weakness whose effects were worsened by a car accident affecting his spine, and he was too heavy. So, his back caused him a lot of pain and constant trouble. He took heavy painkillers; in fact, he ate them daily like candy! Besides starting on a diet to decrease weight that strained his spine, Peter had to reduce the intake of painkillers drastically before starting to exercise. This is an essential measure. Only if the nerve ends and receptors in the connective tissue are not numbed, they are able to send correct information to the PNS (spinal nervous system), which will carry these impulses to the brain within milliseconds and enable it to react naturally, meaning the patient will instantly know whether his movements have a negative or positive effect on his vertebrae, and therefore discs. It was hard for Peter, to say the least; he had to work through his pain, there was no other way! With specific exercises as explained before, we stimulated and strengthened the connective tissue and so improved the mobility of the defected discs and with them the vertebrae enclosing them. At the same time, the supportive muscle groups along the spine were built up and strengthened as well contributing to more flexibility and widened range of motion. Especially through the strengthening of the connective tissue, Peter's pain lessened by 75%! There was no need to take these painkillers every day anymore, and of course, he could enjoy his life a lot more!

There is one more way, however, to treat especially heavily damaged discs successfully and with minimized invasion of the joint's static: Microscopic laser treatment followed by strengthening of the affected area including the connective tissue and muscles through rehab exercises, Yoga, etc. The success is quite remarkable: 50-75% less pain and therefore less medication, not to mention 60-80% less costs–and a lot more joy in life, as long as the patient maintains exercising.

So, there are methods of treatment available. And yet, painkillers are commonly prescribed. Besides having health-endangering side effects, according to the instruction leaflets of most of these medicines very often painkillers also cause the patients' early return to normal activities, because they feel less or no pain and therefore believe they are already fit again–until they stop the medication. This especially happens in pro sport when heavy drugs are involved like Vicardine or–even worse–Cortisone. This substance isolates the affected areas to an extent that even the surrounding muscles are completely numbed and unable to send vital information to the brain. Moreover, it is assumed by scientists that Cortisone can increase the risk of cancer, especially when taken over a longer period!

Despite the facts, thousands of athletes take those types of medicine each year for the 'greater good of the game'. But even worse: At many **high schools with** a high-standard football or basketball team, for example, **they are often given out by coaches and school nurses on a regular basis.** And all those teenagers only too easily overstrain their joints, tendons, muscles or spine–injuring them for life in many cases because they feel no pain. After all, pain is an alarm signal of the body indicating that something is quite wrong! The treatment of people with cerebral palsy, paraplegia etc. often enough includes pain-killers as well; they are supposed to help them moving, which is equally wrong!

One of my favorite challenges has always been to put an athlete back to where he/she had been before an injury, almost as if time traveling. One of those became a dear friend of mine: baseball sensation Luis D. Ortiz who had played with the Red Sox for years and later with the TX Rangers. When I met him, his rotor cuff was badly injured. All MD's and professionals of his organization, as well as other doctors and therapists he had consulted about it, had come to the same conclusion: Reconstructive surgery and early retirement from pro sport. Luis was much too young for that, and I suggested an alternative. After understandable hesitation, he agreed, and we started on a combination of western rehab, isometrics, Tai Chi and good, health improving food. After eight weeks of hard training, his rotor cuff worked again, and even the scar tissue could be reduced! Luis rejoined his old team and was able to provide for his wonderful wife and great little children once again–a great success story.

So, pro sport after rehab is possible on many different levels. Often it becomes a safe haven and a great way to re-invent yourself, as an athlete and/or person. And if conducted properly, there is a good chance to regain previous abilities and personal best form, as in the case of Luis.

*

Quite different and yet strongly related is the story of Master Jamie Cashion the III, a wonderful man and great friend: He was only 17 when he volunteered for the local fire brigade. He loved it. To become a firefighter was his dream, and after passing the test, he did. One day he and his colleagues were called out to an apartment building, which was burning badly. After all inhabitants were rescued, Jamie heard a baby crying, still inside the house. He ran back in and was able to get the little one safely out, but on his way the blazing fire injured him heavily, leaving him with 3rd degree burns on his face and side of his body. So, overnight he had become a hero and victim at the same time. Only one side of his face is burnt, and it can be quite challenging for people who are not used to dealing with someone scarred like that. It has never bothered me, though. Whenever I met him, I could only adore his great personality, big heart and gentle, caring treatment of children. And the children did not mind his looks either; they all just liked him–something we can learn from them, like so many other things!

Jamie Cashion's story humbles me and makes me realize how much we take for granted. Although we hope something like that will never happen to us, we do not normally see how often others put their health and even life in second place and our safety and health in first. Like these wonderful and courageous firefighters and police officers responding to an emergency call. Just remember 9/11 NY. It still makes me shudder whenever I think of this day and its countless heroes on so many levels.

The thought of them leads me once more to the often neglected aspect of mental rehab. Many people do not realize how important this aspect is, simply because they have–thankfully–never been even near to a health-endangering situation. But there are countless men and women out there, not just firefighters, police officers, soldiers and security guards, who have been scarred for life by accidents or violent actions against them, ripped out of their normal circumstances, adding to the immense number of people who are handicapped from birth or due to various diseases. Perhaps it's not easy to imagine just how heavy these negative impacts can be. However, all these fine individuals have the same dreams and wishes, the same feelings and emotions, the same needs, as everybody else. They want to go to school, start dating, get a job, find a partner and get married, have friends and lead a happy, fulfilled life, just like you and me. And if these needs are not met, depression and other serious health problems can aggravate their situation.

Society and even professionals often make it difficult for them–I have received plenty of feedback from my students about that. Exceptions, of course, write the rules, but how many therapists are out there who send their patients home after a few weeks of questionable rehab leaving them to fend for themselves because the Workmen's Comp has run out. I have seen this happening way too often with veteran officers! And how many attorneys are out there, too, who mishandle their clients' affairs in a way that borders on criminal conduct, pressing them into ridiculously low pre-measured settlements and plea bargaining so that they can cash in their retainer. They, and with them many insurance companies, take advantage of their client's often desperate situation, leaving them in many cases without sufficient means to pay for proper treatment and rehabilitation. Should you ever find yourself in circumstances like that, do not forget: You have rights!

*

All these people with special requirements need to be integrated or re-integrated into society's day-to-day life. They need to be an active and productive part of the neighborhood, of social activities, of work, and, emotionally as well as physically, challenged as much and often as possible.

A fine way to start this process is to look at and treat anyone with special needs, limitations or long-lasting injuries just like you want to be treated, as normal, as an equal person, in a kind way. Do not be motherly or overwhelmingly caring. The last thing they need is the impression of being pitied and felt sorry for. All handicapped individuals I have met and, for sure, all I have had the honor to train, teach or rehab, just wanted to be more independent and treated like anyone else. No more no less…

Of course, we do not know how the individual feels and thinks unless there is a close personal relationship, and most of us are no therapists. Therefore, it is a safe bet to handle your handicapped neighbor, colleague or acquaintance just as if there was nothing whatsoever wrong with him or her. You will be surprised about the positive reaction and friendly smiles you will soon get just by saying hello ever so often and showing interest without another agenda behind it. And it is a good opening for getting to know him/her as well, to create a connection and find out about what this person likes or dislikes, about his/her hobbies, activities, visions and dreams for the future. These may be quite similar to your own; you might even know about organizations, foundations or facilities that would be helpful for him/her and so find a basis or denominator for a pleasant and safe friendship. For sure, this approach will make a welcome difference, though there are exceptions, of course.

However, please keep in mind that most handicapped and/or injured individuals, especially the ones who were injured for life, are used to isolation of some kind or other and wrong approaches. Therefore, a little hesitation on their part, particularly if you deal with people emotionally hurt, often children and youths–orphans, for example–is quite common and understandable. So, do not give up on them too fast, take your time and open your heart. You will get positive response, and in the meantime, you already make all the difference in the world for them, whether you know it or not.

*

This brings me back to my own students one more time and to emotional injuries caused by violence and abuse within domestic environment. It is a field widely spread across our cultures and countries, and yet still neglected. As already mentioned, especially women and–even worse, if you can measure this at all–girls have to go through terrible experience only too often and are left not only with physical but with heavy emotional and mental injuries that may not heal in a lifetime. Sadly, again, society and even many professionals, often make it difficult, certainly not much easier, for these victims. This is not really surprising, I believe. Aren't most communities mainly ruled by males? How many men are out there who only pull a face when they are confronted with this cultural downfall? All my female Master Students in the U.S. share this type of history, which makes three out of three, an alarming number. But they all, every single one, prevailed eventually and so show that **you can learn to fight back....and succeed!**

One of them is Michelle who I have already introduced to you. She is one of the most loving personalities I have ever met, with a heart of gold. She had never been a party girl, had never dressed provocatively, which is no excuse for any man to become violent; had studied and worked hard at college and gone home alone. And yet, she had fallen victim to a horrific violent crime that had almost destroyed her. Only through her loving mother and strong family values she survived, but was left with tremendous fears and anxieties, destroying her trust and self-respect. She tried hard to to recover. However, this takes time in every case, and can leave the victim wide open emotionally. Often, men welcome that vulnerability and take advantage, instead of helping to cope and strengthening the woman. My primal goal was from the beginning to counteract that, but it is no exception, sadly, happening very often.

When she was introduced to me, she was extremely shy and reserved, her self-confidence low, and she was very unsure about herself as a woman. We sat down together and she told me a little about her life and what she was looking for. Michelle needed help to find answers for herself, a way to conquer her fears and to reach inner peace and strength in order to break free from her nightmares. Martial Arts provided excellent means to accomplish this. Within a couple of weeks, it became obvious how positively the training influenced her, how much joy it gave her. In fact, Michelle developed a determination and showed an energy-level of a height, that I have hardly ever witnessed in my entire career as a teacher. Being of Pilipino and Thai descent, she found the Arts a natural way for her; and soon, she became so good that I had to watch her closely not to be hit. After only three months of training, her techniques had become so crisp and razor sharp, she would have been able to compete and certainly defend herself against any attacker. Michelle passed her first belt test in an excellent manner, and she was so good that I awarded her the yellow belt instead of the white one, which I have hardly ever done.

Throughout the training, we spent many hours together just talking. It is essential in cases like Michelle's to take your time beyond the actual classes and let your student feel she is accepted as a person and that you really care. The emotional support she needs must not be underestimated. Although Michelle's confidence and attitude as a woman were improving tremendously, she still had a long way to go. One evening we sat together and she told me about the terrible troubles she went through at home, the feelings she had and how she tried to handle her situation. I told her that she was a very beautiful woman and that the ordeal she had to face did not reflect on her looks and for sure not on the inner love she had so much of. And I promised I would make her so strong emotionally as well as physically within a year that anybody trying to get in her way would surely be sorry for it. I was able to elevate her. And to ensure her success even more, I started to teach her Kendo, an excellent tool to learn skills and to lose aggressions at the same time. I could not have been prouder of her: Within the following three months, Michelle was ready to pass her orange belt-test, which she did, again, in amazing fashion. By then she hit the heavy bag so powerfully and with such a speed and timing that people stopped in their tracks just to watch her.

She also started to assist me with my teaching, which had remarkable positive effects, especially improving her self-esteem. Michelle simply loved the work. Teaching and mentoring were definitely her calling, and before long all our students adored her. It was shortly after 9/11 and we had quite a number of older people in our classes who we taught free of charge. It was also the time, when my short film *Close Quarters Combat* was created. Everyone in the gym helped. Clay Lacey Aviation even provided us with a real 727, free of charge. My good old friend Mihran supported us with his team as well as DP Jim Meyer. And Michelle just loved to beat up the 'bad guys'. She had so much fun during the shooting; it was a great joy to see her prospering and becoming stronger.

By the end of the summer, she worked out with me three times a week and helped teaching nearly every day. People who knew her before hardly recognized her any more. Though the same humble, caring young woman, Michelle's outlook on life, her attitude and appearance had changed 100%. Through her re-activated energies and re-awakened 'Inner Chi' she could carry her head high again with open heart and mind, full of thirst for knowledge, wisdom and love. And, as I have mentioned before, she was finally able to break free all by herself and start on a new and independent life altogether, away from any abusive man!

I remember well the dinner with her female friends that followed her green-belt-test, which she passed as all the others in simply glorious fashion. They all told me how much Michelle had changed and that her newfound confidence and self-esteem was tremendous and certainly inspiring. I have always felt most comfortable among a group of women and even liked to go shopping with them. There never was the need for 'macho' behavior and competition; and I simply like to make them smile, feel safe and relaxed. Quite often I have been asked if I was sure I wasn't gay on these occasions (that should tell you males something!). Certainly not. If you are confident in yourself, there is no need to put on a show. Just be yourself…and a real gentleman! And there you have my last secret weapon for success: Love without touch! Simply for the sake of joy and of mentoring these fine women, elevating their hearts and, therefore, spirit, changing their lives for the better.

*

Summing up, there is no such thing as a hopeless case. It is up to **you to take the first step onto a new path in life** and follow it with will power and inner strength. Determination and patience are required. Just remember: Shortcuts, like steroids or other 'enhancing' drugs, are for losers and cheaters. The price has to be paid; your body will remind you of that sooner or later. Besides, what are your achievements worth, your trophy, your title, if you know you only got there because you cheated? And that is exactly what it is: A cheat. You cheat yourself and others! And if your coach, your teacher, even your therapist, suggests anything in that direction, then it is surely time to find yourself someone else. A real, honest coach, teacher, therapist!

Neither I nor any of my fighters have ever taken drugs to win. And how ridiculous this can be nicely shown by one of those 'steroids-athletes' who made a big deal of his approach to break Babe Ruth's home-run record. As many sports commentators had already said before, Ruth did it not being in the best of shapes or even with a huge party-hangover. Well, he was not the best example for any young athlete as far as that is concerned. However, I do not think he ever wanted to be one; all he ever wanted was to play baseball and hit home-runs. And he did just that like hardly anyone else! There will never be another Babe Ruth, no matter how many 'steroids-kids' hit the ball across the field. And there will never be another Bruce Lee, Gene LeBell or Mohamed Ali; another Mark Spitz, Jacky X or Pelè ; another Lance Armstrong or an Albrecht Ginger, just to name a few. All these and many more are unique athletes and sports legends who achieved their records just by themselves. Records are there to be broken one day; otherwise, there would be no records at all. Besides, the first record, especially if it sets a milestone for the next generation, always is and always will be a unique measure for anyone who tries afterwards. It is a lot like in semi-contact kickboxing: The first point counts and sets the lead….

However, when we talk about sport enhancement drugs of any kind, we must consider a vital point that is hardly ever mentioned at all: Drug taking is not just a downfall of the individual. It is also the overwhelming expectations and greed for money that causes those young athletes to be pressured into using them in the first place. This pressure is often handed down from CEO's, team owners and head-coaches, etc. I talked with many retired and still-performing amateurs and pro athletes. All explained it in the same way to me: It is expected. And if you want to move forward with the team or organization, you do not question their methods, you, for sure, do not refuse. Otherwise, you are traded soon and put on the 'black list'. You will most likely never play another game; you will probably never be able to enter a high-standard competition–and therefore the welfare of your family is at stake, as well.

It is a sad fact, that we hardly ever hear about a CEO or a team owner who is put on trial. Only athletes and perhaps their strengthening coaches are singled out, brought before a judge, put through the wringer of the media and marked as guilty by the public. And if they told the whole truth, nobody would probably believe them.

Most steroids, even creatine and so forth, need to be taken for at least eight to twelve weeks, one to three times a year in order to achieve the results the coach and team owner is looking for, especially in strength- and power-sport disciplines like body building, football, boxing, wrestling, as well as in many Olympic disciplines. Otherwise, it would be a waste of time and money. There has to be a break of at least two to three months in between to avoid the serious danger of the body stopping its own hormone production, etc. The consequences for the athlete's health would be immense!

Most of the substances used can be flushed out of the system through herbs and supplements. So, if the athlete keeps off them for three months before the event, they will not be found by conventional testing. Only through regular blood tests and toxic-screening on a quarter-yearly basis those substances will be detected. Therefore, the currently applied system cannot be altogether sufficient. We have to apply proper and far reaching 'drug policies', name GM's and head-coaches and hold them accountable if they cross the line, to solve this problem.

But, of course you can—and you should—enhance your progress, your overall health, your energy and power by taking something: **The right food**—Soul food to go…

Chapter: 9

Nutrition and You... Soul Food to Go

Before diving into the aspects of nutrition, please be advised that most of us are neither MD's nor licensed dieticians. Therefore, a good teacher or instructor only provides guidelines for a change or positive adjustment of eating habits without prescribing a particular diet. For this you need to consult your MD and/or dietician. And if specific features like diabetes, obesity and the like have to be taken into account, this is mandatory before you start to train and change your life in order to ensure your safety, health and success.

There is **NO** form of diet to reduce weight that works safely and with long lasting effects–neither a short- nor a long-term one. **None ever will.** Besides, the average relapse-rate when dieting is between **95 and 99%**.

As an athlete, surely as a teacher, I had to witness many people training like champions but eating like a bird. So wrong and completely unnecessary! For an athlete, may it be on amateur or professional level, it is essential to eat properly, if he/she wants to win gold; certainly, if he/she wants to ensure the previous victory was not the last one! Moreover and even more important, to eat the right food in sufficient quantities is vital for long-term health. It will enable you to enjoy your well-deserved retirement, and it can even save your life. And this does not, of course, just apply to the athlete.

I have eaten and exercised healthily for a very long time, and my strength and energy level is about as high as it was in my late teens/early 20's, even though that is more than 20 years ago! I also recover a lot quicker from illnesses or injuries; my body and soul feel good, and I intend to keep it that way until I am 100 years old or thereabouts! This is **not** exceptional at all!

If you make **eating healthily and regular activities your lifestyle**, success is guaranteed. Choose healthy food, break down your daily intake to **at least three, better five meals a day** and exercise a little at least three times a week, and you are already on your way.

*

The links connecting us with each other and with nature, with our Earth, have already been mentioned. Once again, it is our responsibility–the responsibility of every single individual–to keep the world going round. Vital mistakes have been made in the past–and this is still going on, as we all know: Our air is polluted by industry and daily lifestyle; our soil killed by heavy fertilization, pesticides and over-harvesting; our water poisoned by chemical substances; large areas of nature are destroyed. All this happens in the name of society-development and the 'benefits' of global economy. Our governments, some more than others, lure us into believing they do what they can by establishing laws and regulations supposed to stop the global warming, the fatal change of living-conditions.

Just to give you another example: In California, a law was recently introduced to reduce air-destroying emissions by 20% until 2020. Apart from the fact that this is a ridiculous percentage in the face of the damage already done, before all comply with the new law we will have surely reached 2030 or thereabouts. And before 2020, tens of thousands of new cars, the production of new machines and equipment for the 'modern' world and daily lifestyle, will have increased pollution so that we can safely talk about a maximum of 10% (I believe it will rather be about 5%) before this allusive deadline is met. And this is only a moderate projection, not counting constantly rising energy costs.

And while oil and natural gas resources are exploited and used as if there was no tomorrow–ironically, there might not be a tomorrow if we carry on like that–around the world, although everybody knows they won't last forever, the development and employment of alternative and a lot more environmentally friendly energy-generation only plays a tiny role compared with what can be done. It seems all the people, certainly governments, have forgotten the effects of the oil-crisis in the 1970's. And today we are faced with them again: The costs for transport, food-production, housing etc., and therefore for living, are increasing by the day.

What does this have to do with personal fitness and health? Everything, I believe. And I am not prepared to wait for governments to come to their senses. I try to be as fit and healthy as possible to be able to tackle anything that comes my way, to be able to take matters in my own hand, to be as independent as I can! Do what **you** can–and that is a lot, as we already know–to ensure a happy and healthy life for yourself and your children. After all, again, they are the ones to lead our world into the future; and we are the ones to prepare them!

But be aware: Fitness and healthy lifestyle have become a big business over the past few years. And business very often means it is good for the companies who produce and distribute these so-called 'health- and fitness-items and food' and for no one else, certainly not for customers. We have already talked about (fake) 'research' and this way of advertising. It can also be found in the food-division. One of the largest fast-food restaurant chains, as an example, has decorated its restaurants with an oversized display that tells the customers how nutritious and therefore healthy their food is, claiming this is exactly what the customer needs and wants–according to 'research'.

This display shows a large table packed with the ingredients the meals are made of. But the statements about nutrients and vitamins refer to the items before they are processed, shock-frozen, re-heated, shock-frozen again, and then put into an oven or on a grill. By then, the healthy components are certainly killed. Therefore, these statements could not be further away from the truth! Why the company is allowed to display this, is beyond my understanding.

However, trustworthy information is available, and healthy food can be found in every supermarket. But perhaps some of you might turn to 'home-farming' and grow salads, tomatoes and/or potatoes, as an example. This can be great fun and even a form of therapy, not to mention the money that would be saved considering the increasing costs for our daily food.

*

On our way to a healthy lifestyle, let us walk back down the passage of time to the beginning of mankind first: The human body was designed to adapt to its natural environment, its bio-rhythm following the rhythm of nature with its changing seasons. According to climatic, environmental and food-supply conditions around the globe, it developed certain features, the ability to adapt to heat or cold, for example–characteristics that formed different races, many still apparent today. For a very long time, the early human being was a hunter and collector to provide for his daily meals: He lived by wild stock like deer and fish available in his part of the world and followed the animals on their own search for food in order to ensure his needs could be met. Additionally, mainly in the off-season, when meat was hardly available, he collected fruits and nuts to eat, and therefore you can call him the first vegetarian on the planet, however, only over longer or shorter periods of the year and because he had to.

So, our ancestors mainly lived on meat, fruits and nuts; and if you look up the history of any tribe or culture on our planet, you will find no exception. This is maybe the logical explanation why the human body needs the 'natural' form of creatine, which is, next to calcium, magnesium and ATP, one of the four substances chemically burnt to create energy in the human muscle fibers. This energy is used to generate the body's temperature; it enables the body to move and keeps the other body functions going. Other energy sources are oxygen, protein and complex carbohydrates. If these substances are not regularly provided, the organism will–as last resort–generate energy by burning muscle fiber and body fat sooner or later, in order to survive.

There are only **two creatine-sources** to be found: Red meat and fish with red colored flesh–salmon has the largest concentration. There is no other source! And this is for sure one of the major reasons why full vegetarians and constantly dieting people become tired sooner, why their condition and ability to concentrate is less developed and why they have less muscle-mass, growth and strength depending on their intake of **protein**, which is another source the body needs to build and re-build muscle fiber, no exceptions! Creatine and calcium make up **50%** of the energy compound our body uses for its activities. So you take quite a health risk not only through the lack of energy, but also by depriving your body of vital substances!

I do not think I have to point out that proper food is mandatory, if you want to live a long and healthy life. As said before, burning body-fat and muscle fiber is meant by nature as the **last** resorts to generate energy. It cannot be a natural and therefore healthy thing to do, certainly not for a longer period. Besides, (simplified) to generate let us say one energy point from burning fat, the body actually needs two (!) energy points to do the burning itself. So, it is a bad bargain and one of the reasons why an overweight and de-conditioned person becomes tired so much quicker than a physically fit individual, even to the point of having his/her support system break down altogether. These processes happening in your body are, of course, a lot more complicated, but I would not like to distract or even discourage you by biomechanics and chemical interactions.

There also is, of course, the supply of fluids to be considered; and here we find the experts divided. From one division, at least 8 to 10 ounces (2qts) of fluid per day are recommended. It should mainly be water, but juices, milk or tea, for instance, can be consumed as well (no alcohol!). I am not a happy water drinker myself, although I know I should be; however, I can drink a gallon of milk every day with a smile. The body is able to store fluids in a natural 'reservoir', and that is where our forbearers and their lifestyle, adapted to their environment, come in again. How long the body is able to function without sufficient supply of fluid or none at all, before health problems occur, however, is not quite established. The experts of the other division, and I personally agree more with them, claim it depends on cultural background, climatic conditions, lifestyle and up-bringing as well as health and fitness level of the individual. Consider all those native tribes in Australia, Africa or America: The Australian natives, for example, do not just walk, they run—hunting barefooted—with elegance and speed across deserts and steppes in great heat, hardly ever stopping for rest or a 'coffee break'; the South American Indians do it as well, only their hunting ground is the rainforest.

So, only the 'domesticated' human being, living in 'civilized' countries and cultures is supposed to have a problem, if he does not get his 8–10 oz. of fluids a day? It is not quite accurate and surely depends on the individual. I believe we can safely say that 60-70% of the liquids forming our body weight and reservoir are adjustable to our daily activities and general lifestyle. And so surely is our calorie 'household'. The average male needs about 2000-3000 calories a day, the female about 1800-2500 to keep the body working healthily depending on activities. An athlete, though, may require more than double as much.

Returning to the beginnings of mankind once more, nature had equipped the human body with a so-called **'emergency support system'** with the already mentioned water reservoir and a fat store to ensure life. This system is watched over by a mechanism, a health security guard, a **gatekeeper,** positioned within our digestive system. This gatekeeper counts the calories the body receives, evaluates the quality of food and registers the ingredients needed for healthy functioning. According to this information, it orders the body to react in one way or the other. The support system has been adjusted to lifestyle and environmental conditions across the centuries, but the original purpose has never changed.

Imagine your gatekeeper working along quite happily until you decide to diet—and not just a little, but drastically depriving your body of well needed substances. It will not take long before the alarm is raised; and within 72 hours, the energy reservoirs will be shut down. The time span depends on your overall fitness-level, your body composition, your heritage and origin and—this is a very important aspect—on the quality of food and nutrition you have taken before on a long-term basis! You cannot influence this procedure; you are not able to get around it! That is why it is called an emergency support system. Your gatekeeper has a good memory as well. It will raise the alarm and take necessary steps even earlier, depending on how frequently you diet. In fact, the more often you put your body through the ordeal, the less water and fat you will lose, the less energy is available to you. In the end, your reservoirs will be shut down for good! These reservoirs are located where you want to lose them.

Your gatekeeper does not know why you turned into such a miser all of a sudden. All it knows is there is a large amount of food missing that the body needs, and therefore the life-support-system is in danger. It's afraid you might not be able to 'cross the desert in search for food' and even die. So, it will do everything possible to prevent this from happening. That is the reason why you have such a craving for food while dieting, and put on weight so quickly after you start eating 'normal' again: The reservoirs have to be filled up. And very often they are extended, doubled, even tripled in size, to make sure the next shortage can be survived!

All this in mind, you might ask: "Well, I eat enough, in fact I eat plenty. So, why are my reservoirs extending, why am I so heavy?" Ask yourself: Does my food contain enough vitamins and minerals? Enough creatine and protein? Do I provide my body with the substances it needs to generate energy? Remembering what was said before, then you have your reason: Living on unhealthy junk and fast-food, on processed meals, because they are so convenient, on chocolate, cake and crisps containing little to no complex carbohydrates, let alone all the other vital ingredients, your gatekeeper stores away as much as possible in constant state of alert. The MD's have invented the lap belt, certain types of so-called 'beauty-surgery' and similar treatments instead of recommending the right procedure. Do not even think about them, they are completely unnecessary and only benefit the performing doctors and institutions–unless, of course, health concerns make them necessary and therefore are approved by your personal physician!

However, your gatekeeper is 'intelligent' and can work both ways: As soon as you change your lifestyle and eating habits, it will re-adjust the proceedings in your system and your body will be re-trained. You will benefit almost immediately, and dieting will not be necessary anymore! But, again, there are no healthy shortcuts.

Let us concentrate on what you can do in your day-to-day life to improve your overall health. As said before, every change should be brought about step by step, one day at the time, at a speed that feels comfortable to you. So, after you have taken stock of your eating habits, you can begin to replace food items containing mainly unhealthy substances like certain fats, sugars and simple carbohydrates (fast-food) with products containing vitamins, minerals, complex carbohydrates and other essential ingredients your body needs daily to stay healthy and energetic.

The following 'food-pyramid' starting with the least necessary items (1) illustrates what your daily intake should look like. It is not a prescription, but a guideline recommended by experts for a healthy lifestyle that helps you to choose the right food.

(1)–fats, oils, sweets

(2) milk, milk-products like yoghurt and cheeses–meat, poultry, fish, eggs, pulses, nuts (2-3 servings/day)

(3)–Vegetables–(2–3 servings/day) / fruit (2–4 servings/day)

(4)–bread (preferably whole meal), rice, pasta, cereals (6–11 servings/day)

Now to the life-essential ingredients themselves:

Vitamins:

Many people sadly misjudge and underestimate the importance of these and so neglect them. But vitamin-deficiency causes many health problems in the long run and is the root of quite a few diseases, not to mention less energy, motivation, concentration, strength and therefore less quality of life. The field of vitamins is rather complex and their availability large. So, here is only an outline; a full spectrum can be obtained from a MD or dietician.

Fat Soluble Vitamins – RDA, (IU = international units) / day

Vitamin A, 5000 IU / Vitamin D, 400 IU / Vitamin E, 300 IU / Vitamin K, 70-150 IU /

Water Soluble Vitamins

Vitamin C, 60-100 mg. / Thiamine, 1, 5 mg. / Riboflavin, 1, 7 mg. / Niacin, 20 mg. / Folic Acid, 40 mg. / B 6, 2 mg. / B12, 6 mg. / a day.

You can overdose on different vitamins, like A, D, C and B12, but this, generally speaking, only happens if you take these 4-6 times a day and totally overload your system.

Luckily, our gatekeeper is aware of this problem and most of them simply flush out. However, it can course serious health consequences if done on a long-term basis. After the system is overloaded, the body seems to return to its old settings and needs. So, avoid exaggerations when you start to change your eating habits; a simple good multi-vitamin supplement may be required, but most don't contain enough C and E; a smaller bottle of vitamin E and C will do just fine.

Vitamin killers:

All **industrial sugars**, as well **chocolates**, neutralize most vitamins, if you take them together. Therefore, your body only gets mere traces of these much needed substances, if you take so-called 'vitamin-waters', vitamin-bars, etc. So, opt for products with no industrial sugar at all. You can always sweeten them with natural sweeteners like honey or all fruit sugars. Most minerals are vulnerable to industrial sugar as well. Also, any cigarettes, alcohol and drugs are known to deprive the body of vitamins and minerals.

Minerals:

We distinguish two groups: Group (1) comes in large amounts, group (2) in smaller amounts or just in traces:

Group (1): Sodium, Potassium, Chloride, Calcium, Phosphor, Magnesium.
Group (2): Fluorine, Iodine, Thyroxin, Zink, Iron, Copper.

All minerals have an important function, and you need them throughout the day for cell transport, cell- and bone-growth, tissue repair; they carry oxygen, control the electrolyte fluids household with its flow; they play a major role in the building and support of a healthy immune system and the ability to fight off any infections and colds. Mineral-deficiency will–just like vitamin-deficiency–cause health problems.

Carbohydrates:

The basic structure of a carbohydrate-unit consists of sugar and glucose. We distinguish between simple and complex carbohydrates.

Simple carbohydrates only consist of sugar and glucose and are found in all sweets like candy, ice cream, doughnuts and processed food. These should be consumed with caution and moderation, because the body needs more energy to break them down than it actually gets out of them. That is the reason why you become hungry again rather quickly after you have filled yourself up with sweets and junk-food. The level of usable energy is simply too low.

Complex carbohydrates are rich in fibers. They are processed slowly with maximum energy-generation and long-lasting effects–meaning you will not need other sources of energy for quite a while. Therefore, they are so vital for every athlete! Moreover, they keep your heart, liver, kidneys and arteries healthy. In the liver, carbohydrates are converted to glucose, which is transported to the parts of the body where it is needed by the blood stream. This is called glycogenolysis.

The largest concentration of complex carbohydrates is found in plant-food like green vegetables, citrus fruits, potatoes (all varieties); other sources are rice, pasta, grains and whole-meal bread. They have four major functions:

1. They are the major source of energy.
2. They provide fuel for the brain and central nervous system.
3. They prevent the breakdown of protein (and therefore protect our muscle mass).
4. They are our major source for daily needed fibers.

Therefore, complex carbohydrates should amount to **60-70%** of the total daily calorie-intake +–10%, depending on activities and workload. In our society, carbohydrates have the reputation of being fattening, but it is not true. Just compare the numbers: Carbohydrates = 4 cal/gram, protein = 4 cal/gram, **fat = 9 cal/gram**, fibers = 0 cal/gram.

The following rating shows how much glucose ready to be used by the body can be obtained by particular food: Glucose 100%, potatoes 98%, carrots, steamed 92%, honey (fruit sugar) 87%, corn flakes 83%, white rice 72%, whole meal bread 72%, white bread 68%, raisins 64%, bananas 61%, pasta 51%, oatmeal 49%, orange juice 46%, oranges 43%, grapes 43%, whole meal pasta 42%, apples 39%–just to give an idea what food to choose from as an athlete or rehab client.

Protein:

Protein, generally speaking, is needed for muscle-growth (muscle mass) and maintenance of muscles and skin tissue. It is important for our enzymes, which help to break down our food, to absorb the nutrients through our stomach walls and to send them into our blood stream. Also for hormones and different fluids as well as the structural support of our physiological functions throughout our body. Amino acids are needed to build protein. From 32 different acids, 8 can't be produced by the body and have to be supplied.

The average person needs daily 0, 36 gram/body weight, an athlete 0, 7 gram/body weight and an endurance athlete like a runner, sprinter or Martial Artist up to 10, 0 gram/body weight of protein, which means–as a general rule–about 10% of your daily food should consist of protein. But, again, pro athletes, especially if they do power training and body building, if they need extreme muscle-strength and -growth like weight lifters, hammer-throwers or shot-putters, need more, in many cases double as much.
High in protein are, as examples, fish, lean red meat, chicken, turkey, tofu, soybeans, skimmed milk.

Fats:

Fats with their fatty acids are needed for the body to absorb fat-soluble vitamins, to protect skin, hair and organs as well as to keep the fat-energy-store of the life-emergency-system filled up. The American Heart Association recommends our daily food should contain less than 30% fat. However, to stay below 15% as often as possible would be a safe bet. We distinguish between saturated and unsaturated fats.

Saturated fats contain a high level of **cholesterol**, which can, if consumed in larger amounts, cause heart diseases, high blood pressure and the gathering of plaque on the walls of our arteries. Therefore, our daily fat-intake should contain less than 10% of these.

Unsaturated fats are mainly found in plant food. Therefore, butter and oils based on animal-fat should be substituted with sunflower, safflower or olive oil.

In the average western industrial societies, people consume between 300-500 mg of cholesterol a day. In the U.S., the daily food generally contains well over 40% saturated fat, mainly consumed through junk- and fast-food. In Japan, for instance, the average daily food contains 10-15% fat, of which only about 3-6% is saturated. Therefore, heart diseases and other related illnesses are rare, the life-expectancy is higher and people are generally much healthier than in other countries!

Here a small list of food and their cholesterol contents measured in milligrams: Fruits, grains, vegetables: 0, oysters cooked: 45, scallops cooked: 53, fish, lean: 65, chicken: 65, turkey: 85, lobster: 85, beef: 90, chicken without skin, cooked: 95, egg yolk (one): 270, beef liver: 440, beef kidney: 700.

Apart from the components listed above, there is a large variety of substances mainly found in plants like herbs and vegetables, for example, that have been used **in natural healing** for thousands of years. The healing capacities of many of them have been proved and acknowledged by scientists.

Most of these substances can be taken safely and have **no** dangerous side effects. They can not only contribute to general well-being and health-improvement, but may also substitute medication like painkillers and sleeping tablets in many, especially mild and even medium-heavy cases.

Here are a few examples: All varieties of sun-dried 'cherries' (health food store), contain so-called natural ibuprofen', which is also found in chicken noodle soup–one of the reasons why fever caused by a cold often decreases when you eat it. Ginseng heightens the energy level (without caffeine); green tea 'cleans' the body; peppermint, especially in strong concentration (oil), relieves pain and relaxes; pineapples contain a large amount of enzymes that are needed to break down food in the digestive system; wild brown rice binds excess water and flushes it out of the body. Here a short list of possible foods…

Nutrition Plan for: MMA Students–(moderate muscle gain, with strength)
By Sensei, Anthony v. Sager 4[h] degree BB for info: www.getfit4yourlife.com

Breakfast:
A) Muesli or whole wheat serial with whole full milk and vitamin D.
B) Fresh fruits (cut, or blended) in Mixer/Blender with full milk & Yogurt.
C) Egg omelets (with less jog) 4 eggs but only with one jog. & vegetables.
D) Option (alternate true out the week) large glass of protein w/ fruits & milk.
E) Drinks: fresh made OJ. Shoko Milk, Tea etc.

Lunch:
A) Grilled Chicken breasts, with Cesar salad w/ Italian fat free dressing.
B) Grilled Salmon or Tuna, with green varieties garden salad dressing.
C) Sea food salad or Lunch, with mixed Asian salads.
D) Lean Meat, steak or meat lunch, w/ back potatoes w/ sour cream. etc.
E) Grilled rainbow fish, with vegetables and back potatoes.
F) Hungarian Pusta Goulash, with brown wild rise, vegetable etc.

Dinner:
A) Vegetable pizza with chicken or salami, green garden salad etc.
B) Chicken grilled with wild brown rise and vegetables etc.
C) Steak or chicken fajita on/or w/ corn torttia bread.
D) Goulash sup with wild rise on the side.
E) Vegetable sup, with wild rise on side.
F) Pasta (linguini) with vegetables and/or meat or chicken grilled etc.
G) Back potatoes w/ sour cream etc. and wild rise, and/or meat/chicken.
(Course all Dinner foods ideas should be alternated for your own needs/desire)

This is only a short list of possible food-combinations used by pro fighters and athletes around the globe for decades. Feel free to design your own healthy meals. If you need to gain more muscle mass and weight, increase your protein as well as your carbohydrate intake. If you like to get a little leaner or need to step down a weight division, lower the daily carbohydrate intake and try to eat the heaviest meal before 8 pm. Especially if you would like or have to reduce weight, separate your fat and carbohydrate intake during the day, eat more seafood, fresh fruit and vegetables instead of other foods. And with regular exercises you will be well on your way.

If you would like to know more about nutrition, health food, natural substances and their effects, there is plenty of trustworthy information available by means of books, journals, internet and, of course, through well educated dieticians and/or MD's. So, for a customized nutrition plan see your dietician or MD.

However, you should **never** substitute your prescribed medication with any natural substance without consulting your MD first!

*

Footnote: Through my own personal experiences and the experiences as a teacher, I am painfully aware of the difficulties and problems many people have to face in their lives and the injustice in our world. However, I am an optimist. And if I have 'overdrawn the picture' of a number of issues a little or used strong words, it has been meant to awaken you and anyone who cares to listen. Perhaps we will find new friends and active colleagues and–**together**–find solutions that will make this world a better place.

Peace, Love and Wisdom, Sensei Anthony v. Sager

Chapter: 10

Shin-Tora-Do Karate & Tai Chi, Techniques & Forms, Conditioning, Healing

TEST BOOK
SHIN – TORA – DO   (USA) © TM
From: 9ᵗʰ Kyu – 1ˢᵗ degree SHIN – TORA – DO   Black Belt
SHIN – TORA – DO is a blend in harmony of:
Kadgamala Karate Do:
Gojo Ryu / Kyokushinkai Karate
Hard & soft style, straight, linear movements, simple and direct attacks and defenses.
Aikido / Tai Chi (Chi-Gong):
Soft styles, avoiding flowing, circular and pivoting movements. Emphasis on "Chi", which includes: Throwing, joint manipulation and immobilization.
Savate / Boxing:
Hard styles, using a lot of body energy and force, of body mobility in combinations and techniques. Both styles are hundreds of centuries old and originate in Europe; they go as far back as the Roman Empire where professional competing took place.
Judo / Jiu-Jitsu & Grappling:
Soft style-hard style, using leverage and balance against your opponent for throwing and take-downs, locks, as well immobilization.

Test form for: Shin Tora Do   White Belt 9th kyu.

1. Condition Testing:

10 / 20 / 30	Push-ups.
10 / 20 / 30	Sit-ups.
10 /20 / 30	Jumping jacks.
2 x 2 min.	Jump rope.
1 x 1 min.	Warrior stands.

2. Techniques / Tactics:

10   x   Front – kick   (left & right), (Mai-geri)

10   x   Front – punch (left & right), (Oii-zuki)

10   x   Back – punch (left & right), (Jako-zuki)

10   x   Front – stand & normal stands

10   x   Blocks for head & body (left & right)

3. Defense Techniques and Front – Stand's:

10   x   each side.

4. Self -Defense Forms:

- O -

Time: 0-3 months   *Good Luck, your Sensei.*

Test form for: Shin – Tora Do   Yellow Belt, 8th Kyu.

1. Condition Testing:

15 / 25 / 35	Push-ups.
15 / 25 / 35	Sit-ups.
15 / 25 / 35	Jumping Jacks.
3 x 3 min.	Jump rope.
2 x 2 min.	Warrior Stands (walking without kicks).
Lion walk	2 rounds (20 foot circle).
Bag/pats	2 x 3 rounds of 2 min.

2. Techniques / Tactics:

All techniques from Kyu 9th as well:

10 x Front Kick w/ front & back leg, as well out of forward motion. (L & R)

10 x Roundhouse Kick, front & back, as well out of forward motion. (Mawashi-geri)

10 x Front & Back hand punch, 10 x back fist (L & R).

3. Defense Techniques:

Fight positions, front, side and double stands. As well attention stands.

Fight stand positions, semi, light & full-contact. (L& R)

10 x Maid movements, 10 x active & passive. (L & R)

10 x Side steps, front, side & back. (L & R)

4. Self-Defense / Forms:

Shin-Tora-Do Nage form 1, plus all techniques and movements in harmony with each other, 2 x 2 min. San–Shin in Iron horse.

5. Meditation Techniques:

Hatha Yoga elements & Tai Chi (Chi-Gong), beginner level.

Time: 3-6 months   *Good Luck, your Sensei*

Test form for: Shin – Tora Do   Orange Belt, 7ᵗʰ Kyu
1. Condition testing:
20 / 25 / 35   Push-ups.
20 / 25 / 35   Sit-ups.
20 /25 / 35   Jumping Jacks.
4 x 2 min.   Jump rope.
3 x 3 min.   Warrior walk w/ front kick (L & R).
Lion Walk   3 rounds (20 foot circle).
Bag/pats   3 x 3 rounds of 3 min.

2. Technique / Tactics:
All techniques from Kyu: 8ʰ, 9ʰ, as well:
15 x Front Kick, 15 x Roundhouse & 15 x Side Kick (Yoko-Geri) front and back foot.
As well out of forward motion, plus small foot sweeping (De-ashi-barai). (L & R)
15 x front Punch (Jap), 15 x Back Punch, 15 x Uppercut, 15 x Side Hook, (cross punch).
15 x Back fist forward and with 180 degree turn. All techniques with control. (L & R)

3. Defense Techniques:
All Attention and Fight stands from Kyu: 8ʰ, 9ʰ plus small Turn Steps, as well 90ᵗʰ degree
Side Steps. (Mavate) & De-ashi-barai.

4. Self-Defense / Forms:
Form 1 & 2 (Nage 1, 2) plus 3 min. San-shin in Iron horse.
All techniques, movements and combinations perfect and in harmony together.

5. Sparring / Breaking:
3 x 3 minutes (semi-contact) 2 breaks of 2.5 inch wood.

6. Meditation Techniques:
Hatha Yoga elements & Tai – Chi (Chi-Gong) beginner level.
Time: 6-9 months   *Good Luck, your Sensei.*

Test form for: Shin – Tora Do   Green Belt, 6ᵗʰ Kyu.

1. Condition Testing:

25 / 35 / 45	Push-ups.
25 / 35 / 45	Sit-ups.
25 / 35 / 45	Jumping Jacks.
4 x 3 min.	Jump rope.
4 x 4 min.	Warrior walk w/ Front & Roundhouse Kicks.
Lion walk	4 rounds (20 foot circle).
Bag/pats	4 x 4 rounds of 3 min.

2. Techniques / Tactics:

All techniques from: 7ʰ, 8ʰ, 9ʰ kyu as well:

20 x Side Kick, 20 x Hill Kick, plus out of 360 degree w/ (L & R).

20 x Knee Kick, 20 x Knee Block plus 20 x Shin-Block, w/ (L & R).

20 x Foot Sweep with front and back foot, w/ (L & R).

3. Defense Techniques / Stands:

All techniques from 9ʰ, 8ʰ, 7ʰ kyu. As well:

Defense Steps, and 90ᵗʰ degree Side Steps. 20 x High Block, 20 x Middle Block and 20 x Leg Block. As well with open hand, and re-directing of punches, and foot techniques.

4. Self-Defense / Forms:

Form: (Nage) 1, 2, 3 and San-chin in a 20 foot circle, 4 rounds.

Plus all techniques in movements and combination with each other. Also Chi-Gong/Shin-Tora-Do form 1 and San-chin 6 min. in Iron horse.

5. Sparring / Breaking:

4 x 3 min. (semi contact) 3 breaks of 2.5 inch wood.

6. Meditation Techniques:

Hata Yoga elements & Tai Chi (Chi-Gong) advanced beginner Level.

Time: 12-15 months   *Good Luck, your Sensei*

Seminars: One beginner Techniques Seminar

Test form for: Shin – Tora Do   Purple Belt, 5th Kyu.

1. Condition Testing:

35 / 45 / 55	Push-ups.
35 / 45 / 55	Sit-ups.
35 / 45 / 55	Jumping Jacks.
6 x 3 min.	Jump rope.
6 x 4 min	Warrior walk w/ Front, Roundhouse & Side Kicks w/ (L & R).
Lion walk	6 rounds (20 foot circle).
Bag/pats	5 x 5 rounds of 5 min.

2. Techniques / Tactics:

All techniques from Kyu: 6^h, 7^h, 8^h, 9^h. As well:

20 x Crescent Kick, 20 x Back Kick, also one foot technique as: Jump Kick.

All techniques as demo on partner in full control and harmony. 10 x each leg.

3. Defense Techniques / Forms:

All techniques from: Kyu 6^h, 7^h, 8^h, 9^h. Also 2 Reach-Hands as block, plus 20 x Reach-Hands as technique. (L & R). Also 10 x on partner (L & R) as Nage Form.

4. Sparring / Breaking:

8 x 3 min. (semi & light contact) 4 breaks of 2.5 inch wood.

5. Self-Defense / Forms:

(Nage) Forms: 1, 2, 3, 4 & 5; techniques with partner in harmony and control.

Also; Chi-Gong / Shin-Tora-Do Forms: 1, 2, Sanshin 10 minutes in Iron horse.

6. Meditation Techniques:

Hatha Yoga–Tai Chi (Chi-Gong) inter-medium Level.

Time: 18–-1 months   *Good Luck, your Sensei.*

Seminars: Two Technique Seminars.

Test form for: Shin – Tora Do   Blue Belt, 4th Kyu

1. Condition Testing:

45 / 55 / 66	Push-ups.
45 / 55 / 66	Sit-ups.
45 / 55 / 66	Jumping Jacks.
8 x 3 min.	Jump rope.
8 x 4 min.	Warrior walk w/ Front, Roundhouse, Side & Back Kicks.
Lion walk	10 rounds (20 foot circle).
Bag/pats	6 x 6 rounds of 6 min.

2. Techniques / Tactics:

All techniques from Kyu: 5^h, 6^h, 7^h, 8^h, 9^h. As well:

20 x Double Kick (all Kicks) L & R. plus Spin Hill Kick & Ax-Kick (L & R). 2 Front Kicks as Jump-Kick 20 x both legs.

All techniques as demo on partner in total control and harmony.

3. Defense-Techniques:

All Techniques from Kyu: 5^h, 6^h, 7^h, 8^h, 9^h. As well:

20 x Bear Hands, fingertips, plus both hands as Reach-Hands Block. Also 20 x as re-directing of attack techniques, with open hands.

All techniques with partner 20 x each partner and side. (L & R)

4. Sparring / Breaks:

15 x 3 min. (semi & light contact) 6 breaks of 2.5 inch wood, one stone.

5. Self-Defense / Forms:

(Nage) Forms: 1-6, all techniques w/ partner in harmony with another. Also, Chi-Gong/ Shin-Tora-Do Forms: 1-3, and San-Shin 15 min. w/ movements.

6. Meditation Techniques:

Hata Yoga–Tai Chi (Chi-Gong) higher inter-medium level.

Time: 27-30 months   *Good luck, your Sensei*

Seminars: Two Techniques Seminars, one Side-ring – referee workshop.

Test form for: Shin – Tora Do   1# Brown Belt, 3rd Kyu.

1. Condition Testing:

55 / 66 / 77	Push-ups.
55 / 66 / 77	Sit-ups.
55 / 66 / 77	Jumping Jacks.
10 x 3 min.	Jump rope.
10 x 2 min.	Warrior walk w/ double Kicks, Front, roundhouse & Side Kicks (L&R)
Lion walk	12 rounds (20 foot circle).
Bag/pats	7 x 7 rounds of 7 min.

2. Techniques / Tactics:

All techniques from Kyu: 4^{h}, 5^{h}, 6^{h}, 7^{h}, 8^{h}, 9^{h}. As well:

20 x Triple-Kick (L&R). Also 2 Foot Kicks as Jump-Kick 30 x each leg.

All techniques as demo on partner in perfection and harmony. Each partner and each leg.

3. Defense-Techniques / Forms:

All techniques from Kyu: 4^{h}, 5^{h}, 6^{h}, 7^{h}, 8^{h}, 9^{h}. As well:

Open Hands, defense redirecting of all attacks, scoping and avoiding of all contact. Defense-Kicks, plus Blocks (L&R) plus 2 x 15 min. Chi-Sau (sticky hands) with partner, all techniques in full control and harmony on partner in light and full contact demo. 30 x each arm & leg, both partners.

4. Sparring / Breaks:

20 x 3 min. (semi, light & full contact) 8 breaks of 2,5 inch wood, 1 stone.

5. Self-Defense / Forms:

(Nage) forms: 1-8. All techniques w/ partner in harmony with another. Also Chi-Gong/ Shin-Tora-Do Form: 1-4. Plus Sanshin 18 min. w/ movements, as well:

Chi-Sau (sticky hands) 20 min. with partner as defense as well attack.

6. Meditation Techniques:

Hatha Yoga–and Tai Chi (Chi-Gong) advanced level. Also inter-medium level of Kalarippayat Yoga and the history.

Time: 27-30 months   *Good Luck, your Sensei.*

Seminars: Three Techniques Seminars, one side-ring referee certification.

Test form for: Shin – Tora Do   2# Brown Belt, 2nd Kyu

1. Condition Testing:

66 / 77 / 88	Push-ups.
66 / 77 / 88	Sit-ups.
66 / 77 / 88	Jumping Jacks.
10 x 4 min.	Jump rope.
15 x 2 min.	Warrior walk w/ Double Kicks; Front, Roundhouse, Side, Back-Kick. (L & R)
Lion walk	14 rounds (20 foot circle).
Bag/pats	8 x 8 rounds of 8 min.

2. Techniques / Tactics:

All techniques from Kyu: 3^d, 4th, 5th, 6th, 7th, 8th, 9th. As well:

30 x Quarto-Triple Kick (L&R), four Kicks as Jump-Kicks, 30 x each leg.

All techniques as demo with partner in control, techniques in harmony 40 x each partner, each technique. (L&R)

3. Defense-Techniques:

All techniques from Kyu: 3^d – 9th. Plus 20 x on partner each side, all Nage Forms.

Also Tai Chi as defense, and Chi-Sau (30 min. as attack and defense) w/ partner.

4. Sparring / Breaks:

25 x 3 min. (semi & light contact) 10 breaks of 2.5 inch wood, 1 stone.

5. Self – Defense / Forms:

All (Nage) Forms from: 1-10. All techniques w/ partner in harmony and total control.

Also Chi-Gong/Shin-Tora-Do Forms 1, 2, 3, 4, 5 / Sanshin 20 min. in 20 foot circle.

Also 5 self invented self-defense forms from each partner with total control and harmony.

6. Meditation Techniques:

Hatha Yoga & Tai Chi (Chi-Gong) advanced level, ass. teacher. Also Kalarippayat Yoga and the history of this thousands of years old style.

Time: 42-54 months   *Good Luck, your Sensei.*

Seminars: Four Techniques/Fight Seminars, one side-ring referee certification.

Test form for: Shin –Tora Do   Brown/Black Belt, 1ˢᵗ Kyu

1. Condition Training:

77 / 88 / 99	Push-ups.
77 / 88 / 99	Sit-ups.
77 / 88 / 99	Jumping Jacks.
15 x 4 min.	Jump rope.
15 x 3 min.	Warrior walk w/ Triple Kicks (L&R) Front, Round, Side, Back & Ax-Kick.
Lion walk	18 rounds (20 foot circle).
Bag/pats	10 x 10 rounds of 10 minutes.

2. Techniques / Tactics:

All techniques from Kyu: 2nd, 3rd, 4th, 5th, 6th, 7th, 8th, 9th. As well:

30 x Quarto-Triple Kick, each side. Four Kicks as Jump-Kicks, 30 x each leg.

All techniques as demo on partner, w/ total control & harmony, in light & full contact. 40 x all techniques each side on partner.

3. Defense-Techniques:

All techniques from Kyu: 2nd-9th. All Nage forms w/ partner 30 times each partner.

Also Tai Chi as breathing w/ healing techniques on partner. As well Chi-Sau (45 min. as attack and defense) each partner.

4. Sparring / Breaks:

1.5 hours (semi, light & full contact) 12 breaks of 2.5 inch, 2 stones.

5. Self-Defense / Forms:

All (Nage) Forms: 1-12. All techniques w/ partner in harmony & total control in semi, light & full contact. Also, Chi-Gong/Shin-Tora-Do Form Nr. 1, 2, 3, 4, 5, 6. Plus Sanshin 45 min. in 20 foot circle. And 10 self-invented self-defense demos on partner, with total control and harmony in light & full contact each partner.

6. Meditation Techniques:

Hatha Yoga & Tai Chi (Chi-Gong) advanced level, ass. teacher. Also Kalarippayat Yoga and the history of this thousands of years old style.

Time: 54-70 months   *Good Luck, your Sensei.*

Seminars: Six Techniques/ Fight Seminars, one side & one main-ring referee certification.

Test form for: Shin – Tora Do   1st degree Back Belt

1. Condition Testing:

88 / 99 / 101	Push-ups.
88 / 99 / 101	Sit-ups.
88 / 99 / 101	Jumping Jacks.
15 x 5 min.	Jump-rope.
15 x 5 min.	Warrior walk w/ Quarto-Triple Kicks: Front, Round, Side, Back & Ax- Kick.
Lion walk	25 rounds (20 foot circle).
Bag/pats	14 rounds of 12 min.

2. Techniques / Tactics:

All techniques from Kyu: 1st, 2nd, 3rd, 4th, 5th, 6^{h}, 7^{h}, 8th, 9^{h}. As well:

40 x w/ partner each. Four Kicks as Jump-Kicks both legs 40 x.

All techniques on partner w/ (L & R) 40 x full speed and power w/ total control.

3. Defense-Techniques:

All techniques from Kyu: 1st, 2nd, 3rd, 4^{h}, 5th, 6^{h}, 8^{h}, 9^{h}. As well:

All techniques with partner in harmony and total control in semi, light and full contact. 30 min. Chi-sou as an attack w/ partner, both sides.

4. Sparring / Breaks:

2 hours (semi, light & full contact) 14 breaks of 2.5 inch wood, 3 stones.

5. Self-Defense / Forms:

All (Nage) Forms: 1-14. All techniques w/ partner in light and full contact in total harmony and control. Also Chi-Gong/Shin-Tora Do Forms Nr. 1-7. As well San-chin 1 hour (20 foot circle). Plus Chi-sou (Sticky hands) 1 hour w/ partner as defense.

6. Meditation Techniques:

Hata Yoga in perfection, teacher level. Chi-Gong Tai Chi ass. teacher level. Also: Kalarippayat Yoga and Kadagamala and their history.

7. Teaching / Theory:

2 (kids, adults) classes, teaching of the full spectrum ask by panelists (2 full hours).

Time: 88-100 months minimum.

Good Luck, your Sensei.

Seminars: 8 Techniques/Fight Seminars, 2 main / side-ring referee certifications.

Shin – Tora Do   Self-Defense
Self-Defense 1)

 # 1: Attack from the front with a straight back punch to the head:
  a) **Counter:** Maid movement together with a firm Front-Kick to the lower abdomen, immediately after counter (Front-Kick), twisting the right wrist (from the attacking hand) counterclockwise, taking the opponent to the ground.
  b) **Counter:** Lower Front-Kick, twisting the hand counterclockwise,
  c) **Counter:** Fast with back fist to the temple.

 # 2: Attack from the front with a swinger to the head:
  a) **Counter:** Upper maid movement (after danger passes your head);
     Front-Kick with full force using your hip to full extent, to the groin.

 # 3: Attack with a straight Front Kick to the stomach:
  a) **Counter:** Hip (with side step) moves 90 degree into the attack, catching (scoop) the opponent's kick. Then with a fast back-fist to the face, slide in and over, holding and pushing the opponent's shoulder. At the same time sweeping his standing foot, dropping him hard and fast to the ground.

 # 4: Attack from the front with a side-kick:
  a) **Counter:** With a 90 degree step into the opponent's attack, right elbow or a fast back-fist (depends on distance) at the same time–scoop attacking leg. Then fast elbow drop down, hit attacking leg with elbow into knee, disabling attacking leg. Then grabbing the opponent by the neck or shoulder and immediately continuing kicking to the stomach, groin and head. Always move backwards afterwards.

 # 5: Attack with a straight back-punch to the head:
  a) **Counter:** Maid movement to the right followed by a hard Round-house-Kick to the opponent's ribcage, switch legs, quickly executing a low kick to the kneecap.

 # 6: Attack from behind, squeezing and crushing chest (bear hug):
  a) **Counter:** Stepping down hard on the arch of opponent's feet, same time hit hard backwards with your head to opponent's nose, teeth or chin. Then make a firm step to the side, bending your knees reaching back to the groin of the opponent ripping it hard forwards. Then pushing elbow hard backwards into the solar plexus or chin (depends on your size). Then grabbing backwards his neck or hair, pulling him fast and hard over your extended hip (as well leg) to the ground.

Self-Defense: 2)

 # 7: Attack from behind, squeezing hold in head lock:
  a) **Counter:** Widen your stand eminently reaching with same-sided arm over the top from behind under chin or nose (preacher point) hard and fast, pulling attacker's head backwards. As well sweeping his (closer to you) standing leg, then step fast out with a 90 degree side step. Always step back, in fight stands.

 # 8: Attack from the side, restrain of your hand.
  a) **Counter:** Strong stands, and w/ deep breath counter clockwise with close circle– movement–(always against opponent's thump of the restraining hand) And with explosive circle move–break loose from restrain. Followed by a hard executed Front-Kick to the opponent's groin. Always step back, in fight stands, then leave.

 # 9: Attack with a Round-house-Kick to the head:
  a) **Counter:** Catching the attacking leg (scoop), at the same time using a hard for-

ward palm-punch/strike to the chest or chin of the opponent. Following up with a strong foot-sweep to the opponent's standing leg, throwing him hard to the floor, followed by a hard Front-stamp-Kick to the opponent's head.

 # 10: Attack with a straight punch to the head:

a) **Counter:** 15th degree maid movements to the side and into the movements of the opponent re-directing of his technique as well pushing it down and sideways and counter immediately with a reach-hand or forearm close line (depends on size) to the opponent's throat.

 # 11: Attack with a choke from the front:

a) **Counter:** Snap-Kick to the groin, as well power palm-strike to the chest or chin of opponent (depends on size) followed by double hollow palm-strikes to both ears of opponent (simultaneously). Finish him up with a head-butt to the bridge of his nose. Step back, in fight position – leave.

 # 12: Attack with a head-lock from behind:

a) **Counter:** Finding the opponent's groin (from behind, immediately) rip it hard down (rip it off), then push both arms forwards and even harder backwards, with elbows striking the opponent in his chest or solar plexus (depends on size) followed by a quick 90 degree turn, executing low-kick to his knee and femur immediately.

Self-defense: 3)

13: Attack with a double grab to the nose or throat:

a) **Counter:** Fast Front-Snap-Kick to the groin of the opponent, followed by taking control of attacking hand and followed immediately by low-kick to meniscus (knee). Then with wind-Moeller movement loosening his grip and pulling him sideways and downwards. Followed by a Baseball-Kick from upside down to the forward leaning opponent. Finishing him with an Ax-Kick to the neck. Step back, fight position–leave.

14: Attack with a side-kick to the ribs:

a) **Counter:** First with a fast 90 degree side-step (but into the opponent's attack), simultaneously scoop with open hand the kick out of danger. Letting the danger pass, then with fast back-fist to the opponent's head. Fast leg change with hip and foot turn, execute low-kicks to the standing foot of the opponent, as well a side-kick to his ribcage. Step back, in fight position–leave.

15: Attack with both hands double grab at throat–T-shirt:

b) **Counter:** First take control of attacking hands by grabbing over the same / or wrist. As well get more control by pulling the attacker to you, then suddenly execute hard and fast a head butt to your attacker's nose-bridge or mouth (depending on height).

c) Fast (using the moment of surprise) pull with right or left hand with slide-side-step head down and forwards, and break both strong holds at the same time.

d) Follow up with immediate knee-strikes upwards to the head, while you strongly pull his head down and forwards with both hands.

e) Finally, with a wind wheel drop your opponent to the floor (depending on level of advancement, as well surroundings) step over top and put attacker into a lock or arm bar, or simply walk, aware of your surroundings, away, and call 911.

16: Attack with knife forward trust:

a) **Counter:** Slide sideways, as well turn upper body sideways with forward motion but stay close to attacker, at the same time re-direct the attacking arm (knife)

b) Fast strike with opposite hand, with palm-strike or knife hand to throat of attacker at the same time control with your other hand the attacking knife.

c) Then with both hands re-direct with a wrist throw (counter clockwise) to the floor, throw or kick the knife away from your attacker and quickly go for help or cover.

SHIN – TORA – DO KARATE

Testing grading table, Kyu:

Name:_____   **Date:**_____

Warm up:_____   **Grades:**_____

Condition testing:
Jump-rope:
Push-ups:
Sit-ups:
Lion walk:
Warrior stands:
<u>Techniques:</u>
Techniques:
Tactics:
Timing:
Defense:
Counter:
Blocks:
<u>Self-defense:</u>
<u>Forms:</u>
<u>Meditation/Tai Chi/Yoga:</u>
<u>Rehab:</u>
<u>Pads, focus mittens, heavy bag:</u>
<u>Sparring:</u>
<u>Breaks:</u>
<u>Teaching:</u>
<u>Cool down:</u>

Appendix

Suggested reading and sources for research

Anthony v. Sager: 'Daydreams', Cloud Dancer Production–Media division © 06
Geert Lemmens: Kickboxing – fitness training © 86 ISBN 3 8068 07957
Geert Lemmens: Karate, eine Genese, BoD © ISBN 3-8334-6624-3
Gene LeBells: Grappling World, Pro-Action ISBN 0-9676543-1-9
Dr. Ennio Falsoni: Il magnifico Karate contact e il suo mondo> Master Media,
Dominique Valera: Karate technique full contact, Sedrip> Paris
Benny Urquidez: Training and fighting skills> Unique Productions, Hollywood
J. Corocoran, E. Farkas> Martial Arts Elocipidia, traditio history, Galery Book NY
Dan Anderson: American Free Style Karate> Unique Productions, Hollywood
Bill Walles: Super-foot, fighting techniques
Chuck Norris: Against all odds.
Bruce Lee: Jeet Kune Do
Musashi: The Legend of
Funacochi: Collective work of
Jogon Jamaguchi: Collective work of
Nakayamas: Collective work of
Lao-Tse: the collective work of
ZaZen the Art War:
Mihran Aghvinian: Kadgamala Self-defense www.hyekatchdo.com
Dr. Norman Vincent: The Power of Positive Thinking
Dr. Kenneth H. Cooper: (50 Books) see: www.cooperaerobics.com
Dan Millman: The Peaceful Warrior
William Arnold: Leading from the Zone> Design Group, Roseville
William Arnord: Perfect Courage> Design Group, Roseville
Les Brown: Live your dreams> Morrow/Avon USA
Richard D. Carson: Taming your Gremling, Book & Audio / Nightingale Conant, IL
Morton Rhue: The Wave > Pinguin Publishing & Ravensburger Buchverlag

Useful Links:

www.getfit4yourlife.com
www.Lemmens-ma-de
www.libri.de
www.cooperaerobics.com
www.tigertwins.com
www.kalari-hamburg.de
www.wako-deutschland.de
www.kick-start.org
www.goldenboypromotions.com
www.hyekatchdo.com
www.GeneLebell.com
www.Kadgamala.de
www.superfoot.com
www.Bennythejet.com
www.vallymartialart.com
www.toptencanada.com
www.paulieayala.com
www.Karateus

Acknowledgement

'Get Fit for Life' Systems © 95

The Systems reach far back to my humble beginnings. The idea was born in the dojo of my Grandmaster Geert J. Lemmens in the 1980's, and over more than two decades I have created a summary of the years of research, hard training and gathering experience and called it 'Get Fit for Life'-Systems. Many people have helped me and contributed in one way or the other, but especially my students and friends. They appeared with me in countless radio interviews and TV broadcasts like Bantam/Welter-weight sensation Paulie Ayala. I had met him in a gym in TX. Instantly we became friends and he taught me well in his boxing classes. Once we gave an interview for TV and, would you believe it, introduced each other as world champions, although that still was a dream of both of us back then. Years later, after winning the World title and defending it many times, Paulie declined to come out of his well-deserved retirement because he preferred to dedicate his life to his wife and children, and to the training of future champions–he is one of America's finest! Or former Mister Olympia, the one and only Frank Zane, who appeared with me on a TV-show, as well as Jamie Cashion the III, a wonderful friend.

And after all these years of hard work and training, a long kept dream of mine became reality, when 'Get fit for Life' was shaped into a TV-concept and broadcasted in 1995 and 96. Not long after, I started to produce my DVD with a training program for anyone with special needs. Everybody was helping: Marine Clinton Cloudle's self-defense routine with me was shot, Timothy, Jonathon, my stepdaughter Jenae, Doreen, Heidi and her boyfriend, attorney Chat Berry, Dr. Richard Chamberlin, J. Pat Burleson. They all 'played' their 'roles' beautifully, or were simply there with loving support. WBA World Bantam Champion Paulie Ayala let us use his private gym and even made a special appearance; and my old friend Cliff Browns provided us with his back yard. So, the idea to create a program for anyone with the need to be in a better place in life, that I had kept in my mind many years, was finally realized as well. It was teamwork at its best!

And not to forget Tim Mc Coy and his son Timothy, who had been a fine student of mine for years, despite his physical disability and learning- and speech-difficulties, which were supposed to slow him down and forbid him to do as well as he did–not Tim, happy .and amazing from the start with full support from his dad within all of my endeavours. Both, his dad and wife were always on our side with loving spirit. I wish, many parents would do just half as much. Their children would prosper in ways most parents can only dream of.

A big thank you to all my teachers and students for all those years of support. And I do apologize if I left out someone. This was surely not intentional!

"Get Fit 4 Life Systems" ™
Rehab Plan

The following two programs are meant as replenishment to the book for anyone in need:

The program consists of 12 classes, 45 minutes each, one month. It is designed to train children and adults who are handicapped from birth or by an accident, and its concept addresses a wide range of limitations.

1. Class (paraplegics) Wheelchair:

a) Teach handicapped youth/adults power to continue and better their life (after accident)

b) Accepting of their handicap, their body and surroundings

c) Meditation

d) Re-learning to relax and breathe, to learn and concentrate

e) Respecting their mothers and fathers, teachers and country

f) Before any Martial Arts are learned, the student must have accomplished point a)-e)

g) Basic Martial Arts training, modified for the individual's needs

h) Basic self-defense

2. Techniques for Meditation and Relaxation

A

Close your eyes, relax and rest your arms and legs. Focus on a point in your head and let that energy point flow through your body evenly; concentrate on each part of your body as your focus point flows. You cannot jump from one side to another around your body. Keep it evenly and on its path within yourself. For the beginner: You must concentrate on the words of your teacher. As an advanced or Master Student; you simply listen to your heart and follow your inner journey.

B

You will learn to relax and breathe more easily. When this is more improved we will move on, and as next step, Anthony selected the Sun-Greeting from the Okinawa Karate System. Relax and simply follow your teacher's instructions: We start with the relaxation technique A. Then, again, please close your eyes and breathe with ease, concentrate again on the cosmic energy (or also known as Inner Chi) Now slowly open your hands and move your arms upwards in a half circle like albatross wings and let your fingertips meet above your head. The center of your hands will form a triangle. Slowly move your arms down in a half circle again, and let your fingertips meet once more in front of your legs. Repeat the two movements 5 times, inhale when you move your arms up, exhale, when you move them down. Control your breathing and the coordination of your hands.

C

Bring your arms before your rib cage and inhale. While exhaling, move your arms away from your body in a straight line. Push your last breath strongly out as you reach the point of furthest extension of your arms possible. Now twist your arms and turn your hands, palms facing away from you, fingers stretched upwards, and straighten out. Repeat at least 5 times with deep breathing. Chi-exercise.

D

Please sit up and relax with your eyes closed for two minutes.

E

Begin with your left arm extended, palm facing down. Flex the biceps and pull your arm up towards your head ending with the palm facing up and elbow bent. At the same time, your right arm is bent at the elbow with the palm facing up and your biceps flexed. Switch position and movement of arms. Continuously watch your breathing, inhaling slowly, exhaling smoothly. This exercise should be repeated at least 10 times.

F

Moving your right arm into the right side of your body, extend the arm straight out while you exhale and then return your arm to the center of your body. When you push your arm out your fingers will point towards your body. When you pull your arm in towards the body, your fingers will point towards your body as well. Repeat these moves with the left arm and then again with both arms extending in front of your body and over your head. Always concentrate on your breathing, inhale slowly and exhale smoothly. This exercise should be repeated at least 5 times with left and right arm.

Basic Karate Techniques:

G

Gyaku Zuki, Oi Zuki (Shudan) Punches (paraplegic)

With the left, as well as right, hand. Start position: Left hand next to your chin. The left hand will punch straight to the opponent and the right hand then quickly follows up, same target. This basic exercise should be done at least ten times with each hand, concentrate on punching directly on target and the correct hand position. Don't forget the correct breathing! Inhale on the way back, exhale on the way to the target.

H

Shotei and Haito-Uchi–right hand (inside and outside) (Ridge hands). First to the left side of your neck, then your ridge hand technique will be executed to the right side of your neck. The other hand will be in fight position protecting the other side of your body and face. This exercise should be done at least 10 times each hand. Concentrate on your breathing, by executing the ridge hand fast exhale, on the way back smoothly inhale.

I

Tate Zuki–Short front punch. Start position: Hands will be first in front of your body. Punch extending your hands directly in front of your body, do not twist your arms. Punch and exhale at the same time. This should be done at least 10 times each hand.

J

Ura Zuki–Cross-hook. Start position: Fight position, right hand on the head, protecting the face, left hand coming out in an angle and within 45 degrees, executing a cross hook to the opponent's face or ribs (depending on his height). Head target should be temple or side of the chin, to the body should be the short ribs or Solar Plexus, depending on angle and height. For people in a wheelchair it is most important to execute and

reach their target with great accuracy, most likely having only one window for execution.
K

Upper cut. Start position: Arm is by the face, the other arm is at the side and must do a half circle, and its ending position must be a straight upwards line in front of your head until the upwards faced fist hits the opponent's chin or nose; even though the student is sitting in his wheelchair it is still recommended that he comes (slightly) forwards and upwards. Control your breathing, inhale on the way down, exhale on the way up. This exercise should be done at least 10 times each.
L

Back-fist. Start position: With elbow pointing towards your target, extend the attacking arm to strike until your wrist hits the opponent's nose or temple/head. Before impact, extend your wrist and pull the same backwards fast. With these mechanisms the impact triples and shocks your opponent. The other hand of course must protect your side and head. This exercise should be done at least 10 times each.
M

Basic Blocks: Age–Uke, upwards head-block. Start position: The forearm should be at a 45-degree angle and two to three inches in front of your forehead. The other arm should be at the other side of your face and the turn of the same should go inside of the switch as the upper arm is on the way down; as the block reaches its peak the forearm turns and with a thrust reaches its final point as the opposite arm reaches its final point as well on the side of the head. Repeat with each arm 10 times.
N

Soto–Uke, scoop-block (inside-block): The Forearm should be at a 45-degree angle, the wrist facing upwards coming from below, the other arm protects the side of the face and ribs at the same time. Make sure when you execute the block just before coming to a halt, turn the lower end of your forearm/elbow down to the center with a thrust to ensure the technique/block will push the on-coming attack out of its set course and the technique out of danger. You should execute this block with both arms at least 10 times each.
O

Utchi-Uke. Hammer fist-block. Start position: The forearm must be in a 45-degree angle and should start out behind the ear, coming from behind and down fast and hard to ensure the same effect as with Soto-Uke to push the attacking punch out of danger. As usual, the other arm protects the other side of the head and ribs. This exercise should be done at least 10 times each arm.
P

Juji-Uke. Cross-block. Start position: Thrust both arms outwards simultaneously crossing at about two inches below the wrist to make an "X". Make sure at the end of the technique to put a good thrust into it. This exercise should be done at least 10 times with strong exhale when technique comes to a halt. Inhale on the way back.

*

When the student masters the above rehab/Karate beginner plan, then he can move slowly on to other forms of self-defense for handicapped children/youths/adults by Anthony:
A

Attack: Hammer fist. Defense: Highblock with power, grab the wrist with the same hand you use to high-block. Strike the throat and then grab the attacking hand, twist the same sideways, until the attacker goes or is thrown to the floor.

B

Attack: Slap to the face from the side. Defense: Cross-block and then slide smoothly down the arm, holding the hand while you elbow-strike (or back-fist, depending on height) to the head of the attacker with power and thrust. Then hit the elbow down and break your attacker's elbow. This exercise should be done at least 10 times each arm.

C

Attack: From the back in a choke hold. Defense: First break the little finger and try to get under the attacking arm, as well grab the hand and bend the wrist and then elbow at a 45-degree angle pushing the same with the wrist in your hand (and control) to the floor. This exercise should be done each partner and side 10 times.

D

Attack: From the front with a stick. Defense: Block with a cross-block at the forearm. Grab the attacking arm, twist and push it in a fast half sideways motion. Then counterattack with a palm-strike to the head–shin or temple–hard (depending on height). This exercise should be done 10 times each partner and side.

E

Attack: With stick from the side. Defense: Before the stick hits your head, move to the side and grab the attacking wrist, as well push on the same elbow, hyperextend it and move attacking arm down sideways out of danger. Hold attacking arm down by pushing it down and twisting it downwards. This exercise should be done at least 10 times each partner and side.

F

Attack: To the head from behind with a stick. Defense: Before stick hits your head turn and move slightly sideways and with an X-block move attacking arm sideways, then smoothly take wrist and block at the same time as you turn the wrist down sideways, blocking the stick. At the same time hyperextend the elbow and push the attacking arm all the way down. His body will follow. Hold on to the wrist and take the stick out of the hand and use when you need it. This exercise should be done 10 times each side and partner.

G

Attack: From the side with a knife. Defense: Just before the knife hits, you block it sideways away from your body, then grab the attacking wrist and twist it hard; at the same time counterattack with a back-fist or a palm-strike to the head/throat (depending on height). Also well to use is a ridge-hand to the throat, then push the opponent with a double palm-strike to the floor and quickly leave (for advanced students: Use the same knife and control the opponent until help arrives) these exercises should be done ten times each side and partner.

End of beginner to inter-medium training plan for anybody with special needs

'Get Fit 4 Life Systems™
Anthony Martin von Sager

Sport Rehabilitation and Muscle Strengthening Plan for Athletes with post-traumatic injury © 88/98

For Board of Examiners of Germany Sports Assoc., by Anthony Martin von Sager
    Anthony Martin von Sager started Martial Arts in 1980 under Grandmaster Geert J. Lemmens in N. Germany. Due to his personal handicap and therefore the large obstacles he needed to remove from his path Anthony devoted a major part of his time to helping injured and handicapped athletes and anyone in need to be in a better place in life from the beginning of his Martial Arts journey. In 1986 he was voted into the position of Sports Referent for handicapped youths and athletes within the German Sports Association (DSSV, DAKV, DSB) (until 1993)

*

    Most athletes, especially pro athletes, have many enhanced sports capabilities at their disposal. With this in mind, the following recommendations are addressed to athletes who suffered physical traumata caused by accidents during sportive activities or work. They show how to safely rehabilitate them to avoid short-term physical disability. For illustration a case example is used: An athlete, let's call him Bob.

    During a competition Bob heavily injured one of his knees. He was in hospital for two weeks after surgical treatment of his cross-tendons that stabilized the knee's structure. Now, the functional capabilities and range of motion of Bob's knee are extremely reduced, and its surrounding muscle group heavily atrophied. Affected are the ischio curale and the vastus lateralis (quadriceps), also known as knee stretcher that controls the depression of the knee-joint. At the same time the biceps femoris (controls the elevation of the lower foot) is mildly inflamed.

    Bob needs a sport-rehab program that addresses the knee's structure as well as its functions to be synchronized and implicated for pain-free use. In order to prevent chronic tendonitis the static posture of the knee needs to be re-integrated in the surrounding support muscle group and its tendons, which have to be rebuilt and strengthened. As form follows functions, the program will increase the specified and selected capabilities of the athlete in his field of sport and ensure his safe and soon return. As a result Bob will be physically and mentally balanced. A part of the program will include nutrition and food supplementation recommendations to enhance his internal healing as well. The program's duration is 8-14 weeks, 2-3 sessions per week, each session 45 minutes.

Sport Rehabilitation and Muscle Strength Plan for post-traumatic injury, part 1

1) The first exercise is a slow bending of the knee and therefore as well the stretching of the hamstrings. A goal is to activate involvement of the patient, if necessary with a knee brace, and for eliminating the pain ice packs. Depending on the degree of injury and pain this should not be done longer than 10-15 minutes in one session, no more than two sessions a week within the first two weeks after injury, and not to be increased until mobility and free movements improve and the pain decreases.

2) After stretching is completed, the mobility of the knee has increased and the pain decreased. The mobility and strength of the surrounding muscles have improved, (quadriceps as well hamstrings) and come to a balance. We will now introduce increased resistance / isometric training. This will condition Bob's muscle tone and increase his lost muscle mass. At this point we start to educate the client about recovery enhancing nutrition: A higher protein intake will increase muscle growth, and healthy Carbohydrates will improve endurance and strength.

3) Kneeling or standing before the client, the therapist holds the injured leg on his shoulder or in his hands (depending on height) and bends it slowly and carefully into the bodyline. The client's back and hip must fully rest against a wall as the therapist reaches the knee and brings it over his shoulder. Above the knee joint the same-sided arm stretches and stabilizes the lower leg and so prevents it from snapping out of its designated position so that it is not overstretched! **Attention reader and therapist**: You need to be extremely careful (especially at the beginning) not to overstretch the injured leg's cross-tendons and hamstrings, etc. This rehab exercise is continued at least 10-12 weeks and done to **both** legs to create more balance.

4) The next exercise is the so called 'air bicycling': The client lies on his back resting his hands (palms to body) comfortably underneath his hips, lifts his legs in a right angle, knees slightly bent, and moves them as if riding a bicycle. **Attention:** Make sure the client does not have an arched low back, and adjust the angle of the legs if needed until the back rests on the matt to protect the low back.

5) After successful performance of the first 3 exercises, Bob will relearn to use his ligaments and to stabilize his tendons like the meniscus as well as the strengthening of his hip flexors with this exercise: Bob rests on his back; the therapist, kneeling in front of him, elevates Bob's leg, then holds it by the ankle and asks Bob to push it against his hands; as he pushes in, Bob pushes out. The same routine is applied the other way: Bob pushes in as the therapist pushes out. These two exercises should be done at least 12-15 times in 2-3 sets each leg, unless the patient experiences pain or discomfort, and if so the treatment should be stopped momentarily. There is the option of so called negative resistance work with "rubber band" instead.

Sport Rehabilitation and Muscle Strength Plan with post-traumatic injury, part 2

In the past 3-4 weeks of Bob's rehabilitation, his knee should have become more stabilized and strengthened. If that is hopefully the case, we will be able to proceed to the next step...

6) Which will be a combination of fitness-, rehab- and strength-training. In most cases (like my own) only resistance or even negative resistance exercises will be possible at first, until the pain in the joint is manageable. Often it will take 1-2 weeks before the patient is able to move to just resistance and very light weight with negative motion (meaning the therapist helps to elevate the weight) to strengthen the injured muscle groups (like hamstrings or quadriceps) and to re-build injured muscle fibers. This will lead to a re-programming of the injured muscle groups, and therefore the so called 'muscle memory' will kick in and take over. Eventually these muscles will work smoothly and normally again; and in a later stage the muscle groups will work 100% efficiently, all muscle fibers and tendons combined. This rehab exercise should be done 2-3 times a week, 3 sets each.

*

When the patient is ready we will extend the strength-training to 3 times a week. The following exercises are to be performed for the next 4-6 weeks.

7)–a. Leg extension station: At the beginning with help of the therapist on the positive way and with none or very little weight on the machine. This exercise will be done between 10-12 times each leg, 3-4 sets each.

7)–b. Leg curls station: At the beginning same procedure with help of the therapist on the positive way and with low or none weight at all, just correcting motion and form. The routine has to be done with at least 10-12 reps at 3-4 sets each leg.

Attention reader/therapist: We have been told for a long time that the back should not be arched in order to help with the exercise and/or to perform it with heavier weight (which would be a cheat). This is completely wrong as long as the exercise is done correctly and with accurate body posture, the back (especially the low back) even has to arch a little in order to ensure a successful contraction of the hamstrings! By this the patient also keeps away stress from the lower back.

8) Bob is ready for the next challenge: Stationary or static squats. Standing with his legs double-shoulder width apart, he bends his knees slowly to squat down between 10-25% depending on fitness and injury.

For his safety, several measures can be taken: First, have a bench or chair behind your client so that he can sit down if necessary; Second, stand in front of your client and hold his hands when performing this exercise.

and success.

The well balanced nutrition-plan includes a high amount of complex Carbohydrates and protein, many vitamins and minerals (salads and corn products), such as a high weekly dose of vitamin E (500-1000 mg), F, B6, and B12, vitamin C, Calcium and magnesium. (Please be advised that this is a recommendation. Only a dietician or MD is able to pre-scribe a nutrition plan). After completion of this rehab plan with physical as well as mental training and nutrition guidelines, Bob should be back in top form (after successful operation and treatment) and therefore return highly motivated to his pro sport in less than 3-4 months (depending on heaviness of injury and possible complications). Good luck Bob, and we'll see you soon back in action with hope for a successful next season.

Translated and notary by: Meleia Waschka 9-16-1997 (lice. State of TX till 06-06-98)

Testimonials:

Dear Anthony, thank you for coming to our class, we hope you can come and see us again…love, the class. (*Marina Middle School, L.A., CA*)

Dear Anthony, thank you for your having taken the time and lighten our spirits. Please come back soon, *Ms. Lopez*

Dear Anthony, I think what you are doing can help anyone, please keep up the good work, you inspired me a lot today. *Eden*

Dear Anthony, thank you so much for coming, and sharing your life's ups and downs with us. I was truly inspired, keep up the hard work. Sincerely, *Ms. Wilson, Teacher*

Thank you for taking your time and coming to Pace University, you are truly an inspiration to me. Your strength and courage were evident when we met you. I wish to meet more people like you. Your passion, strength and authenticity are greatly appreciated. Thanks, *NYC* ☺ *Sheena*

Thank you for taking time to come to NY and speak with us. Thank you for your teaching me that anything can happen and to believe in yourself to make the impossible, possible! *Helen Cheng*

Thank you for taking the time to speak to our class. It has been wonderful and inspirational to hear from your experience. I hope this was not the last time we hear from you. *Polina Ovcharova*

Thank you so much for taking the time to come to our class. You are truly inspirational to us all. I just hope you enjoyed your time in NYC; I'm looking forward to hearing from you again. *Lucy A.*

Your Speech was truly inspirational, inspired me to move forward. *Pamela, NYC Student*

First off, thank you very much for taking the time out to share your amazing story with us. It's people like you who make a different in this world and encourage people like myself that anything is possible. Your love and dedication to make people happy is a true inspiration to me. Thank you for being so true to your self, to make such an impact in the lives of others. *Sophia Garcia*

I learned to today that it is not just about setting goals; it is about loving yourself! Success happens because of devotion, passion, desire and love. Without these elements, success is unachievable. Being true to you is the only way to life. As a side note, you are the most genuine and inspirational speaker I have ever heard. Thank you so much, Anthony. *Ryan Muddleston*

Anthony, I learned so much from you today. It was always my dream to open my own clothing business, and after listening to you today I really feel this is something I can do. You have inspired me to go outside my comfort zone and to achieve my dreams. Thank you, *Kristin McClune*

Before I met you I was thinking, it would be unstoppable for me to walk down the same path as my brothers, and I just came from the ER where we rushed my brother after overdosing. After meeting you, listening to your accomplishments and obstacles you had to overcome, I'm inspired to break free and to find my own path, healthier and stronger. Thank you for making me break the board…! *OO7* (I feel his name should be protected and his courage honored. Anthony v. Sager)

"To my friend Anthony, you are a true warrior of life, your perfect courage in action, of your life truth! Truly inspiring, thank you." *(Bill) William W. Arnold, Professor, Pace University, N.Y.*

What the Legends have to say:

You are the man, truly inspirational to all of us.
Gene LeBell, L.A., CA, '04

You are an inspiration; your work especially with handicapped/injured individuals has always been amazing & inspiring for all of us. I always admired your, "Yes I can!" mentality.
Geert J. Lemmens, L.A., CA, '04

You are an inspiration. Your work and accomplishments in the Budo world are well known. I am proud of you.
Toni Bader, 2000

I have known Anthony nearly all my life. A great role-model and inspiration, not just for himself, but helping countless others over the years.
Mihran Aghvinian, '03

Your work and relentless search for the truth, your involvement and engagement for your students, especially for handicapped children, is truly inspirational and amazing.
Jamie Cashion, TX, '93

You are amazing, a true inspiration. You made a big difference in my life!
MLB baseball sensation, **Luis D. Ortiz**, TX, '97

You are an inspiration, to a good friend.
Chuck Norris, TX, '94

You are amazing, all the best.
Bob Wall, L.A., CA, '93

I saw you teaching for years around town, your work is truly amazing and inspirational!
Wesley Snipes, MDR, CA, '03

To: "The Man" – your are, an inspiration to all of us, keep up the great work!
Dan Inosanto, MDR, CA, '04

Keep on kicking, nice to hear from you, old friend.
Bill Super-foot, Florida, '04

You are amazing; keep going and all the best.
Benny the Jet, L.A., CA, '05

Your Video *Get fit for Life* and programs are for anybody with the need to be in a better place in life!
J. Pat Burleson, TX, '93

Thank you for all your support, you are an inspiration, keep up the good work.
WBA Bantam World Champion **Paulie Ayala**, TX '96

I met sensei Anthony through my cousin Renshi Mihran Agvinian after several motorcycle and training accident's and he's been essential in my rehabilitation and training .Through his guidance and teachings in his book I have learned allot about my own injuries as well as helping other with disabilities.

He has been a inspiration to me and all around him.

WITH LOVE AND RESPECT
Sensei, George Manoukian, 1st Dan

Martial Arts & Fitness movements and forms:

There a few basics & inter-medium martial arts, yoga, tai-chi as well as fitness training moves.
Please train carefully, always warm-up properly, stretch and eat well. Have fun!

Sempei Michelle with me

After a great event once again

Brother Renshi Mihran & me

At Hye-Katch-Do our champions start young
Narek Mkrtchian five years old

The Warrior Stand
Sensei, George Manoukian, 1st Dan

The Warrior Walk w/ Front-Kick   (shin-tora-do karate

The American Eagle Stand w/ full movements   (shin-tora-do karate)

The American Eagle Touch the Sky w/ full body-extension

The Flamingo Stand

(Shin Tora Do Karate)

Flamingo stand w/ foot forwards

Sanshin

(Goju-Riu / Karate)

1.

2.

Sanshin – cont

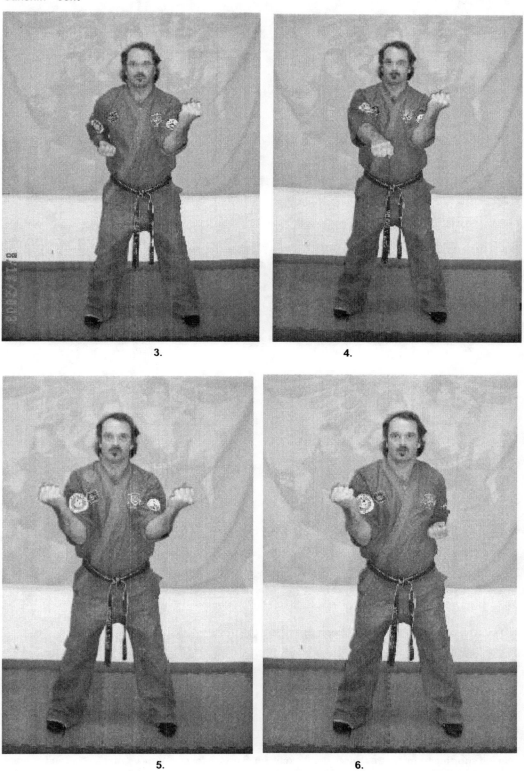

3.

4.

5.

6.

Sanshin cont

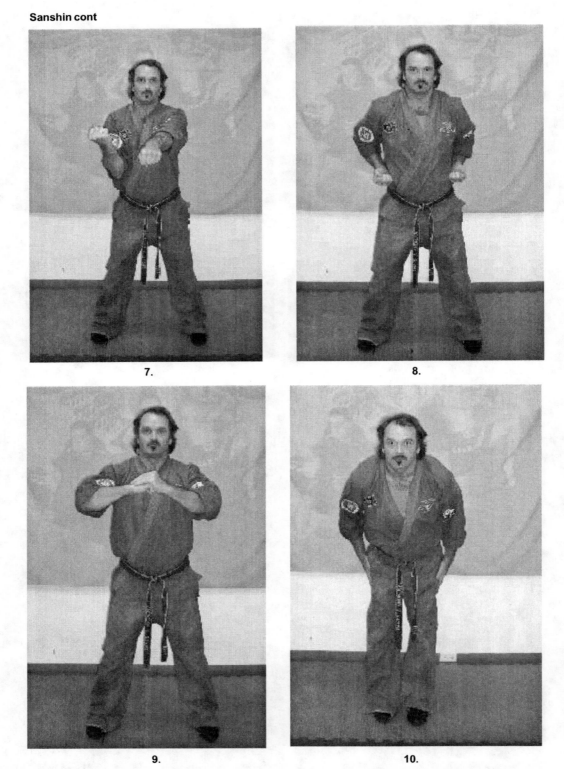

7.

8.

9.

10.

(We did shorting form, for this photo shot: excellent exercise for strength, concentration and overall conditioning, improve breathing and lung capacity)

Chi-Sou (sticky hands)   **(Wu-Shu)**

Pushing four corners of the wind   **(Chi-Gong)**

Pushing against the sky (Chi-Gong)

26. Pushing against the sky (sideways)

Splashing Energy River (Chi-Gong)

1. begin
Ed & Lorayne Helin, both age of 79

2. finish
tai-chi & yoga students (3 months)

Barrel of Life Stand   (Chi-Gong)

Lion Stand   (Gojo-Riu)

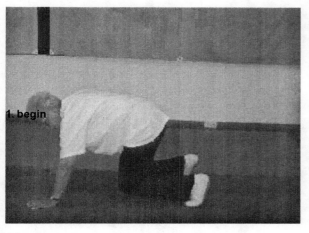

1. begin

1. begin

2. end

Shoulder exercise / boxing form　　　　　　　　　**(MMA & Fitness)**

Reps 5-25 x 3 sets depending on fitness and goal

1. (Left & Right alternation)

Side shoulder exercise

Death lift, shoulder / neck

end of form

1. begin
Uppercut shoulder workout

2. end

Push-ups   **(universal)**

Leg raises   **(universal)**

1.

2.

(universal)

Power crunches

3. from leg raise's into power crunch

Back pull-ups

1.

2.

Cobra stretch / upper facing dog   (Hata Yoga)

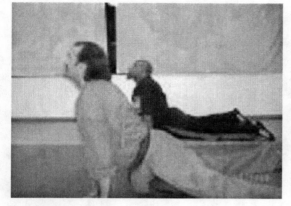

Child Position

1.

Child position change into Lion stands

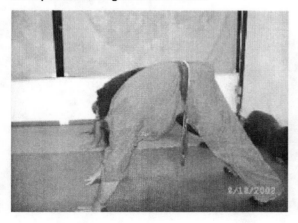

Squats with and without kick   **(cardio kickboxing)**

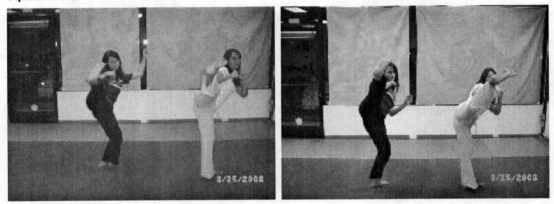

Partner workout, focus box-techniques

Jack knifes / isometrics   (low)   **(universal)**

Jack knife (high)

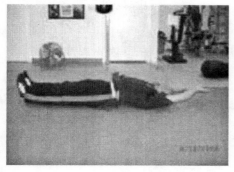

1.

(universal)

2.

Jump-rope – for:
Warm-up or cool down

Stomach warm-up a la Renshi

Heavy bag, just arms

Heavy bag work-out boxing & kickboxing

Sensei, Jeannette 3x World champion

& Sempei Maral Aghvinian

Focus mittens training, for anyone's safely   **(boxing)**

Jab or front punch

Focus mittens training cont.

Cross hook

Focus mitten training cont.

Front kick / with front and back leg

Sparring / shadow boxing / kickboxing

(boxing, Chinese boxing)

Basic stretching and cool downs

1.

2.

Basic stretching and cool downs

3.

4

Za-Zen Meditation  **(karate do)**

Hye-Katch-Do MMA Champions – Gokor grappling challenge 08
For more info see: www.hyekatchdo.com or www.gokor.com

Five competitors, four Gold, one bronze & one Grand Champion!

Rock-star work at its finest, with Shihan J. Pat Burleson TX

Tai-Chi in the park at Sensei, Cliff Browns' home TX

Sempei Jessi, Rock-star work

always will fight for our stars

TOP FOUR HURRICANE FIGHT TEAM USA

14 x TX State champion, 7 x U.S. National, 8 x World Champion

Some of my personal heroes, friends and idols:

Antonio,
To a good friend
Chuck Norris

At Walker TX Ranger Set 93

Hye-Katch-Do—grand opening

Kancho Lemmens & Family

Sempei Jessi Beach action

At the Legends 97 TX

My Dojo (TX) w/ Luis De Ortiz 96

Benny the Jet, at HKD

Paulie Ayala

WABF Champ–Ayala

Visiting with Bob Wall 93

Super-foot lecture on roundhouse kick NBL WM 2000 GA

Visit with Sifu Dan Inosanto's central dojo MDR, CA

With Patrick Swayze at Planet Hollywood, Dallas TX

With Troy Dorcey at the Legends 97 TX

Shihan Toni Bader

Frank Zane 93

Simon Kim   **Al Dacascus at NBL-WM * 2000 GA**

(* WM – World Martial Arts Champion chips)
For more legends see: www.getfit4yourlife.com
A little action around the world…

Anthony Martin Sager

CITY HALL
LOS ANGELES, CALIFORNIA 90012

JAMES K. HAHN
MAYOR

December 14, 2001

Anthony Martin von Sager
Cloud Dancer Productions
P.O. Box 1773
Venice, CA 90294-1773

Dear Mr. von Sager:

Thank you for sending me your video, *Get Fit for Life*. I appreciate it and I'm sure I'll enjoy watching it. You're a great inspiration to disabled children.

Best wishes and happy holidays.

Very truly yours,

JAMES K. HAHN
Mayor

JKH:bhn

THE WHITE HOUSE

WASHINGTON

June 24, 2002

Mr. Anthony Martin von Sager
Cloud Dancer Productions
Post Office Box 1773
Venice, California 90294-1773

Dear Mr. von Sager:

Thank you for your letter to President Bush requesting sponsorship. The President appreciates the strides you have made in your life and the example you are setting for others.

Unfortunately, the White House generally does not get involved in the awarding of financial assistance or federal grants to particular individuals or projects. By law or under the rules of specific grant issuing entities, those decisions are left to others.

A resource that may be of interest is the Catalog of Federal Domestic Assistance. This online, searchable database, accessible at www.cfda.gov, lists more than 1,400 assistance programs administered through federal agencies.

We appreciate your understanding. The President sends his best wishes.

Sincerely,

Desiree Thompson
Special Assistant to the President
and Director of Presidential Correspondence

C. A. Kotsanis, M.D.

**DFW EAR, NOSE &
THROAT ASSOCIATES
& ALLERGY CENTER**

Baylor Medical Plaza
1600 W. College St., Suite 260
Grapevine, TX 76051
Metro (817) 461-6342

September 11, 1997

To Whom It May Concern

Re: Anton Sager
      7208 Meadow View Terrace
      North Richland Hills, Texas 76180

I have had the pleasure of knowing Mr. Anton Sager for the past several weeks. I have had the opportunity to work with him professionally in my office for about a week and was able to observe him for his skills in massage and also Tai-Chi. I found Mr. Sager to be a very highly ethical individual with excellent skills in the field of physical therapy.

At this point, he is seeking full employment with his skills as a massage therapist/physical therapist. I feel that his skills and his accomplishments along with his work ethic would be very helpful to any individual or department. I therefore recommend Mr. Sager highly to anyone who is seeking an individual with such talents.

Sincerely,

Constantine A. Kotsanis, M.D.

CAK:T+343

Diplomate, American Board
of Otolaryngology
Ear, Nose and Throat Surgery
Head and Neck Surgery
Facial Plastic Surgery
Allergy
Hearing Aid Center

GEMEINSCHAFTSPRAXIS
FACHÄRZTE FÜR ORTHOPÄDIE

DR. MED.
THEO WEGMANN
SPORTMEDIZIN
PHYSIK. THERAPIE

DR. MED. UNIV. ZU LEUVEN
PHILIP DE HERT
SPORTMEDIZIN

APENRADER STR. 4
24939 FLENSBURG
TELEFON 0461 / 4004
TELEFAX 0461 / 44579

PRAXISZEITEN:
MO - FR 7.30 BIS 18.00 UHR
ODER NACH VEREINBARUNG

27.06.1996

To whom it may concern.

DATUM:

Mr. Kay Sager, born: 03.07.63, has been in my orthopedic threatment since 1984.

In spite of his handicap, he has shown to be an extraordenary cooperative patient. With energy and endurance he engaged himself in a sports- and fitnesscenter, where he - as far as I know - developed programms for sportsorientated young people.

He has allways shown a great intrest in caring for and motivating young sportsmen, especially young people with a physical handicap.

We hope Mr. Sager will continue to work on this same basis and wish him all the best for his further career.

Dr. De Hert

Dr. Wegmann

THE POWER FROM WITHIN BUSHIDO

TWENTIETH CENTURY FOX
A NEWS CORPORATION COMPANY

P.O. Box 900
Beverly Hills, California 90213-0900
Phone 310 369 3288 • Fax 310 369 8925

Carlos Kotkin
Creative Executive
Production

June 17, 1998

Anthony Martin Sager
P.O. Box 1773
Venice, CA 90294-1773

Dear Anthony,

Thank you for both your letter and tape, "Get Fit for Life." I enjoyed reading your story as well as the accompanying articles. Your determination and optimism are truly inspirational, and I congratulate you on your many accomplishments.

Unfortunately, at this time there is little room in the studio's feature and television slates to pursue this project. However, we appreciate your time and effort in sharing your material and would like to return your tape so that others may watch it as well.

I commend your hard work and dedication and wish you the best of luck in all of your endeavors.

Sincerely,

Carlos Kotkin

cc: Sanford Panitch

July 22, 1996

Anthony Martin Sager
7209 Meadowview Terrace
N. Richland Hills, FW Texas 76180-2622

Dear Mr. Sager,

   Thank you for your letter to Steven Spielberg requesting a meeting and forwarding a synopsis for your television show and novel.

   Although our feature film and television development slates are currently full, we wanted to thank you for sending your important and inspirational story to Steven Spielberg.

   Because we are aware of the high cost of duplication we are returning your material to you so that you may share it with others.

   One of Steven's hopes for the film, "Schindler's List," was to show that one man could make a difference to the lives of many. You obviously believe the same thing and have worked hard to aid others in their own lives.

   Thank you for your letter to Steven. We wish you all the best.

Sincerely,

Kris Kelley
Director of Public Relations

KK/tr

Maria Shriver

August 4, 1999

Dear Anthony,

I was so moved and so grateful to receive your kind note about John. I can't tell you how much it meant to me that you took the time to think about me and my family during this heartbreaking period.

I will always remember your kindness, and please keep our family in your prayers.

Love,

Maria

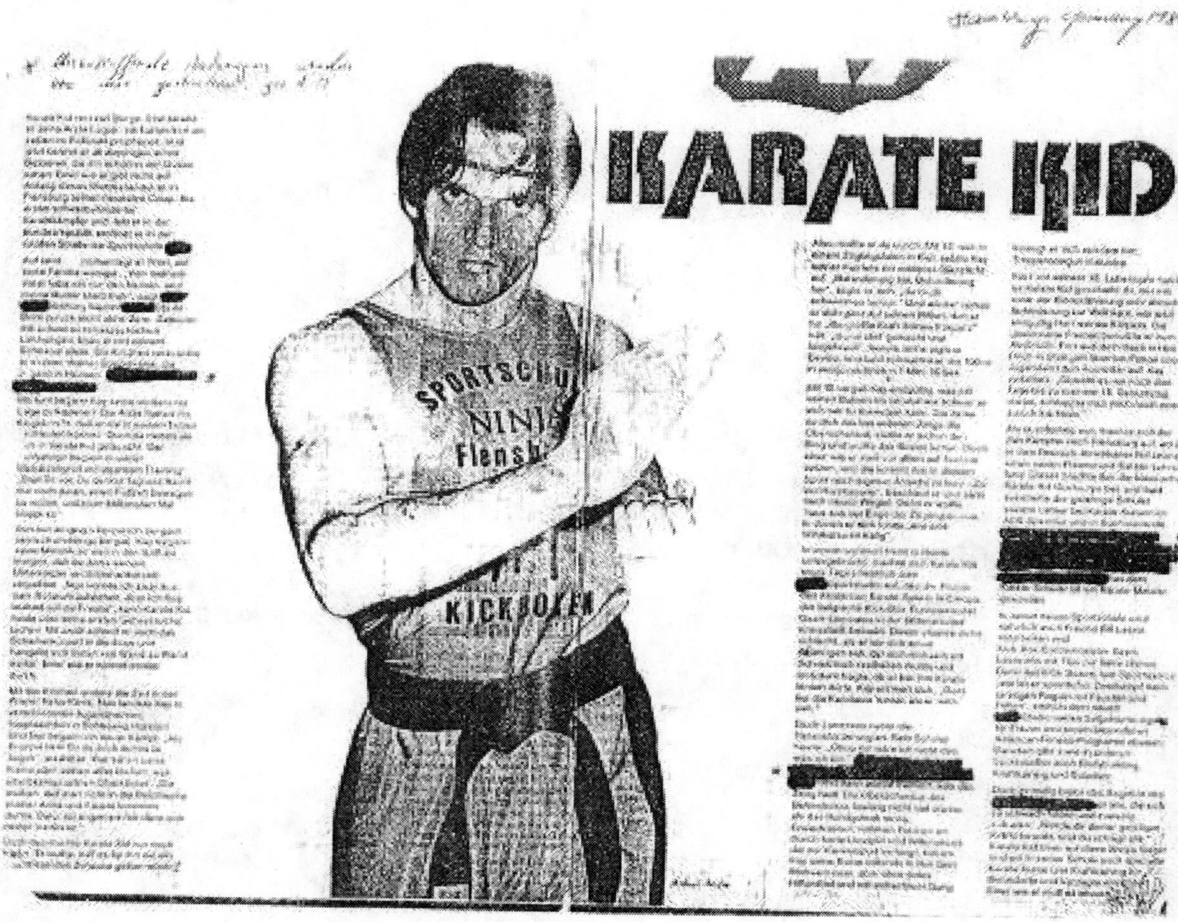

KARATE KID

Los Angeles Times

Sunday
Final

SUNDAY, OCTOBER 24, 1994

Beating the odds

Martial arts master Anthony von Sager, practicing his technique at the Marina Fitness Club in Marina del Rey, once came in first to become a world karate champion.

(Body text illegible.)

ODDS

CONTINUED FROM 11

(Body text illegible.)

SEE ODDS, PAGE 12

The Dallas Morning News

ONE MAN'S THERAPY

Martial arts used to enable disabled

Recall pe target W: City Cou

Five stand by to terminate

Karate helps teacher, disabled